# On Being
## *Presbyterian*

D0980165

# On Being
# *Presbyterian*

*Our* **BELIEFS, PRACTICES,** *and* **STORIES**

SEAN MICHAEL LUCAS

P U B L I S H I N G

P.O. BOX 817 • PHILLIPSBURG • NEW JERSEY 08865-0817

© 2006 by Sean Michael Lucas

All rights reserved. No part of this book may be reproduced, stored in a retrieval system, or transmitted in any form or by any means—electronic, mechanical, photocopy, recording, or otherwise—except for brief quotations for the purpose of review or comment, without the prior permission of the publisher, P&R Publishing Company, P.O. Box 817, Phillipsburg, New Jersey 08865-0817.

Unless otherwise indicated, Scripture quotations are from The Holy Bible, English Standard Version, copyright © 2001 by Crossway Bibles, a division of Good News Publishers. Used by permission. All rights reserved.

*Page design by Lakeside Design Plus*
*Typesetting by Dawn Premako*

Printed in the United States of America

**Library of Congress Cataloging-in-Publication Data**

Lucas, Sean Michael, 1970–
   On being Presbyterian : our beliefs, practices, and stories / Sean Michael Lucas.
      p. cm.
   Includes bibliographical references and index.
   ISBN-13:   978-1-59638-019-6 (pbk.)
   ISBN-10:   1-59638-019-5 (pbk.)
   1. Presbyterian Church in America. I. Title.

BX8968.52.L83 2006
285'.1—dc22

                                                                    2005057515

To Sara

*for joining me on this journey*

# Contents

# Preface

THE IMPETUS FOR THIS PROJECT came from a larger historical work in which I have been engaged for over three years now, tentatively titled *For a Continuing Church: Conservative Dissent in the Presbyterian Church in the United States, 1934–1974*. That larger work focuses on the conservative movement within the southern Presbyterian church that led to the formation of the Presbyterian Church in America (PCA), the denomination of which I am a part. That work could be viewed as a type of historical archeology; in it, I attempt to seek out the lineaments of the "conservative Presbyterian mind" by uncovering many of the bones of its history in the subterranean layers of Presbyterian newspapers and old personal files, church session records, and General Assembly minutes. As I have been doing this work, the questions that I have kept in the forefront of my mind are: How did the PCA come to be the way it currently is? What is the connection between the way the conservative movement in the old southern Presbyterian church developed and the way the PCA lives and breathes as a church of God doing kingdom business today?

These historical questions have led me to a more pressing question which I have faced as a teaching elder in the PCA: Do conservative Presbyterian churches, as represented in my denomination, embrace their Presbyterian identity? Or do other ideas, practices, and narratives serve to shape them? One way to read the history of the PCA, which I will explore more fully in my larger historical argument, is a movement, by fits and starts, from an essentially conservative evangelical, or even fundamentalist, identity to one that is more distinctively Presbyterian. In other words, one could read the history of the PCA as an attempt to answer the question: What does it mean to be a (conservative) Presbyterian in the postmodern age?

It is no wonder that conservative Presbyterians wrestle with this issue today. The past thirty years, which coincide with the whole of the PCA's existence thus far, have not been friendly to denominations of any stripe. On the one side is the extreme hemorrhaging of the old-line Protestant denominations. And on the other side is the rapid growth of nondenominational or loosely affiliated churches. Nowhere is this contrast better illustrated than in Louisville, Kentucky, where I lived for several years. Louisville is the home of the Presbyterian Church (USA) headquarters, with its bloated bureaucracy and public hand-wringing over membership losses. But it is also the home of one of the largest nondenominational churches in America, Southeast Christian Church, with a membership of over twenty-two thousand; on Easter Sunday in 2003, Southeast drew over thirty-five thousand attendees, dwarfing the attendance of all the old-line Protestant churches in the city put together.

This trend toward nondenominationalism has produced several responses. From within old-line Protestantism, there have been a number of books seeking to shore up denominational identity. In the late 1980s, for example, Lilly Endowment Inc., sponsored a series of six books, called *The Re-forming Tradition*, which sought to address the old-line Protestant decline as it played out within the PC (USA). More recently, the PC (USA) publishing house has offered books such as *To Be a Presbyterian* (1996), *What Unites Presbyterians: Common Ground for Troubled Times* (1997), *Presbyterians: A Spiritual Journey* (2000), *Being Presbyterian in the Bible Belt* (2000), and *This We Believe: Eight Truths Presbyterians Affirm* (2002). Still, the church loses members at an astonishing rate. In other denominations, such as the Southern Baptist Convention, this search for identity has been pronounced. Two books titled *Why I Am a Baptist* were published within a year of each other by rival groups within that denomination, each presenting a different vision of Baptist identity. Likewise, the Lutheran Church-Missouri Synod recently published *Why I Am a Lutheran* (2004) in an effort to explain to insiders and outsiders what Lutheranism is all about.

Within conservative Presbyterianism, there have been differing responses. The PCA, for example, spent several years developing a strategic plan for the denomination, which was finally presented at the 2003 General Assembly. However, it is not clear that the plan has widely impacted denominational life outside the church's offices in Atlanta. At the local level, a number of PCA churches leave "Presbyterian" out of their name, for fear of being confused with the much more theologically progressive PC (USA). This move has the by-product of making PCA churches look and feel more like nondenominational churches. Others re-traditionalize conservative Presbyterians by emphasizing their difference with mainstream evangelicalism to such a degree that "evangelical" becomes a dirty word. Still others, both within and outside the PCA, claim that being Reformed is not enough, leading to revisions of Presbyterian worship and doctrine in directions suggested more by Vatican II and postliberal theology than by John Calvin, the Westminster Assembly, or even American Presbyterian history. Hence, the quest for a conservative Presbyterian identity has either moved *toward*, *away from*, or *beyond* evangelicalism, especially as represented in its nondenominational or parachurch forms.

The question of identity becomes particularly pressing on the local level, as people from other Protestant traditions join a conservative Presbyterian church. The common story for many PCA members is that they were raised in baptistic churches, came to Christ there or in other venues, came to understand "the doctrines of grace," and found those doctrines taught clearly in a PCA church, which they then joined. Yet many of our church members, and even some officers, do not have a solid understanding of what it means to be Presbyterian. In exchanging one church for another, they have not yet learned the narratives, distinctives, and practices of their new spiritual home. As a result, our members often find themselves somewhat at a loss to explain to their friends and families why they belong to a Presbyterian church and why their friends should come and join their church as well.

This book is meant, then, as a primer on Presbyterian identity. It is not written for specialists or scholars; it is written for church members, ministerial candidates, ruling elders, and, especially, potential Presbyterians. This is not a polemical work promoting a particular point of view in areas where conservative Presbyterians have legitimate differences of opinion (for example, in the area of worship styles). Rather, I intend to stick fairly closely to the Bible, PCA constitutional documents, and official position papers in laying out what Presbyterians believe, do, and say about themselves. In the "For Further Reading" sections, I will list books that represent a wider-range of perspectives and allow the reader to explore issues more deeply on his or her own. And since this book is meant to be useful for new members' classes as well as for Sunday school or officer training venues, I have provided questions for thought and review at the end of each chapter.

I also do not intend to maximize the differences between Presbyterians and other evangelicals. As I see it, the label "evangelical" means to communicate a certain "gospel-oriented" attitude or style; evangelicals recognize the world-historical significance of the death and resurrection of Jesus Christ for their lives and they long for others to enjoy communion with him. This recognition that the gospel of Jesus changes everything lends a certain style to the ministry of "evangelical" churches, regardless of confessional stance or label used. Presbyterians are evangelicals in that we have a gospel orientation which expresses itself in our preaching, witnessing, and life together. That being said, as Presbyterians, we have some perspectives and practices that are different from other evangelicals; we also have a story that is part of the "evangelical" story, but distinct as well. Recognizing the differences will help in understanding what it means to be Presbyterian.

No one ever makes an important journey alone. I am no exception. My parents, Steve and Susan Lucas, are also now members of a PCA congregation, having come through their own journey to this place.

Though we did not start out Presbyterian, I am thankful for their love for the triune God and his Word, leading us all on this journey, though by different paths. I am also grateful for the support of my parents-in-law, Ron and Phyllis Young, who are not Presbyterian but who remind us of the love of Christ and the larger communion of the saints.

Important also have been those friends who have provided encouragement along the way. Steve Nichols, my dear friend from seminary, has been part of this journey as well. D. G. Hart, my mentor at Westminster Theological Seminary, taught me to love the Presbyterian stories. Bruce Keisling supported my work as I went through deep waters. Shawn Slate, Jonathan Medlock, and John Roberts all lived out Presbyterianism with and for me. My friends and colleagues at Covenant Theological Seminary have taught me about grace-centered Presbyterianism; it has been a delight to be here. Wayne Sparkman, director of the PCA Historical Center, lent me a hand often in the course of writing. I am grateful to Bryan Chapell, D. G. Hart, Robert Peterson, and Michael Williams, who read parts of this book in its early stages and gave valuable feedback.

I thank those churches that have been willing to interact with this material. In this regard, I especially thank my friends at Community Presbyterian Church (PCA), Louisville, Kentucky, where this project had its first incarnation, and The Covenant Presbyterian Church (PCA), St. Louis, Missouri, whose interaction led to a refinement of the material. I have been blessed to serve both of these churches as well as to learn Presbyterianism at the feet of two fine churchmen and pastors, David Dively and George Robertson.

In God's grace, my family worships within the bounds of the PCA. With deep gratitude, this book is dedicated to my wife, Sara, who told me when we first were married not to leave her behind in my intellectual and spiritual travels, but always to make sure we walked side by side. It was a wise charge, and, by God's grace, we have walked this way together. What she may not realize is that in God's providence I could not have walked this way without her. Our four covenant children—Samuel, Elizabeth, Andrew, and Benjamin—have joined us in this journey, memorizing catechisms, learning hymns from the Trinity and RUF Hymnals, singing psalms from the Trinity Psalter, and participating in the life of the visible church. It is my prayer that our life together will lead them to teach their own children about the beliefs, practices, and stories that we as Presbyterians hold dear— especially the graceful gospel of our Lord Jesus—

> that the next generation might know [it],
>     the children yet unborn,
> and arise and tell [it] to their children
>     so that they should set their hope in God. (Ps. 78:6–7a)

# Abbreviations

| | |
|---|---|
| BCO | Presbyterian Church in America, Book of Church Order |
| *Inst.* | John Calvin, *Institutes of the Christian Religion*, ed. J. T. McNeill, trans. Ford Lewis Battles (Philadelphia: Westminster Press, 1960). |
| LC | Westminster Larger Catechism |
| PCA | Presbyterian Church in America |
| PC (USA) | Presbyterian Church (United States of America) |
| PCUS | Presbyterian Church in the United States |
| OPC | Orthodox Presbyterian Church |
| SC | Westminster Shorter Catechism |
| WCF | Westminster Confession of Faith |

# Introduction: Presbyterian Identity in the Postmodern Age

WHEN YOU THINK ABOUT WHO YOU ARE, what comes to mind? If you are like me, you could come up with a number of descriptors. For example, I am a son, raised in a typical American, upper-middle class family: my parents had two kids; we lived in the suburbs; my dad worked in cities; and my mom stayed at home with us. Because of my dad's work, we moved around a bit, mainly up and down the northeast corridor between New York City and Washington, D. C. (though my marriage license notes that my residency was Los Angeles County, California, when I got married). I am a husband and a father of four children. I am a pastor with a scholarly bent. I am a historian with a pastoral calling. I became a Christian when I was a teen, was a fundamentalist Baptist, but am now a Presbyterian. I am a writer. I am a voracious reader whose favorite authors include Mark Twain and Wendell Berry. I am a gardener. I am a sports fan, cheering mainly for teams from the state of Indiana. My favorite sport is baseball, but I follow all sports fairly closely. I am a fan of Bruce Springsteen and U2, but I also like country and bluegrass music. I prefer trucks over cars or minivans and manual transmissions over automatics. I only buy Fords, but when I follow NASCAR, I cheer for drivers of Chevys, particularly Jeff Gordon.

All of these descriptors hang together in Sean Lucas; together they combine for an identity that is unique to me. Indeed, we could say that my personal identity describes "the real me," my own personality. The way this identity develops, the way I became attached to the various descriptions above, has a lot to do with the way my life has

1

played out and intersected with others' lives. In other words, my *story* and my family's story have a lot to do with who I am and what I consider essential.

In addition to my story, I have done certain things and not others. In fact, certain things I do could almost be considered "rituals" because I do them with such regularity. Part of this, I am sure, has to do with being a guy. My wife and I used to laugh at the way I used to visit the same tollbooth on exit 26 of the Pennsylvania Turnpike (number eight, which was the center booth, and placed me in the proper position to get on US 1 heading north). More important practices for shaping who I am, though, must include the fact that I was an early reader; that I played baseball every spring and summer from age eight to eighteen; that my father generally purchased Fords and my father-in-law works for a Ford subsidiary; that my mom would stay up with me to watch the World Series every year; and that, from the time my parents professed faith in Christ when I was 9 or 10, I've rarely missed a Sunday worship service. Many of these *practices* have continued on with my own children and will shape their own sense of identity as they grow up.

Most important in shaping who I am have been my *beliefs*. I believe that marriage is a divine institution, that I promised to be faithful to my wife, and that divorce is not an option for us. I believe that God is the giver of life in the womb and that children are a blessing from the Lord. I believe that, while all lawful callings are God-ordained, those who desire to be pastors desire a good calling, a calling that is chief among equals, given its importance in the household of God. I believe that history can tell us a lot about who we were, who we are now, and what we ought to do and be in the future. I believe that we hold the creation as a stewardship, that God placed us here to be producers and not simply consumers, and that hard work is good work. Other beliefs are not as important, such as: the greatest and most difficult game invented by humankind is baseball (although golf is a close second on both counts); that I will catch a lot of flack from my family if I ever buy a vehicle other than a Ford; and that people (and sports teams) from Indiana tend to be superior to those from the rest of the nation (as evidenced by my wife). These beliefs lead me to do certain repetitive practices, which in turn reinforce a story about who I am and to whom I belong.

When we say someone is having an "identity crisis," we mean to say that he has become disillusioned or is experiencing dissonance within the core of who he is. Perhaps he is questioning his fundamental beliefs, his core values. Perhaps the practices that defined him are now unfulfilling or have been taken away due to sickness or loss. Perhaps he finds out that the story by which he has lived does not make sense of reality as he now knows it. Whatever the case may be, this individual will begin searching for new beliefs, practices, and stories that will provide him with a stable identity. Not to do so would classify this person as having a "breakdown," leading to some sort of "dementia" (a form of mental insanity in which someone "lies" to himself, as in when someone goes around telling people that he is Superman). The most obvious type of identity crisis is what we call a "mid-life crisis," in which a man who has spent fifteen or twenty years in the work force finds that the beliefs, practices, and stories he had when he was first out of college are no longer sufficient or fulfilling. And so, this individual sometimes buys a fast car, flirts with younger women, or changes careers, all in an effort to find a new identity.

One more thing about identity. Our current "postmodern" age prides itself on promoting fluid identities. In premodern or even early modern societies, identity was created by social relations and family connections (e.g., John, the oldest son to a blacksmith, is raised in the family business in which he provides horseshoes for the village in which he lives; he in turn expects to pass this trade to his son, etc.). However, in the present, due to the mobility of society, the influence of technology, and the loss of family ties even within the "nuclear" family, identities are forged rather than inherited. As a result, postmodernity loudly proclaims that it is possible to create or recreate your identity countless times. Perhaps the best contemporary example of this is the pop singer Madonna, who, over the course of twenty years, has transformed herself from a "boy toy" to a Marilyn Monroe replica to tawdry woman about town to Jewish spiritualist. The

4

result of all of this identity creation is that people no longer hold core beliefs or master stories or shared practices; all that is left are identities that imitate sound-bites and thirty-second commercials, here today and gone tomorrow.

Now, why have I gone on at length about this issue of identity? And what does it have to do with "Presbyterian identity"? Those are fair questions. First, I wanted to describe "identity," because it is one of those words that we use frequently without pausing to think about what we mean. This is particularly true when we talk about "religious identity." But I also want us to begin to see how a particular type of identity is formed, as the confluence of *beliefs*, *practices*, and *stories*. And I needed to alert you to how, in our contemporary situation, this issue of identity is quite conflicted due to the "postmodern turn" of our society.

Above all, I want to suggest in the rest of this book that Presbyterian identity is formed through shared beliefs, practices, and stories. These three things work together to forge what one nineteenth-century Presbyterian theologian called the Presbyterian idiosyncrasies of mind.[1]

## PRESBYTERIAN BELIEFS

By Presbyterian beliefs, I am referring to "doctrine." In fact, sometimes you will hear someone refer to the fact that Presbyterians are "confessional." What we mean by that is that Presbyterian churches summarize their beliefs in confessions of faith. As opposed to those who have a limited statement of faith or those who have a "book of confessions," conservative Presbyterians take the Westminster Confession of Faith very seriously. Perhaps you know that conservative Presbyterian churches require their pastors, ruling elders, and deacons to subscribe to the Westminster Standards, a seventeenth-century document that contains a thirty-three-chapter confession of faith and two catechisms, one "larger" and one "shorter." By "subscribe," we mean that we ask our officers to claim the beliefs of the Standards as their own, as their confession of what they believe the Bible teaches. While our churches do not require church members to affirm the beliefs contained in the Westminster Standards, you should expect the preaching and teaching to conform quite closely to them for the simple reason that the officers have said in good faith that the beliefs contained in those documents are their own.

Of course, a large body of what Presbyterians believe is quite similar to beliefs of other evangelical Protestant churches. For example, conservative Presbyterians, along with other evangelical Protestants, believe in the inspiration and inerrancy of Scripture, the Trinity, and the great doctrines of salvation, such as justification by faith alone, adoption, sanctification, and glorification. We also affirm together the divine-human nature of Jesus Christ, his substitutionary death on the cross, his physical resurrection from the tomb, and his ascension into heaven. All evangelical Protestants believe in the necessity of good works, an organization called the church, the reality of heaven and hell, and Jesus' eventual return in glory. As noted in the preface, that is why I think Presbyterians *are* evangelical, because we hold to the centrality of the gospel, to the way it has transformed our lives, and to a deep desire to have other lives transformed by it as well. We have this gospel in common with all who believe that they are sinners and who are trusting in Christ's blood and righteousness alone for their salvation—that is, with all who are *evangelical*.

It is important to state this simply. Too many who go under the label of "Presbyterian" or "Reformed" doubt whether other evangelicals really believe the gospel because they don't speak it with a Presbyterian accent. Such was the case with one Presbyterian denomination in the 1950s that refused to join a council of churches because its membership included Baptists and others who believed that faith preceded regeneration, rather than the other way around. As a result, these Presbyterians concluded that their evangelical brothers believed a defective gospel and hence may not be brothers after all! Such an attitude is out of bounds. While we might have differing levels of fellowship and intimacy based on theological commonality, still we have to say that all who claim Jesus as Savior and Lord are our brothers and sisters in Christ. We also should want to say that we have a great body of truth in common with all those who are followers of our Lord.

6

That being said, there are several beliefs—several doctrines—that distinguish Presbyterians from other evangelicals. I will be explaining them in part 1. Presbyterians tend to stress five big ideas.

First, we believe in *God's sovereignty*. In other words, God is the King who created all things, governs over every sphere of life, and works together all things for our salvation. When we pray, "Our Father who art in heaven," we are praying to the King (in heaven) whom we have come to know as "our Father." We didn't deserve this relationship—far from it. Rather, this relationship is rooted in God the King's free choice to save. As a result, Presbyterians emphasize *the priority of grace*. God's amazing grace meets our deepest need: we are sinners who need mercy. We don't deserve God's mercy, but God shows it to us supremely in Jesus' death and resurrection on behalf of sinners like us. But God doesn't stop with saving us from his wrath; he also transforms us by his grace so that we more and more bear the image of Jesus. And this grace keeps on working to lead us safely home.

Our individual stories, which God the King is working out in our lives by his grace, connect with his one big story, which he is working out in Scripture and history. That's what we mean, preeminently, when we use the word *covenant*. We want to say that, in Holy Scripture, God is telling us one big story of redemption, focused on one people of God, that starts in the garden of Eden in Genesis and ends in the City of God in Revelation. We sometimes use the term *covenant of grace* to describe this story. There were some differences in the way this story took place in the Old Testament and in the New. The Old Testament, we could say, was a time of promise, and the New Testament is a time of fulfillment. But even with these differences, it is all one story that focuses on one person, Jesus Christ, the Redeemer of God's chosen people, who has inaugurated God's reign on earth—God's kingdom—through his death and resurrection. And this story focuses on God's promise to meet our needs in grace through Jesus Christ—his promise to be our God and for us to be his people. This story of God's unfolding promise leads to the establishment of his reign in this world and among his people, the church.

Presbyterians understand the *nature of the church* a little bit differently from other evangelicals. We describe the church in a number of ways: as a people shaped by the Trinity and by the gospel, but also as a people defined in terms of space, character, and marks. Above all, we rely heavily on the distinction between the church as God sees it and the church as we see it. This gives rise to the language of the "visible" and "invisible" church. As we will see, the distinction is important not only for the way it helps us reckon with a number of thorny pastoral issues—particularly the problem of "apostasy"; it also provides a solid rationale for seeing our children as members of the visible church. Rather than upholding the ideal of "regenerate church membership," like our Baptist brothers and sisters, we believe that the church that we can see, the visible, is made up by professing adults and their children.

Because this is the case, children of professing believers ought to receive the sign of initiation into God's visible people—baptism. That means, of course, that Presbyterians embrace a different view of *the sacraments* from baptistic fellow believers. When it comes to baptism, we believe that God's purposes have centered on households. In Genesis 17, God made promises to Abraham as the head of a household and gave him a covenantal sign—circumcision—that extended to his entire household and sealed those promises to his posterity. In Acts, the same thing is done, except now the covenant sign is baptism: God's promise to grant Abraham's blessings is given to believing heads of households, and the covenantal sign is extended to all the members of the household. Presbyterians also have a different understanding of the Lord's Supper. We believe that, for those who receive the Supper in faith, something *happens*: namely, we enjoy the presence of the Lord himself. This does not happen through a transformation of the bread and wine into something they are not. Rather, it happens through the work of God's Spirit in lifting our eyes and hearts to heaven where Jesus is in his glory. This is probably more than what most evangelical Protestants believe; they tend to think of the Supper as simply a memorial, a time of remembering that Jesus died. We believe that, too; but we also believe that the Supper is more than that.

8

These beliefs don't stand in isolation from the rest of our lives as nice intellectual toys with which to play. Rather, these beliefs shape our practices and in turn are reinforced by those practices. When we talk about practices, what we mean are those repetitious actions through which our beliefs about God and his purpose for us are reinforced. You can think about practices as those activities which you do every day in your line of business. For example, every day when I reach my office, the first thing I do is check my e-mail. If there are any messages to which I need to respond, I do. In the midst of writing a response, the phone might ring. I always answer it the same way: "Hello, this is Sean Lucas." If there is an internal matter that comes up, I use the memo template in my word processing program to crank out my thoughts for others. I try to go down to the seminary library once a week and walk through the serials section, checking to see if there are any new journals in my field. I am sure that in your business, there are practices in which you engage every day as well. My beliefs about what my work should look like shape my practices and my practices reinforce these beliefs.

We can think about religious practices in the same way. Perhaps we can say that there are practices that we use as "we do business" with God and those which we use when "we do business" as the church. In the former, we engage with God through *practices of piety*. What we will find is that these practices of piety are profoundly tied up with corporate worship. The way we experience union and communion with God in Christ by the Spirit is through the preached Word, the sacraments, and prayer. But it does not stop there—we also move toward the world in service for others. We serve not because we can somehow earn favor with God. We serve out of profound gratitude for the grace that we have been shown by God the King. And so, these beliefs intersect with our practices of piety to shape the way we engage and are engaged by God for the sake of the world.

As we think about corporate *worship*, Presbyterians have generally held that worship is to be regulated by Scripture. What that means is one of the hotly debated topics of our day, but at the minimum it must mean that Scripture norms the "elements" of the worship service. In the movement from being called into God's presence to confessing our sins to hearing God's Word and participating in God's sacraments, we participate in the renewal of God's covenant promises and the retelling of God's gospel story. As a result, our beliefs deeply influence the way we worship and are reinforced by our worship practices.

Most of the time in worship, Presbyterians like to do things "decently and in order" (1 Cor. 14:40). But our penchant for orderliness really comes through as we do the business of the church. This brings us to another set of practices, which could be lumped under the heading *church government*. Because God is the King and he rules especially in the church, Presbyterians have thought quite a bit about how God's authority is granted to the church, how it is mediated, and how it is to be used. As a result, we argue that God in Christ is King over the church and he gives elders as gifts to Christ's church to oversee and shepherd his people. These elders are responsible not only for their own local congregations, but for all of the churches in a given geographical area. The elders gather in higher "courts" of the church— such as presbytery and General Assembly—in order to express their care for the work of the whole church.

Another aspect of church government that sets us apart is that we have a document that regulates what we as Presbyterians can and cannot do as churches. This is called the Book of Church Order (usually abbreviated BCO, which you may hear some people pronounce as "Boco"; you'll also find that Presbyterians love acronyms and abbreviations). The BCO regulates everything from the nature of a mission church to the calling of a pastor, from the process for ordination to the process of church discipline, from the resignation of ministers to the dissolution of local churches. As elders, we try very hard in our various meetings to root everything we do in the BCO (the underlying principles of which are, in turn, rooted in the Bible). It is not unusual, when some difficult question is before a session (the local church's body of governing elders) or presbytery, for all of the men present to consult various sections of their own copies of the BCO.

This sets us apart from many evangelical churches that have limited constitutions, which are rarely consulted. It means that we may do things a little slowly and in line with the niceties of parliamentary procedure, but we are all doing the same thing "decently and in order." Even more, these practices reinforce our belief that we are not the kings of the church; rather, God in Christ is the King and he is ruling in our midst through his Word and Spirit. Our practices are informed by our beliefs and our beliefs are reinforced by our practices.

## PRESBYTERIAN STORIES

As a historian, I probably lean toward believing that this may be the most important part of our Presbyterian identity. That, of course, is not true; what we believe is more important than the stories about we who believe(d). Yet the stories that we tell about ourselves provide clues for what beliefs and practices we cherish and why we cherish them. One temptation we must avoid is to conclude that the larger Presbyterian story is unimportant. Because conservative Presbyterians had to leave the old-line Presbyterian Church (USA) to form new denominations, we may think that the *really* important part of the story is that which led to the creation of our own denominations. Not only is this line of thinking terribly naïve, but it also robs us of what is rightfully ours: we are Presbyterians, and we have as much right to stand in the line of Presbyterian teaching and life that goes back to John Calvin, and beyond him to the apostles, as those who belong to the old-line Presbyterian church.

That is why the third part of this book will briefly remind us of the Presbyterian story. This is vitally important for understanding why our churches are the way they are. John Calvin, John Knox, and the Westminster divines—theologians who lived in the sixteenth and seventeenth centuries—directly influence the way things are done in the PCA today. Do you doubt that? Listen to any sermon preached in a PCA church and you will more than likely hear a quote from Calvin or a statement from the Westminster Standards. You will also hear thoughts from Jonathan Edwards, the eighteenth-century sometime

Presbyterian pastor, or Charles Hodge, the nineteenth-century Presbyterian theologian. Not only are old, dead Presbyterians quoted often in the PCA, but their thoughts and conflicts have shaped both the beliefs that the church holds dear and the way in which the church did and does its business of worship and government.

And then, of course, there is the entire story of how conservative Presbyterian denominations came to exist during the last century, through the heroic efforts of ministers like J. Gresham Machen and Robert G. Rayburn in the North and ruling elders like Jack Williamson, Kenneth Keyes, and Bob Cannada in the South. How our churches came into existence influences how we do things today; in the PCA, this is demonstrated in everything from our denominational "askings" from the local churches (instead of per capita taxes) to our belief that congregations control their own property for their own purposes and not for those of the denomination. We will not be able to get into all the ways in which our story shapes who we are today; that will have to await the bigger book to which I referred in the preface. But we will make a few suggestions about this and, hopefully, you will be able to think about others in your own context.

It is my prayer that this book will help to explain to you what being Presbyterian is all about—what beliefs move us, what practices shape us, what stories we tell about ourselves. In the end, the most important thing is not that your identity is Presbyterian, but that your identity is shaped by Jesus Christ. For if you put your wholehearted faith in Jesus, you are united to him and receive all the benefits of salvation: you are declared right with God, you are adopted into his family, you are set apart and are made holy in God's sight, and you are glorified. This union with Christ is spiritual, mystical, real, and inseparable—it marks you with a *Christian* identity, as belonging to God the King by his amazing grace. It places you in the unfolding story of God's people of promise, stretching back through the history of the church to the story of Israel. It points you forward to God's reign finally manifested fully on earth at the end of the age. And it places you in God's blood-bought people, the church. That identity—believer united to Jesus Christ—is the most important; and if that identity is not yours, then you should speak with a friend, loved one, or pastor who can show you from Scripture how to enter into right relationship with God through faith in Jesus. You will begin a journey of faith that I hope will lead you to walk with faithful Presbyterians around the world and in your own neighborhood for God's glory.

# PART ONE

# »Presbyterian Beliefs

# CHAPTER 1

# God Is King:
# The Sovereignty of God

WHEN YOU THINK ABOUT THE PHRASE "God's sovereignty,"
what comes to mind? I asked this question of a Sunday school class
recently and got a number of solid answers: omnipotence and
omnipresence; maker and master planner; total and absolute control;
comforting presence. All of these answers hit at significant aspects of
the idea. However, I would suggest that we could sum up all of these
by thinking about the word *sovereignty* itself. After all, the word
derives from *sovereign*, which can denote a person who exercises
supreme, permanent authority. To put it simply, when we talk about
God as sovereign, we mean that God is King.

Our God is more than *a* king. Rather, our God is *the* King, the
supreme King who created all things, rules and directs all things
to their proper ends, and exercises his will supremely in every area
of life. There are many places in Scripture that articulate this vision
of God as the King, but one of the best is Daniel 4. In many ways,
this is a strange chapter in Daniel; it presents itself as a kind of
affidavit from Nebuchadnezzar, ruler of Babylon and conqueror
of Israel and Judah. Nebuchadnezzar has a dream, which Daniel
interprets for him. In the dream, God tells the king that though
Nebuchadnezzar was great and his kingdom extended throughout the "known world," he would be humbled until he learned
"that the Most High rules the kingdom of men and gives it to

whom he will" (Dan. 4:25). A year after this dream, Nebuchad-nezzar boasts in his own heart over his kingdom; immediately, a voice from heaven rearticulates what Daniel had told him. The king loses his reason, is driven from other men to live with field animals, and is made to eat grass like an ox; his hair and finger-nails grow long and animal-like; and he is humbled. Finally, the king "lifted [his] eyes to heaven, and [his] reason returned to [him]" and this is what he confessed:

I blessed the Most High, and praised and honored him who lives forever,

for his dominion is an everlasting dominion,
and his kingdom endures from generation to generation;
all the inhabitants of the earth are accounted as nothing,
and he does according to his will among the host of heaven
and among the inhabitants of the earth;
and none can stay his hand
or say to him, "What have you done?" (Dan. 4:34–35)

God the King stands over all other kings of this world; his will is supreme and no human can contradict or challenge his desires. One hymn text puts it this way:

O Father, you are sovereign
in all the worlds you made;
your mighty word was spoken
and light and life obeyed.
Your voice commands the seasons
and bounds the ocean's shore,
sets stars within their courses
and stills the tempest's roar.

O Father, you are sovereign
in all affairs of man;
no pow'rs of death or darkness
can thwart your perfect plan.

All chance and change transcending,
    supreme in time and space,
you hold your trusting children
    secure in your embrace.

O Father, you are sovereign,
    the Lord of human pain,
transmuting earthly sorrows
    to gold of heav'nly gain.
All evil overruling,
    as none but Conqu'ror could,
your love pursues its purpose—
    our souls' eternal good.

O Father, you are sovereign!
    We see you dimly now,
but soon before your triumph
    earth's every knee shall bow.
With this glad hope before us
    our faith springs up anew:
our sovereign Lord and Savior,
    we trust and worship you![1]

As this hymn teaches us, God is the King over his creation. He brought the worlds into existence by his powerful word and as the Creator has rightful claim to the creation's obedience. God is also the King over every sphere of life. He guides and directs both the macro-story—the movement of human history—and our micro-stories—each of our individual lives; everything happens in accordance with his plan. Even the pain we feel and the sorrows we know come under the King's rule. Finally, God is the King over human salvation. God the King is unfolding a story, a plan, that involves the salvation of a people for his own glory and that focuses attention on the God-Man, Jesus.

This belief that God is the King raises some difficulties; we will treat these briefly in the proper place later in this chapter. However, perhaps the greatest difficulty is existential: the way we feel about God's

rule over every part of our lives. Even Protestant saints like Jonathan
Edwards struggled existentially with the reality that God is the King.
In a narrative of his conversion meant to encourage his son-in-law,
Aaron Burr Sr., Edwards reflected on how he had long objected to the
doctrine of God's sovereignty; in fact, he said that "it used to appear
like a horrible doctrine to me." Yet there came a time when he was
convinced that this belief was biblical and, hence, true. Edwards was
never able to give an explanation for it, save for the "extraordinary
influence of God's Spirit." Yet his mind was able to "rest in it" to such
a degree that this belief became "a *delightful* conviction." Edwards
would go on to claim that "the doctrine of God's sovereignty has very
often appeared, an exceeding pleasant, bright and sweet doctrine to
me: and absolute sovereignty is what I love to ascribe to God."[2] Even
someone like Edwards struggled to understand how God could be the
King; this was not only an intellectual struggle but a profoundly *personal* one. It points up to us, I think, that this belief that God is the
King is just that: a *belief* toward which we will not necessarily reason
our way. Rather, it is a belief in which we must rest.

## GOD IS THE KING OVER HIS CREATION

From the very beginning of time, God the King has been working out a story, one that focuses on manifesting his glory in his creation. Ephesians 1 tells us that God "chose us in [Christ] before
the foundation of the world" and that this was "according to the
purpose of him who works all things according to the counsel of
his will" (1:3, 11). Because of passages such as these, Presbyterians believe that "God from all eternity did, by the most wise and
holy counsel of his own will, freely, and unchangeably ordain what-
soever comes to pass" (WCF 3.1). Right from the get-go, the issue
of God's kingship over all his creatures and all their actions is
joined (WCF 5.1). Is God truly sovereign from the beginning of
time or is he not? Is God the one who began and who is directing
human history, or are some other forces in charge?

That issue becomes particularly pressing when we talk about creation. As Presbyterians, we confess that "it pleased God the Father, Son, and Holy Ghost, for the manifestation of the glory of his eternal power, wisdom, and goodness, in the beginning, to create, or make of nothing, the world, and all things therein whether visible or invisible, in the space of six days; and all very good" (WCF 4.1). When we confess this, we mean several things. First, we believe that God the King created all things in the world out of nothing. God spoke all creation into being by the power of his Word and Spirit (Gen. 1:1–3; John 1:3; Heb. 1:3). Next, we also believe that God the King created for his own glory. In creation, God highlights his power, wisdom, and goodness (Rom. 1:20; Ps. 19:1). Third, we mean that God the King *was* before anything else was. Before time began, God was; in fact, God is the one who created time as well as matter. As a result, God does not depend upon his creation; rather, God's creation depends upon him. Finally, we can say that, because God the King created, he has ownership over his creation (Ps. 24:1–2). God has rights over his creation in the same way that a painter has ownership rights over a piece of art or an author has ownership rights over his manuscript.

All of these points argue that God the Creator is King over his creation; God is the "Sovereign Lord who made the heaven, and the earth and the sea and everything in them" (Acts 4:24). As creatures, we are dependent upon God and distinct from him. Even when we pretend to live our lives independently from God and ignore his will, still God is our King and his will is our law. All humankind is responsible to God and will be judged by God; this is right because God is the Creator and King over humankind. The apostle Paul makes the point that Gentiles, who did not have the written law of God, "show that the work of the law is written on their hearts, while their conscience also bears witness, and their conflicting thoughts accuse or even excuse them on that day when, according to my gospel, God judges the secrets of men by Christ Jesus" (Rom. 2:15–16). The upshot of God's sovereignty over his creation is that he is both King and Judge over it.

## GOD IS THE KING OVER EVERY SPHERE OF LIFE

The question that might arise from believing that God is the King over his creation is whether or not God the King continues his involvement with it. Is God the blind watchmaker, who, having once created the world and its laws, then leaves it to run on its own? Or does God involve himself directly in the day-to-day movements of his creation?

Presbyterians believe that, in fact, God continues to exercise his role over every sphere of life. One of the ways we typically express this belief is through the idea of *providence*. We confess that

> God the great Creator of all things doth uphold, direct, dispose, and govern all creatures, actions, and things, from the greatest even to the least, by his most wise and holy providence, according to his infallible foreknowledge and the free and immutable counsel of his own will, to the praise of the glory of his wisdom, power, justice, goodness, and mercy. (WCF 5.1)

In other words, we believe that God the King is bound to and involved with his creation. The fancy theological words here are *transcendence* and *immanence*. We do believe that God is not like his creation; he is "holy" and "wholly" other; he is *transcendent*. But we also earnestly believe that God loves his creation and is near to it; he is intimately involved with it, guiding its affairs and governing his creatures; he is *immanent*. We want to say that providence has to do with four types or categories of divine activity: upholding, directing, disposing, and governing. God the King is *upholding* "the universe by the word of his power" (Heb. 1:3) in such a way that, if he were to stop doing so, the world would cease to exist. Another way of putting this is that "in him all things hold together"; in a way that we don't really grasp, God in Christ is sustaining the world so that we live and move and have our being "in him" (Col. 1:17; Acts 17:28).

God the King is also *directing* the events of human history. Most importantly, God orchestrated human history so that "when the fullness of time had come, God sent forth his Son" (Gal. 4:4). All of ancient history led up to the moment of the incarnation of Jesus Christ: the preservation of the Messianic line, the administration of the old covenant and Jewish kingdom, the movement of world powers to return the Jews to Palestine, even the call for the worldwide census that brought Mary and Joseph to Bethlehem from their native Nazareth—each event was part of God's directing of human affairs. God the King continues to fit together his larger story of salvation with our smaller life-stories in such a way that it is a grand mosaic proclaiming his glory.

Further, God the King *disposed* events to turn out a certain way in line with his perfect and secret plan. God disposed that it would be Isaac, not Ishmael; Jacob, not Esau; Moses, not Aaron who would uniquely lead his people. God disposed that Pharaoh would react in certain ways so that God would demonstrate that he alone was the true God (Ex. 4:21). In ways that we cannot fully understand, God even disposed that Adam would sin in the garden of Eden and thus begin the entire story of redemption (WCF 5.4).

Finally, God the King *governs* human beings and their actions. We can say this because Presbyterians claim that no part of God's creation is exempt from God's providence. It is not as though Pharaoh was under God's control, but Adam was not; or Cyrus was under God's control, but Augustus Caesar was not. *All* of God's creatures are under his control. Even inanimate objects and forces are under God's control. David sang about this in Psalm 68:

> O God, when you went out before your people,
>     when you marched through the wilderness,
> the earth quaked, the heavens poured down rain,
>     before God, the One of Sinai,
>     before God, the God of Israel.
> Rain in abundance, O God, you shed abroad;
>     you restored your inheritance as it languished;
> your flock found a dwelling in it;
>     in your goodness, O God, you provided for the needy.
>         (Ps. 68:7–10)

God was the one who caused the rain to replenish the land and to provide for the flocks; he is the one who controls the storms and the droughts of life. Nothing stands outside God's control.

This providential activity on God the King's part is rooted in his unerring foreknowledge and irreversible purpose. God's foreknowledge is not merely his looking down the corridor of time and seeing that something is going to happen. Rather, God's foreknowledge implies God's foreordination—God knows something is going to happen because he is the one who has determined such a thing will happen (Rom. 9:11). This foreknowledge is both exhaustive and unerring. There is simply nothing in human existence that takes God by surprise because God has purposed irreversibly that such an event would happen. As difficult as it is for us to understand, the evil that happens in our world is under God's control. Immediately, Joseph's words to his brothers should come to mind: "As for you, you meant evil against me, but God meant it for good, to bring it about that many people should be kept alive, as they are today" (Gen. 50:20). In the same way, the central day in the Christian faith is one we call "Good Friday," a day in which an unmistakably evil action was used for God's glorious good purpose of saving his own. Peter himself noted this in his Pentecost sermon: "This Jesus, delivered up according to the definite plan and foreknowledge of God, you crucified and killed by the hands of lawless men" (Acts 2:23). Peter did not let the religious leaders off the hook—they had certainly done evil in crucifying the Lord of Glory; yet this happened in accordance with God's plan. And God was able to use this unmistakably evil act to bring about the ultimate good: the redemption of God's people.

One of the difficulties with understanding providence is relating God the King's governance of all things with responsible human agency. If God is sovereign, then in what sense are human actions free and, hence, morally accountable? In order to get at this, we have to step back to reaffirm that God's kingship over all his creatures is all-inclusive. Human beings cannot limit God's authority or his freedom. But even more, God's kingly authority *establishes* human existence and, hence, human choice. When God created human beings and granted them dominion over the rest of creation, he delegated to them his authority to make decisions about creation. That delegated authority or rule did not come to an end with the fall of Adam and Eve; humans still have the authority to make those decisions and choices and to exercise rule (Ps. 8:6). Now, though, human beings must deal with an additional factor—the corruption communicated to us by virtue of our first parents' sin. Hence, our minds are clouded by sin and our wills are bound by our own sinful self-interest. As a result, when humans make choices, not only are they limited by God's prior delegation of authority and by his sovereign administration of his creation, but they are also limited by their own sinfulness.

There are some very practical implications that result from this broad understanding that God is King over every sphere of life. One thing we would want to say is that human history has both purpose and direction. This is certainly true for the big story that God is working out. God is guiding human history to a specific goal: the full and final salvation and liberation of his people and his creation (Rom. 8:18–30). But it is also true for our smaller stories. Events that happen to us are not purposeless, but full of meaning, granted to us from the hand of God. As a pastor friend of mine, David Dively, has well said, "God has made this moment for me and me for an eternity of these moments." This is the case because our smaller stories are knit together by God into his larger purpose and plan to bring about glory.

Because this is God's story, nothing happens to us by luck or chance. Indeed, one of the sins forbidden in the first commandment is "ascribing the praise of any good we either are, have, or can do, to fortune, idols, ourselves, or any other creature" (LC 105). Rather, we have the faith of the hymn writer:

> Whate'er my God ordains is right:
>     his holy will abideth;
> I will be still whate'er he doth,
>     and follow where he guideth.

He is my God; though dark my road,
    he holds me that I shall not fall:
wherefore to him I leave it all.

Whate'er my God ordains is right:
    he never will deceive me;
he leads me by the proper path;
    I know he will not leave me.
I take, content, what he hath sent;
    his hand can turn my griefs away,
and patiently I wait his day.

Whate'er my God ordains is right:
    though now this cup, in drinking,
may bitter seem to my faint heart,
    I take it, all unshrinking.
My God is true; each morn anew
    sweet comfort yet shall fill my heart,
and pain and sorrow shall depart.

Whate'er my God ordains is right:
    here shall my stand be taken;
though sorrow, need, or death be mine,
    yet I am not forsaken.
My Father's care is round me there;
    he holds me that I shall not fall:
and so to him I leave it all.[3]

Our loving God and Father so directs our paths that, though our road be dark, he upholds us. We can trust that the path on which he places us is the proper one, and so we can be content in his providential leading. And our only hope is in his comfort, mediated by the Spirit and the Word, reminding us that God's care will never leave us nor forsake us. Human history has a purpose and direction: it will result ultimately in the full and final salvation of us and of the church as a whole.

Although God the King is directing our stories and his larger story for his own glory, it may not be clear to our human eyes what God is doing in the daily events of our lives or in the broader sweep of history. As God told Israel when the people prepared to enter the Promised Land: "The secret things belong to the Lord our God, but the things that are revealed belong to us and to our children forever, that we may do all the words of this law" (Deut. 29:29). It may be difficult to understand what God is doing in our lives; we may wonder whether God has a purpose in it all. We can rest certain that he does, but we may not be able to discern what that purpose is in this life. The same goes for understanding what God is doing in the larger sweep of contemporary events and recent history. It is very tempting for us to think that we can say what God meant in a particular war or in allowing the rise of a particular world leader. Stephen J. Nichols, a theologian friend of mine, once wrote a brilliant essay on the folly of attempting to name the Antichrist. Surveying church history from the early church forward, Nichols cataloged the many different suggestions that biblical students have made for who the Antichrist was, ranging from Constantine to the Pope to Ronald Reagan! Even when it comes to the study of history, some advocate a kind of "providential history" in which religious figures are divided up into righteous and unrighteous teams and the effects of their actions are granted theological significance. To be sure, we must seek to understand human motivations in the writing of history. But identifying certain events (ones we like) as "the work of God" while failing to recognize other events (ones we don't like) as being equally God's work ironically represents a significant misunderstanding of God's providence. All of life is under God's control; all of it is for the praise of his glory; but the *hows* and the *whys* may be harder to grasp in this age.

Finally, because God the King is governing every aspect of our lives, our daily work and callings are granted great significance. Our callings, our "vocations," *are* the way God exerts his rule in this world. As a result, whether you are a housewife, a lawyer, a teacher, or a minister, what you do is vitally important in God's scheme of things. You are extending God's rule wherever you are, for you are a child and an agent of God the King. Some Presbyterians argue that this means God's rule must be extended to every sphere of human existence, such as science, art, or politics. Abraham Kuyper, a Dutch Reformed theologian who founded the Free University of Amsterdam and eventually served as Prime Minister of the Netherlands, held that Presbyterian beliefs (summed up under the heading of Calvinism, after their most prominent developer, John Calvin) provided a worldview that could alone grant a coherent rationale for human endeavor. Kuyper famously expressed his belief in God's kingship over the world by proclaiming, "There is not a square inch in the whole domain of our human existence over which Christ, who is Sovereign over all, does not cry: 'Mine!' "[4] He also claimed that God's sovereignty had to be expressed by "a *Science* which will not rest until it has thought out the entire cosmos; a *Religion* which cannot sit still until she has permeated every sphere of human life; and so also there must be an *Art* which, despising no single department of life adopts, into her splendid world, the whole of human life, religion included."[5] Kuyper suggested that Presbyterian and Reformed believers could construct a coherent "world and life view" that approached every sphere of knowledge from the standpoint of God's kingship and law. This understanding has led many Presbyterians to pursue their vocations under God's direction, seeking to extend his reign in every sphere of life.

## GOD IS THE KING OVER HUMAN SALVATION

There is one further question that might come to mind: If God the King governs every aspect of our lives, does he also direct our stories of salvation? This is where the rubber often hits the road, for when most people talk about God's sovereignty, they particularly refer to God's right as King to save whom he will in the way he wills. The whole complex of theological words for this point—*predestination, election, foreordination*—serves as an important identity marker between Presbyterians and many other evangelicals. And yet, the truth that God is the King over human salvation flows naturally from what we have already seen: if God is the King over his creation, having ownership rights over what he has made; and if God is the King over every sphere of life, upholding, directing, disposing, and governing all his creatures and all their actions; then does it not follow that God demonstrates the fact he is King over his creatures by saving whomever he desires to save?

As we have already noticed, all human beings since the fall start their lives in rebellion against God. From the time of our first parents, Adam and Eve, humans have sought to live independently of God, making their own evaluations of what is good and evil. Because of this rebellion, God could rightfully damn all humans to experience his eternal wrath and justice. No one deserves salvation. The fact that anyone experiences mercy is solely because of God's grace. Not only this, but as the result of the fall, our wills are bent away from serving God. As Paul put it so memorably in Romans:

> None is righteous, no, not one;
>     no one understands;
>         no one seeks for God. (Rom. 3:10, quoting Ps. 14)

Because no one seeks after God, and because our wills are set against God, someone outside of us needs to intervene if we are to receive divine mercy and forgiveness.

That is why Presbyterians confess that

> those of mankind that are predestinated unto life, God, before the foundation of the world was laid, according to his eternal and immutable purpose, and the secret counsel and good pleasure of his will, hath chosen, in Christ, unto everlasting glory, out of his mere free grace and love, without any foresight of faith or good works, or perseverance in either of them, or any other thing in the creature, as conditions, or causes moving him thereunto: and all to the praise of his glorious grace. (WCF 3.5)

Now, that section of the Westminster Confession of Faith sounds like it was written by a lawyer. Let's see if we can break it down into more manageable ideas. The key thought is that God the King has chosen in Christ those whom he will save for his own glory. Everything else is descriptive of the way in which God the King chose: he did it before the foundation of the world; he chose according to his own irreversible purpose and his own good pleasure; he did this out of his freedom, not because of any obligation placed upon him by the creature; and this choosing has as its end goal the praise of God's glorious grace.

Another way of putting this might be that God the King has chosen us out of his own freedom and for his own purposes. The apostle Paul, in 2 Timothy 1:8–9, made this point: "Therefore do not be ashamed of the testimony about our Lord, nor of me his prisoner, but share in suffering for the gospel by the power of God, who saved us and called us to a holy calling, *not because of our works, but because of his own purpose and grace, which he gave us in Christ Jesus before the world began*" (emphasis added). Here we have many of the components of God's sovereignty in our salvation: God did the choosing in Christ out of his own freedom before the world began and not because we placed God under obligation by our works. Another straightforward place where the Bible speaks to this is Romans 8:29–30, where Paul writes that "those whom he foreknew he also predestined to be conformed to the image of his Son, in order that he might be the firstborn among many brothers. And those whom he predestined he also called, and those whom he called he also justified, and those whom he justified he also glorified." Each of these texts claims that God is King over our salvation—he is the one who chooses us and he does so out of his own freedom.

Even further, God the King takes all the steps necessary for our salvation. As we confess, he has "foreordained all the means thereunto" (WCF 3.6). He was the one who secured the salvation of his people by sending Jesus to die on the cross and to rise on the third day from the tomb. He was the one who caused us to be born in a certain place and time. He was the one who brought us into contact with the gospel at the right time. He was the one who poured out the Holy Spirit to use his Word to call us effectively to faith in Jesus. He is the one who grants us every spiritual blessing in Jesus: justification, adoption, sanctification, and the promise of glorification. If God did not do these things, no one would be saved. Truly, as the apostle John points out, "We love because he first loved us" (1 John 4:19).

There are those who claim that Presbyterians cannot share the gospel effectively with their neighbors because no one can know whom God has chosen. But when you think about it, this is a weak objection, because the same sovereign God who chose to save also chose the way in which to save—by neighbors sharing the gospel with their neighbors, parents teaching the gospel to their children, pastors preaching the gospel to their congregations, missionaries declaring the gospel to people groups who have never heard it. That is what the Great Commission is all about: as you go through life, make disciples. Another reason this objection does not hold weight is that, though God knows whom he has chosen, we do not. Therefore, we are called to share the gospel without distinction and with everyone we meet. The apostle Paul, on Mars Hill, declared that "the times of ignorance God overlooked, but now he commands all people everywhere to repent, because he has fixed a day on which he will judge the world in righteousness by a man whom he has appointed" (Acts 17:30–31). This was Paul's message everywhere he went, in the synagogue and in the marketplace, on Mars Hill and on the Temple mount. He didn't try to discern who the "elect" were; rather, he preached the gospel to all, believing that God was calling out his own in every group of people.

To be sure, sometimes our friends get themselves wrapped around the axle trying to sort out how predestination "works." We confess that "the doctrine of this high mystery of predestination is to be handled with special prudence and care" (WCF 3.8). Sometimes people have shipwrecked their faith because they have not been able to figure out whether their dying neighbor or their co-workers were elect. Again, this misses the point. The identities of those who were chosen before the foundation of the world are known only to *God*; what *we* know is this: "Believe in the Lord Jesus and you will be saved" (Acts 16:31). Further, the belief that God is King in matters relating to our salvation is not meant to lead us to despair, but to assure our hearts. It should lead us to rejoicing. That is certainly the way Paul uses it in

Romans 8. Writing to believers who were experiencing the deep "suffering of this present time," Paul tells them that nothing can separate them from God's love, nothing can turn God against them (8:18, 31). Why? Because, Paul writes, those whom he foreknew he also called, justified, and glorified (8:29–30). As a result, we can rejoice in the "the love of God in Christ Jesus our Lord"—in him, we are more than conquerors (8:37–39).

Our rejoicing is rooted in an understanding that God as King does not *have* to save us. We, God's creation, have rebelled against God; we seek to live independently from him; we do not seek God at all. But God sought us, sent his Son to die for us, and grants us his Spirit to turn our wills toward God. As Isaac Watts put it:

> How sweet and awesome is the place
>     with Christ within the doors,
> while everlasting love displays
>     the choicest of her stores.
>
> While all our hearts and all our songs
>     join to admire the feast,
> each of us cries with thankful tongue,
>     "Lord, why was I a guest?"
>
> "Why was I made to hear your voice,
>     and enter while there's room,
> when thousands make a wretched choice,
>     and rather starve than come?"
>
> 'Twas the same love that spread the feast
>     that sweetly drew us in;
> else we had still refused to taste,
>     and perished in our sin.[6]

Our salvation is not due to our own goodness or our own ability. Our salvation is solely the result of God's mercy. This is undeserved favor—this is *grace*. And it is grace rooted in God's actions as King over his creation, working his will in providence and redemption.

## »Questions for Thought and Review

1. Was there ever a time when you struggled with the belief that God is the King? What was the turning point in seeing this as a "delightful conviction"?

2. All evangelicals affirm that God created all things visible and invisible, but probably most have not thought about the implications to which this affirmation leads. How do the affirmations about God's independence from his creation and his ownership over creation confirm or challenge your views of God?

3. Do you feel at times that God is distant from his creation? How does the affirmation of God's providence comfort you in the midst of pain and struggle?

4. Why is the affirmation that "nothing stands outside God's control" important? If there were people or forces outside God's control, what would that do to your view of God?

5. How does "Good Friday" challenge your view of God's control of evil? If God planned to bring the ultimate good out of such terrible evil, how does that challenge our understanding of the evil of our lives?

6. This chapter says that "God's kingly authority establishes human existence and, hence, human choice." How does this understanding revise the typical confusion over God's sovereignty and human responsibility? If God did not establish human existence, how would humans make meaningful choices?

7. How does the Presbyterian commitment to God's providential control over life provide us with confidence, assurance, and meaning as we look at our lives and human history? How do we relate our confidence that God is in control over all events in our lives with our inability to discern necessarily God's intent in these events?

32

8. In what ways do God's rights as King in your salvation encourage you in God's grace? How does this strengthen your assurance in God's care for you?
9. How would you answer a friend who claimed that Presbyterians cannot share the gospel effectively with their neighbors because no one can know whom God has chosen?

## »For Further Reading

Boettner, Loraine. *The Reformed Doctrine of Predestination*. Philadelphia: Presbyterian and Reformed, 1966.
Edgar, William. *Truth in All Its Glory: Commending the Reformed Faith*. Phillipsburg, N.J.: P&R, 2004.
Helm, Paul. *The Providence of God*. Downers Grove, Ill.: InterVarsity Press, 1994.
Kuyper, Abraham. *Lectures on Calvinism*. Grand Rapids, Mich.: Eerdmans, 1948.
Murray, John. *The Free Offer of the Gospel*. Phillipsburg, N.J.: L. J. Grotenhuis, n.d.
Sproul, R. C. *Chosen By God*. Wheaton, Ill.: Tyndale, 1994.

# CHAPTER 2

# The Priority of Amazing Grace

IT IS NOT A STRETCH TO CLAIM THAT "Amazing Grace" is the most familiar hymn to Anglo-Americans. Music critic and historian Steve Turner told the song's story in his book *Amazing Grace: The Story of America's Most Beloved Song*. Turner pointed out that during the period of national mourning after September 11, 2001, the hymn appeared to be everywhere. "One of the most poignant images of the shock and grief," he wrote, "was that of people of all ages joining hands or linking arms and softly singing the words." Throughout that time, the song appeared at funerals, church gatherings, tribute concerts, and other venues. For a nation grieving, the attempt to remember God's grace in the face of tragedy was a necessary and important step.

This does not mean that everyone necessarily understands what *grace* means. Peter Jennings, the ABC news anchor, observed during President Reagan's 2004 funeral that the hymn "Amazing Grace" was appropriate because it spoke of one who had been low and ended up victorious against all odds. Others have shared similar sentiments. Judy Collins, whose 1971 version of the hymn was a chart topper, claimed that the song was "about letting go, bottoming out, seeing the light, turning it over, trusting the universe, breathing in, breathing out, going with the flow." Joan Baez, another 1960s performer who sang the hymn, thought that grace was "the loveliest way to say a form of enlightenment or a form of real gratitude, of giving." Grace in this secular understanding is tied to self-improvement that comes through an enlightened understanding that works with the forces of this world. As Collins put it, "We're always in the path of this power and my own feeling is that agnostics, atheists, spiritual people, and devoted churchgoers alike all have the same experience because it is talking about forces unseen which are always around us."

But these secular understandings seem to be far away from the Christian notions of grace as summarized in the famous hymn. Bono, lead singer of the supergroup U2, points this out when he says: "It's a powerful idea, grace. It really is. We hear so much of karma and so little of grace. Every religion teaches about karma and what you put out you will receive. And even Christianity, which is supposed to be about grace, has turned redemption into good manners, or the right accent, or good works, or whatever. I just can't get over grace." John Newton's hymn text does not speak about one who is "low," but a wretch, one who was lost and blind, fearful, experiencing dangers, toils, and snares. And salvation comes not through any amount of self-effort or self-enlightenment, but is rooted in God's promise, originating in his own good pleasure and extrinsic to one's own abilities or worth.[1]

Grace is more than effort or enlightenment, good works or good karma. It isn't something we do or earn. Grace is shown to us and done for us by someone outside of us. We don't deserve grace; it is a gift. As a result, a biblical understanding of grace is tied into what we have already considered: God the King's working to save a people for his own glory. Such salvation is completely undeserved—"while we were still sinners, Christ died for us" (Rom. 5:8). Indeed, while the acronym of grace that speaks of "God's Riches At Christ's Expense" may seem a little hokey, it expresses something fundamental—salvation does not belong to us by right or self-effort; rather, salvation is granted to us only out of God's mere good pleasure, his undeserved favor. Even more, salvation does not come through enlightenment or "going with the flow." It is rooted in God's self-revelation in Jesus Christ, who came to this world and lived the perfect life that we could not live, died a death that satisfied God's wrath, and was raised again to justify sinners. By faith alone in Jesus, we are saved from God's wrath—which we fully deserve—and we are granted all the riches of Christ's benefits—which we plainly do not deserve. And this glorious exchange is the crowning example of God's undeserved favor toward sinners like us.

In this chapter, I would like to explore the biblical meaning of grace as Presbyterians understand it. In order to help us think this through, we will be guided by John Newton's most famous hymn. When Presbyterians meditate on what grace means, we believe that grace meets our needs. Certainly, God's grace satisfies our most "basic" need: salvation from sin, death, and wrath. But God's grace is shown to all humankind in general: it sustains life by ensuring the regular operation of nature and by motivating us to be creative. We also confess that grace transforms us from the inside out. We are not saved by grace and made pure by works—rather, it is all of grace, from beginning to end. Finally, we cling to the hope that God's grace will lead us home to know fully the glory of God's presence.

## GRACE MEETS OUR NEEDS

Amazing grace!—how sweet the sound—
    that saved a wretch like me!
I once was lost, but now am found,
    was blind, but now I see.

'Twas grace that taught my heart to fear,
    and grace my fears relieved;
how precious did that grace appear
    the hour I first believed![2]

The amazing-ness of grace is deeply rooted in the fact that we are sinners who deserve God's wrath. Think about texts like Ephesians 2: there Paul tells us that we are "dead" and we manifest this death by "following the course of this world," living according to its dictates and satisfying "the desires of the body and the mind." As a result, we are "by nature children of wrath": we are those who deserve the full justice of God. Why? Because all of our sin is ultimately against God the King (Ps. 51:4), and the King has the right and the necessity to execute justice in order to uphold his rule. Hence, what we sing is really true: we are "wretches," "lost," and "blind."

Yet God did not leave us under his wrath. Ephesians 2:4 turns everything around with the glorious word "but," as in: "*But* God, being rich in mercy, because of the great love with which he loved us, even when we were dead in our trespasses, made us alive together with Christ." The renowned preacher and teacher Martyn Lloyd-Jones once remarked that the little word "but" is the greatest word in all of the Bible, for it signals the turn from God's wrath to God's mercy and grace. What did we deserve? Wrath. What do we receive? Undeserved mercy. What is this called? Grace. And so, we who were once lost are now found, we who were once blind can now see. And we owe this undeserved mercy completely to the free choice of God our King. That, in a nutshell, is the glorious, the amazing, the indescribable nature of grace.

Now, in our effort to preserve the grace-centered nature of Christianity, Presbyterians have often referred to many of our foundational beliefs as "doctrines of grace." These doctrines specifically refer to what have come to be known as the "five points of Calvinism." Ironically, the so-called "five points" were originally a response articulated by the Dutch Synod of Dort in 1618 to the "Remonstrants," a group of theologians originally led by James Arminius, who protested (or remonstrated, hence the name) the dominant religious teaching in the Dutch universities and churches. The Remonstrants offered statements on five key areas where they believed the mainstream Calvinist teaching to be inaccurate. They contended that:

- God's choice of human beings was conditioned by their foreseen faith;
- human depravity was mitigated by God's grace, which was extended to all human beings to enable them to believe;
- this grace could be resisted by some men and women, resulting in their damnation;
- it was possible for some believers to sin and to lose God's grace;
- God's grace was extended to *all* because Jesus had died for every individual human being.

In response to these teachings, the Synod of Dort condemned "Arminianism" (named after the teacher of these beliefs) and set forth a document with five parts. These five parts have been boiled down to "five points" that typically get remembered under the acronym TULIP (which is appropriate, since that is a Dutch flower!): *T*otal depravity, *U*nconditional election, *L*imited atonement, *I*rresistible grace, and *P*erseverance of the saints. When people think of "Calvinism"—a summary of Presbyterian beliefs—they typically think about these five points. While there is much more to Presbyterian beliefs than these five points, they are a helpful summary of our understanding of God's grace demonstrated in his redeeming us from our sin. Let's look at each one of these beliefs.

*Total depravity.* This belief does not mean that human beings are as bad as they could be. Rather, it means that we are corrupted both at our cores and through and through. Even the apparent good we do is tainted to a greater or lesser degree by sinful motivations. Not only this, but we also confess that "we are utterly indisposed, disabled, and made opposite to all good, and wholly inclined to all evil" (WCF 6.4). Our minds, hearts, and wills are bent toward our own desires, appraised apart from God's will and evaluated for their own utility for advancing ourselves. When it comes to spiritual things—to glorifying God and enjoying him forever, as our catechism says—we are incapable. As we saw in Ephesians 2, we are not ill, very ill, or dying; we are *dead*. We are unable to turn to God because we are corrupted in our very being, alienated from God and turned toward our own selfish, sinful desires.

*Unconditional election.* As we have already seen, if humans are to be saved from deserved wrath, God would have to be merciful. And so, God the King chose a people for himself to be saved (Ex. 19:5–6; 1 Peter 2:9–10). This choice was made out of God's own freedom. It was not conditioned on anything that God saw in you or me—our qualifications to be saved, our future faith or obedience or ministry. God's choice was contingent on nothing save God's own good pleasure as King (Eph. 1:3–10).

*Limited atonement.* Not only did God choose a people to be saved, but he secured their salvation by sending Jesus to die a sinner's death in their place. Hence, Jesus' atonement was "limited" in its *intent*—it was intended for God's chosen people. That is why it is probably better to talk about a definite or particular atonement, rather than a "limited" one: Jesus died for a particular people, namely, the people that God had chosen. As theologians Robert Peterson and Michael Williams argue well:

> We believe in particular substitutionary atonement because Scripture implies it when it speaks of Father, Son, and Spirit working harmoniously to save the people of God (Eph. 1:3–14; John 17:2, 9, 9–10, 19, 24; cf. 1 Pet. 1:1–2). We hold to definite atonement because sometimes when the Bible speaks of Christ's saving death, it excludes some persons (John 10:11, 15, 26; 17:2, 9, 19). We teach limited atonement because Scripture describes the cross as effective, not making salvation possible for all, but actually securing salvation for multitudes (Rev. 5:9; cf. 1 Pet. 1:18–19).[3]

*Irresistible grace.* Because human beings stand opposed to God, in rebellion, corrupt through and through, under his wrath, God had to act in order for anyone to be saved. In acting, God, out of his mere good pleasure as King, chose a people to be saved; he sent his Son, Jesus, to purchase their salvation by bearing God's wrath on the cross; and he sends his Spirit to call these chosen ones to himself and to apply salvation to them. This "effectual" call is not universal, made to all human beings indiscriminately; rather, it is extended only to those whom God has chosen to save: "All that the Father gives me will come to me, and whoever comes to me I will never cast out" (John 6:37); "No one can come to me unless the Father who sent me draws him" (John 6:44). This call is "irresistible" in the sense that God's grace *will* bring his chosen ones to salvation and salvation to his chosen ones.

God the Spirit does this by "enlightening their minds spiritually and savingly to understand the things of God; taking away their heart of stone, and giving unto them a heart of flesh; renewing their wills, and by his almighty power determining them to that which is good, and effectually drawing them to Jesus Christ." Yet this drawing is not against the sinner's will; rather, individuals "come most freely, being made willing by his grace" (WCF 10.1).

*Perseverance of the saints.* Because God has worked for our salvation at every point—election, atonement, effectual calling—he will certainly bring it to consummation so that we enter into the fullness of eternal life. Our perseverance is tied to God's preservation: "He who began a good work in you will bring it to completion at the day of Jesus Christ" (Phil. 1:6). Our final salvation is in *God's* hands, just as the rest of our salvation is. Therefore, salvation is certain because it is based firmly on *God's* purpose and promise. If it were possible for God's purpose in predestination, calling, and justification to fail, then it might also be possible for God's promise to preserve us and enable us to persevere to fail as well. But since that is clearly impossible—for "if God is for us, who can be against us?" (Rom. 8:31)—we can trust that God's grace *will* carry us to the end.

Taken together, these "five points"—which center in God's purposes and actions—highlight God's grace. They spell out what the apostle Paul claimed: "For by grace you have been saved through faith. And this is not your own doing; it is the gift of God, not a result of works, so that no one may boast" (Eph. 2:8–9). But they all take their place because what we said in the beginning of this section is true—we were dead, under God's wrath, without hope in this world; and God in his undeserved mercy made us alive, granted us forgiveness, and gave us hope in this world and the world to come.

Not only does God's grace meet our need for salvation, but it also extends to every area of our lives. We sometimes call this "common grace." Some branches of the Reformed world deny that there is such a thing as common or general grace, but it seems clear that God's determination not to destroy rebellious humankind is itself a demonstration of undeserved favor. Even more, in Genesis 8:21–22, after the flood, God promised to sustain life so that "while the earth remains, seedtime and harvest, cold and heat, summer and winter, day and night, shall not cease." God continues to shower humankind with his kindness and love, as Jesus observed: "But I say to you, Love your enemies and pray for those persecute you, so that you may be sons of your Father who is in heaven. For he makes his sun rise on the evil and on the good, and sends rain on the just and on the unjust" (Matt. 5:44–45). Because God shows his common grace to humankind in the regular provision of the necessities of life and the preservation of the uniform laws of science and nature, humankind is able to grow and develop and progress and investigate. Scientists are able to discover how DNA works; farmers are able to use "advances" in biochemistry to fight weeds and grow crops; artists explore the human condition in photography or paintings. In each of these areas, sinful human beings are able to find and know "truth," even when they deny or are in rebellion against the God of truth.

Even more, Christians are able to work beside nonbelievers in the realms of science, history, art, and nature (the realms of "general revelation," that is, God's truth shared with all humankind in creation) because God's grace is general or common. There are "surface" truths on which Christians and non-Christians are able to agree, basic principles of operation that are common to us all. As a historian, I am able to engage with historians who specialize in the American South, and we are able to speak meaningfully to one another because God's common grace shows us "truth." And so, God's undeserved mercy envelops all human beings, sustaining us, enabling us to provide for our families, motivating us to explore his good creation. Surely, as a famous hymn reminds us, "he shines in all that's fair," calling out to his creatures in his kindness to repent of their sin and love him as their royal father (Rom. 2:4).

Thro' many dangers, toils and snares,
    I have already come;
'tis grace has brought me safe thus far,
    and grace will lead me home.

The Lord has promised good to me,
    his Word my hope secures;
he will my shield and portion be,
    as long as life endures.[4]

Grace not only sustains our lives with the regularity of God's good creation, which meets our most basic needs. And not only does it shout to us the glorious news of Christ's death and resurrection, which meets our need for God's forgiveness. Grace also upholds us throughout our journey here in the world, in our struggle with sin and our battles with the devil. Through the dangers, toils, and snares of this life, grace sustains. But grace does more than bear us up and help us to put one foot in front of the other. God, through his undeserved favor, *transforms* us: his promise to remake us into Christ's image has begun in Christ and will continue throughout our lives.

This may sound strange to us. Although our salvation is from beginning to end the result of God's grace, we tend to think that we need to become more like Christ through our own strenuous self-exertion. We are saved by grace, we think, but made holy by the law, our effort, our work. Only in recent days have Presbyterians begun to understand that, like every other aspect of our salvation, our holiness depends on our faithful resting upon God's grace alone.

First of all, it is important for us to recognize that, through faith in Jesus Christ, we are spiritually united to him. Paul says, "I have been crucified with Christ" (Gal. 2:20). We are united to Christ in his death (Rom. 6:1–4), and so we are dead both to the reign of sin and to the curse of the law (Gal. 2:19; 3:10–14). Christ's death becomes our death, his righteousness is ours, and his life is

42

ours ("it is no longer I who live, but Christ who lives in me," Gal. 2:20). As the familiar hymn by Augustus Toplady put it:

Rock of Ages, cleft for me,
    let me hide myself in thee;
let the water and the blood,
    from thy riven side which flowed,
be of sin the double cure,
    cleanse me from its guilt and pow'r.

Not the labors of my hands
    can fulfill thy law's demands;
could my zeal no respite know,
    could my tears forever flow,
all for sin could not atone;
    thou must save, and thou alone.

Nothing in my hand I bring,
    simply to thy cross I cling;
naked, come to thee for dress;
    helpless, look to thee for grace;
foul, I to the Fountain fly;
    wash me, Savior, or I die.[5]

By our union with Jesus, his death is the "double cure" for our sin—sin's guilt and power are both dealt with in Christ's death. By our union with Jesus, God's wrath against our sin is turned away, not by way of the works of the law, but by way of Jesus' death for us. By our union with Jesus, our clinging to his cross, we receive "dress," namely the righteousness of Jesus; we receive grace; we receive cleansing.

In addition, not only are we united to Christ in his death, but we are united to him also in his resurrection. Paul wrote to the Roman believers:

For if we have been united with him in a death like his, we shall certainly be united with him in a resurrection like his. . . . Now if we have died with Christ, we believe that we will also live with him. We know that Christ being raised from the dead will never die again; death no longer has dominion over him. For the death he died he died to sin, once for all, but the life he lives he lives to God. (Rom. 6:5, 8–10)

In God's sight, there is a new reality about each one of us. Once we were dead, now we are alive; once we were bound to sin, now we are set free; once we were rebels against him, now we are obedient sons and daughters. God has "made us alive together with Christ—by grace you have been saved—and raised us up with him and seated us with him in the heavenly places in Christ Jesus so that in the coming ages he might show the immeasurable riches of his grace in kindness toward us in Christ Jesus" (Eph. 2:5–7). We are new creations—united to Christ in his death, raised with him to walk in newness of life—and we foreshadow in our very beings what God is doing in this world: creating a new heavens and a new earth.

Because these things are true about each of us, we are called to live in accordance with this new reality. In Presbyterian and Reformed circles, we sometimes talk about keeping the proper order between the "indicatives" and the "imperatives": *because* certain things are true about us in Christ, we are called to live in certain ways. Because we are new creations, united to Christ in his death and resurrection, the great thing we are called to do is to "present yourselves to God . . . and your members to God as instruments for righteousness" (Rom. 6:13). Or, as Paul puts it elsewhere, "I appeal to you therefore, brothers, by the mercies of God, to present your bodies as a living sacrifice, holy and acceptable to God, which is your spiritual worship. Do not be conformed to this world, but be transformed by the renewal of your mind, that by testing you may discern what is the will of God, what is good and acceptable and perfect" (Rom. 12:1–2). Because we know God's mercy in Jesus, we present ourselves to God in gratitude.

Historically, Presbyterians and Reformed believers have recognized this. While many people tend to think of John Calvin as a grumpy, cold theologian, he was actually a "theologian of piety" or a "theologian of the Christian life." His coat of arms, which he developed himself, had at its center the image of a heart, often aflame, offered on an outstretched hand. Around that seal were the words, "I offer my heart, Lord, promptly and sincerely." In Calvin's most popular little book, *On the Christian Life*, he observed that "it is the duty of believers to 'present their bodies a living sacrifice, holy, acceptable unto God': this is the only true worship." The reason for this, according to Calvin, was "that we are consecrated and dedicated to God; it means that we may think, speak, meditate, or do anything only with a view to his glory." Indeed, Calvin went on to say:

> We are not our own, therefore neither our reason nor our will should guide us in our thoughts or actions. We are not our own, therefore we should not seek what is expedient to the flesh. We are not our own, therefore let us forget ourselves and our own interests as far as possible. But we are God's own; to him, therefore, let us live and die. We are God's own; therefore let his wisdom and will dominate all our actions. We are God's own; therefore let every part of our existence be directed toward him as our only legitimate goal.[6]

*Because* we are not our own but belong to God in Christ, *therefore* we live wholly to God. By virtue of our union with Christ, we present ourselves to God to live as he desires according to his mercy and grace.

We are enabled to present ourselves to God because we recognize that he has already granted us "every spiritual blessing in the heavenly places" (Eph. 1:3). By virtue of our union with Christ, we are as *justified* as we will ever be—our status has been changed in God's sight forever. By virtue of our union with Christ, we are as *righteous* as we will ever be—not inwardly, which is increasing more and more as the Spirit uses his Word to transform us into Christ's image, but in God's sight because we are clothed in the perfect righteousness of Christ (Gal. 3:27). By virtue of our union with Christ, we are as *adopted* as we will ever be—we cannot become more "children" than we already are; we have been moved from the status of slaves to beloved children of God (Gal. 4:4–7). And, by virtue of our union with Christ, we have the greatest of all spiritual blessings—we have *Christ* himself, through communion with him by the Spirit and Word. All of these blessings come to us through grace—the undeserved favor of God.

As a result, we are freed from the trap of beginning with grace and finishing by works. Too many of us are tempted to believe that, while God has saved us and may be pleased with us, he would be even happier if we were missionaries or pastors, if we could do some extraordinary service for him. Then, we mistakenly believe, *then* God would be satisfied with us. But this perspective fails to understand two important truths. First, we are still, at best, sinners saved by grace. We confess that our best works, which proceed from God's Spirit, "are defiled, and mixed with so much weakness and imperfection, that they cannot endure the severity of God's judgment" (WCF 16.5). Second, God is not satisfied with us because of what we have done or can do. In fact, we can't do *anything* that would satisfy God. We believe that "we cannot by our best works merit pardon of sin, or eternal life at the hand of God" (WCF 16.5). Rather, God is satisfied with us only because he sees the perfect work of his Son. Because our persons are "accepted through Christ, their good works also are accepted in him; not as though they were in this life wholly unblamable and unreprovable in God's sight; but that he, looking upon them in his Son, is pleased to accept and reward that which is sincere, although accompanied with many weaknesses and imperfections" (WCF 16.6). Even as Christians, our best works are accepted only by virtue of our union with Christ; God continually looks at us in his Son and thereby accepts our works as flawed as they are. We begin by grace and we continue by grace.

This recognition of God's grace as we pursue holiness also frees us from believing that our sins could separate us finally from his love. All too often we are motivated to live by our *guilt*, rather than by God's *grace*. We recognize our failings, we feel the conflict within us because of our remaining corruption, we know the opposition of Satan, and we hear his accusations ringing loudly in our ears: "You call yourself a Christian and you did *that*? You screamed at your children or at your spouse. You envied your co-worker's success to such a degree that you sought to sabotage his rise up the ladder. You shaded the truth so that it became a lie, and you did it to make yourself look good. You lusted in your heart and dreamed about having someone else's spouse." What we tend to do with these accusations is to use them as a motivation to make amends, to placate God with promises of repentance and good behavior. We fear God's response to our sins; we fear that he will walk all over us with his God-sized cleats. We are like children who fear our parents' discipline, but not our parents' distress. And so, we use this guilt not to drive us to Christ and his mercy, but to drive us to self-righteous achievement. We begin to measure our spirituality by what we don't do, what sins and transgressions we avoid, and what external righteousness we manage to accomplish. All of this we do as an attempt to keep God happy with us. Meanwhile, we are far from communion with him, far from a deep love for him, and far indeed from understanding the grace and mercy of God.

When we understand God's grace, we answer the accusations of the Enemy far differently. We confess, "Yes, I am a sinner and I fail my Lord in many ways. But my God is rich in mercy—in Jesus Christ, he has covered all my sins. Even these sins, as heinous as they are, are covered by Jesus' blood. God may discipline me for my good, but he will not do so with vengeance—that wrath was fully satisfied by Jesus' death." Out of this confession, rooted in a deep trust in God's mercy, we offer ourselves anew to God out of a profound gratitude for that mercy. We understand that we are united to Christ by faith in him, and we are assured that nothing can separate us from the love of God in him (Rom. 8:31–39). And we trust in his enduring grace for strength to live for him (2 Cor. 12:9). This grace transforms us, makes us new creatures, and enables us, by the power of the Spirit, to live lives that are pleasing to God.

## Grace Will Lead Us Home

And when this flesh and heart shall fail,
 and mortal life shall cease,
I shall possess within the veil
 a life of joy and peace.[7]

Grace begins our journey in the Christian life, and it sustains us throughout. God's undeserved mercy comes to us in Jesus Christ and saves us, pointing us always to the blood and righteousness of Christ as our only hope for salvation. Throughout our journey, God's grace also transforms us. It reminds us of our new identity in Christ and calls us to live in the light of this new identity. And, finally, grace brings us safely home—God's undeserved favor finishes what it starts. God our King continues his good work in us until we are brought home safely to God. This perseverance and preservation of the saints is a distinct mercy and a real grace: we can certainly trust that at the end of our journey, when this flesh and heart shall fail, God will enable us to cross within the veil to the life of joy and peace promised to us in Jesus. Grace will indeed lead us home.

In the midst of this life, God promises to enable us to persevere. As Presbyterians, we confess that those "whom God hath accepted in his Beloved, effectually called, and sanctified by his Spirit, can neither totally nor finally fall away from the state of grace, but shall certainly persevere therein to the end and be eternally saved" (WCF 17.1). This is the argument of Romans 8—if God has known us before the foundation of the world, chosen us, called us, and justified us, nothing can separate us from his love. But, notice further that Romans 8:30 says that God has *glorified* us—past tense. How is this the case? The apostle Paul tells us that our future glorification is absolutely certain because, from God's perspective, it has already happened. It is similar to what Paul says in Ephesians 2—from God's view, we are made alive together with Christ, raised up with him, and seated with him in the heavenly places: we are *already* glorified. And yet, we also await in hope our final unveiling as the children of God. Grace sustains us and enables us to persevere to the end.

To encourage us, the triune God graciously gives us strong evidence that he will accomplish his purpose. We are pointed to the "immutability of the decree of election, flowing from the free and unchangeable love of God the Father" (WCF 17.2). God the King does not change his mind, nor is his love wishy-washy—those whom he has chosen to save, motivated as he is solely by his unchanging

48

love, he *will* save. This should give us great courage and confidence as we struggle with sin, looking toward the finish line of our lives. We also look to "the efficacy of the merit and intercession of Jesus Christ" (WCF 17.2). Jesus' life and death are fully effective for saving us: his blood makes full payment for our sin and cleanses us from all unrighteousness; he clothes us in his righteousness so that it becomes our covering in the presence of the Father. Likewise, Jesus' continuing intercession at the Father's right hand is another line of evidence to strengthen our hearts: "He is able to save to the uttermost those who draw near to God through him, since he always lives to make intercession for them" (Heb. 7:25). A third gracious comfort to us as we persevere in the faith is "the abiding of the Spirit and of the seed of God with them" (WCF 17.2). The fact that we have the Spirit living within us empowers us to persevere in the call of God. Though we may falter and fail at times, the Spirit witnesses with our own spirits to strengthen us in our perseverance. And finally, God grants us grace to persevere by directing us to "the nature of the covenant of grace" (WCF 17.2). As we continue in the journey of life, and as we near the end of the race, we cling to the promises God has made in the gospel. God will surely keep his promises to us: "If we endure, we will also reign with him" (2 Tim. 2:12).

In our last days, God also gives us grace to die well. We share the same confidence that the apostle Paul had: that "the Lord will rescue me from every evil deed and bring me safely into his heavenly kingdom" (2 Tim. 4:18). Perhaps the greatest picture of this grace given to believers in their dying is found in John Bunyan's *The Pilgrim's Progress*. As the traveler, Christian, starts to cross the dark river of death, he begins to falter. His friend, Hopeful, urges him to feel the bottom of the river where it was firm and points him to the promises of the gospel; yet, Christian seems determined to shake Hopeful off and to claim that those promises were not for him. But when Hopeful proclaims the gospel of grace to Christian one last time—"Be of good cheer, Jesus Christ maketh thee whole"—God's gracious light breaks through Christian's heart and enlightens his eyes. He exclaims, "Oh, I see him again! and he tells me, When thou passest through the waters, I will be with thee, and through the rivers, they shall not over-flow thee." With this grace-centered confidence, both travelers "took courage" and they make it safely to the other side of the river: for "Christian therefore presently found ground to stand upon, and so it followed that the rest of the river was but shallow. Thus they got over."[8] As it did for Bunyan's Christian, God's grace brings all Christians safely into his heavenly kingdom. We need not worry or fret as we die, for the same God who called us out of darkness and raised us from the dead in Christ, the same God who shapes us into the image of Christ and enables us to live Christ-centered lives, this same God will bring us safely into his kingdom where, in his presence, we will enjoy delights and pleasures forevermore (Ps. 16:11). What amazing grace this is! Thanks be to God for his indescribable gift of grace!

## »Questions for Thought and Review

1. We have to be honest enough to admit that the belief that human beings deserve God's wrath is a "hard sell" in today's world. What are some points of contact or some illustrations that might help your unbelieving friends and neighbors understand the spiritual position they are in?

2. We say that total depravity does not mean that people are as bad as they could be, but that people are corrupted through and through. How is that different from the way many secular people view human nature? What are some practical ramifications of these different views of humankind?

3. Many evangelicals believe that it is not possible to share the gospel with unbelievers unless we tell them that Jesus died specifically for them. What are some answers that you might give to that claim?

4. If God did not call sinners to himself in an irresistible fashion, would unbelievers come on their "own"? Why not?

5. One possible response that people might make to the "five points of Calvinism" is that they are profoundly unfair. How would you answer this objection?

THE PRIORITY OF AMAZING GRACE

6. Have you ever met folks who denied "common grace"? Have you ever thought about the fact that God shows his undeserved favor to all creation—those who disobey him as well as those who obey him? How does common grace provide a basis for scientific thought and exploration?
7. Have you ever been tempted to try to finish your salvation by works? What are some natural consequences of placing too much emphasis upon your performance as a means of gaining or keeping God's favor? Can anyone truly do "good works"? How does God accept our works as good?
8. Think about the Calvin quotation on page 44. How does the fact that we are not our own but belong to Jesus Christ enable us to give ourselves freely to God? What is the great motivation for presenting ourselves to God, according to Romans 12:1?
9. How does the certainty of God's purposes in Romans 8:29–31 strengthen our assurance that he will enable us to persevere to the end?
10. Have you ever known someone who "died well" in the Christian faith? How was God's grace evidenced in the way that person died?

## »For Further Reading

Boice, James M., and Philip G. Ryken. *Doctrines of Grace: Rediscovering the Evangelical Gospel.* Wheaton, Ill.: Crossway, 2002.

Chapell, Bryan. *Holiness by Grace.* Wheaton, Ill.: Crossway, 2001.

Horton, Michael S. *Putting the Amazing Back into Grace.* Rev. ed. Grand Rapids, Mich.: Baker, 2002.

Mouw, Richard J. *He Shines in All That's Fair: Culture and Common Grace.* Grand Rapids, Mich.: Eerdmans, 2001.

Peterson, Robert A., and Michael D. Williams. *Why I Am Not an Arminian.* Downers Grove, Ill.: InterVarsity Press, 2004.

Sproul, R. C. *Grace Unknown: The Heart of Reformed Theology.* Grand Rapids, Mich.: Baker, 1997.

Turner, Steve. *Amazing Grace: The Story of America's Most Beloved Song.* New York: Ecco, 2002.

# CHAPTER 3

# God's Story, Promise, Reign: Covenant and Kingdom

"There is a fine line between the use and the overuse of a word," Richard Phillips of First Presbyterian Church, Margate, Florida, once observed. He went on:

> The same is true with public figures. When someone is getting exposure, we are excited for them. But when they are over-exposed we are embarrassed for them. In my view, the word *covenant* has crossed that line in Christian circles. As such, one often hears it applied in dubious ways. We have gone from covenant people and covenant children to covenant schools and covenant businesses. I recently was given a bag of covenant coffee beans, which, by the way, I received as an effectual means of grace. Today, if you want to express zeal to be distinctively Christian, and especially if you are Reformed-leaning, you are very likely to apply the word *covenant* to your activity or group or product. In the process, the word has begun to lose definition and take on little more than a vague nimbus.[1]

I could not agree more. And as you have come to interact with Presbyterians, you have probably experienced this confusion with the overuse of the word *covenant*.

It shouldn't be this way. As we saw in the last chapter, covenant describes God's voluntary condescension to cross the divide between Creator and creature, to relate graciously with finite human beings, and to enter into a relationship with them. This very act of God's accommodation is gracious. And particularly after the fall, God made "*the covenant of grace*; wherein he freely offereth unto sinners life and salvation by Jesus Christ" (WCF 7.3). God's covenant is the way he relates to human beings in general and to his chosen people in particular.

And yet, coming up with a basic definition of the word *covenant* is notoriously difficult. Perhaps the best is from theologian John Murray, who argued that "a divine covenant is a sovereign administration of grace and promise."[2] I think this works best because it does not exclude other important ideas that typically get associated with covenant—such as whether covenants are based on conditions, whether covenants are mutual arrangements, what exactly is offered in covenants, whether a covenant has "contractual aspects," whether merit is involved in covenants, and so forth. Rather, the definition brings the idea of covenant down to several key thoughts, some of which we have already seen: it is a *divine* covenant, that is, it starts with God and his rights as King; it is a sovereign *administration*, and so it suggests God's rules for relationship, which as King he has the right to set up; this administration displays God's *grace*, from first to last, in allowing finite human beings to have God "as their blessedness and reward" (WCF 7.1); and it is based on God's *promise*.

In fact, this definition sets the stage for understanding what Presbyterians believe about the covenant and God's kingdom. God's covenant, this sovereign administration, is a *story* of redemption. It began in the garden of Eden with one covenant, a "covenant of works," which Adam failed to keep. It has continued on since the fall with a second covenant, a "covenant of grace," which Jesus established in his death and resurrection. This covenant of grace, this story of redemption, had two "phases" or "dispensations," whether called "law" and "grace," or "old covenant" and "new covenant." And this story is moving toward a climactic ending, in which God's reign is made manifest over the whole world in Jesus Christ. This reign is what we mean by God's kingdom; and so, God's covenant seeks the establishment of his kingdom, his reign, throughout the entire earth—that's why we pray, "Your kingdom come." The reason we can trust that this story is moving toward the manifestation of God's reign on earth is that this story is rooted in and reveals God's *promises*, made all the way back in Genesis 3:15 but made most importantly to Abraham in Genesis 12:1–3: God promises to bless all the families of the earth through Abraham's seed, Jesus (cf. Gal. 3:6–9, 16). This story of promised redemption, resulting in God's reign and blessing the whole earth—this is what Presbyterians mean when they talk about God's covenant and kingdom.

## GOD'S COVENANT IS A STORY OF REDEMPTION

In the aftermath of the first phase of the Great Awakening, Jonathan Edwards was concerned to place the recent revival in a larger framework. And so, in 1739 he preached a thirty-unit sermon that he entitled "The History of the Work of Redemption." Drawing in part from the new interest in "epic history" and the rising historical consciousness in the West, Edwards's sermons attempted to tell the great story of redemption from before the foundation of time to the consummation of the age. He suggested that the Northampton revivals of 1734–35 were part of the engine that God was using to drive history. The cyclical movement of history from revival to degradation to revival would bring history to a final outpouring of God's Spirit in revival and final apostasy before Jesus would return to conquer all his enemies and usher in the millennial age. While we may want to quibble with some of Edwards's theology in these sermons, they are valuable for the way in which he spoke of God's covenant. Throughout these sermons, Edwards set forward a "covenant theology" under the rubric of God's work of redemption. The story of God's work of redemption is what Presbyterians often mean when we talk about "covenant." We mean to account for how God, from the very beginning of human history, has been working out the redemption of a chosen people for his own glory.

This story begins in the garden of Eden with Adam and Eve. In the garden, God's relationship with humankind ran through Adam, who acted as a representative for his entire posterity. God condescended to relate to Adam so that, if Adam were to obey God's commands perfectly, he and his posterity would receive promised life as a reward (WCF 7.2). This covenant relationship was pictured especially in the tree of the knowledge of good and evil: "And the Lord God commanded the man, saying, 'You may surely eat of every tree of the garden, but of the tree of the knowledge of good and evil you shall not eat, for in the day that you eat of it you shall surely die'" (Gen. 2:16–17). God's command, his law, came to Adam requiring obedience; if man disobeyed, judgment in the form of death would come; and the implication was that, had Adam obeyed, he would have received life and blessing.

As we are all acutely aware, Adam failed and broke the "covenant of works" (some people call it the covenant of life, or the covenant of creation, or the Adamic administration; the name is less important than the idea). Yet, after Adam's fall, the story does not end. Rather, God gives Adam and Eve a promise that their offspring would bring redemption for humankind: "I will put enmity between you and the woman, and between your offspring and her offspring; he shall bruise your head, and you shall bruise his heel" (Gen. 3:15). Adam's offspring, or "seed," would triumph over sin and its consequences. Further, this promise points toward God's covering the shame of human beings through the life of another creature (Gen. 3:21). The story of redemption has begun through God's promise of redemption: Adam's Seed would come to reverse the curse; the shame of women and men would be covered by another's blood.

God continues to unfold this story of redemption in the story of Noah. Adam's progeny demonstrate that God's curse has come true: human beings die both physically—through natural and violent means (Gen. 4–5)—and spiritually (Gen. 6). By Noah's day, "the wickedness of man was great in the earth, and every intention of the thoughts of his heart was only evil continually" (Gen. 6:5). God is determined to bring judgment upon humanity, but he remembers the promise he made to Adam and Eve—he keeps his promise and continues the story by showing grace in preserving Noah and his family. Even more, God's preservation of Noah demonstrates his concern to redeem his entire creation (Gen. 9), and the story of redemption continues on.

Moving from humankind in Adam to a particular portion of the human race in Noah, God narrows this story of the promised Redeemer in selecting one family—that of Abraham. In Abraham's story, the story of redemption that is bound up with God's promise becomes more specific: "I will make of you a great nation, and I will bless you and make your name great, so that you will be a blessing. I will bless those who bless you, and him who dishonors you I will curse, and in you all the families of the earth shall be blessed" (Gen. 12:2–3). God promises Abraham several things: Abraham's children will comprise a great nation; Abraham's name will become great so that he will be a blessing; and through Abraham all the families of the earth shall be blessed. To put it more simply, God promises Abraham a Seed, land, and universal blessing. The story of redemption, then, focuses on Abraham's family—his physical offspring— but, more importantly, his spiritual offspring.

Out of Abraham's progeny, we find that the story of redemption continues on in Isaac, not Ishmael; in Jacob, not Esau. God's purpose in the story of redemption is strange to readers from the ancient Near East: the younger is preferred above the elder. And yet, God's story of redemption emphasizes that God's sovereign choices move this story forward. While he uses means (remember what we said about God's providence), God is still the one directing this drama. And so, Isaac and Jacob are the children of promise. Isaac is surprising because he was born to a hundred-year-old man; Jacob is surprising because he appears to be such a scoundrel. And yet, God transforms Jacob the supplanter into Israel the prevailing one (Gen. 32:22–32). And among Jacob/Israel's children, the story focuses on Judah, not Reuben the firstborn, for God promises that "the scepter shall not depart from Judah, nor the ruler's staff from between his feet, until tribute comes to him; and to him shall be the obedience of the peoples" (Gen. 49:10).

After the people's exile in Egypt, the story focuses on the crowning and typical work of God's redeeming purpose. The exodus sets forth God's determination to redeem his people from slavery. In doing so,

God triumphs over all the gods that human beings set up, which are no gods at all, and he does so by means of the bloody sacrifice of a spotless lamb. As such, this points forward to the real point of God's deeds—the perfect, sinless Redeemer who would come to save his people from slavery to sin by means of his bloody sacrifice upon the cross. The story moves on through the giving of the law, which was to serve as a tutor and restrainer for Jacob's children (Gal. 3:23–26). As Presbyterians, we confess that

> under the law, it [i.e., God's covenantal story of redemption] was administered by promises, prophecies, sacrifices, circumcision, the paschal lamb, and other types and ordinances delivered to the people of the Jews, all foresignifying Christ to come; which were, for that time, sufficient and efficacious, through the operation of the Spirit, to instruct and build up the elect in faith in the promised Messiah. (WCF 7.5)

God raises up Moses the prophet and Aaron the priest to lead God's people, but they are deeply flawed men. They point to God's Redeemer, who would be a perfect prophet (Deut. 18:15; Heb. 1:1–2) and a perfect priest (Heb. 5, 7, 9–10).

After forty years in the wilderness, God leads his people into the Promised Land. For several generations, they are ruled by judges who operate as chief clansmen, leading the different tribes. As social order disintegrates, with everyone doing what is right in his own eyes, the people come to believe that they need a king. They choose Saul, a Benjaminite; but he is a failure. Finally, God brings forward the great king—David, from the tribe of Judah, a man whom God loves deeply. Through David's reign, God's story becomes even more specific: David's son would reign over a kingdom that would last forever (2 Sam. 7). Yet, neither David nor David's immediate son, Solomon (whom God calls his beloved son in 2 Sam. 12:25), was the hero of the story; both were deeply flawed, and both pointed beyond themselves to a perfect King who would rule over God's people.

Throughout the rest of the story, God's people lose sight of God's promises. God sends prophets to remind the people of the storyline, but he also gives hints about how the story will continue to unfold. For example, the prophet Isaiah proclaims that God's sign for his people's deliverance would be the appearance of a virgin-born child who will be "God with us" (Isa. 7:14). It will be upon the shoulders of this child that the government of God's people should rest, for he shall be the "Mighty God" (Isa. 9:6). This Spirit-empowered child will restore David's throne after a time of exile; when David's tree has been cut down, a "branch" shall grow in its midst, and he shall rule over a kingdom of peace and righteousness that will encompass all peoples (Isa. 11:1–10). Yet, the means for such an enthronement are surprising—it would happen not through military triumph, but through suffering (Isa. 53); in apparent defeat, the one who will be the true Israel would strive and overcome.

Finally, "when the fullness of time had come, God sent forth his son," Jesus (Gal. 4:4–5). Jesus came as the promised Seed; the perfect prophet, priest, and king; the suffering servant who would redeem God's people through his death and resurrection. And Jesus had been chosen by God from before the foundation of the world for this role: "It pleased God, in his eternal purpose, to choose and ordain the Lord Jesus, his only begotten Son, to be the Mediator between God and man; the Prophet, Priest, and King, the Head and Savior of his Church, the heir of all things, and judge of the world" (WCF 8.1). Jesus was the focus of this unfolding story of redemption that God told throughout the Old Testament; it is *one* story focused on *one* people who focused their faith on *the* Redeemer of God's people "by whom they then had full remission of sin, and eternal salvation" (LC 34).

And yet, Jesus does not destroy his enemies and bring the story to an end immediately, nor does he accomplish redemption in the way that God's people expected. And before the cross and the resurrection, he tries to alert his disciples to this startling reality: good and evil would grow up side by side in the world until the judgment; the number of those under God's reign through Jesus would be small to start, but that number would grow steadily larger, so much so that their influence would one day spread over the whole world; the good news of salvation by faith alone in the crucified and resurrected Jesus would be preached throughout the world; and then Jesus would return to bring his story of redemption to an end. And so, Jesus' kingdom, his reign, begins spiritually: he grants his Spirit to his "new community," ascends to heaven, and awaits the time of his return. In the meantime, the story continues: God redeems individuals as they place their faith in Jesus Christ and live out their place in this story. We await the end of the age when the story of redemption will come to a close.

This unfolding history of redemption is what we often mean when we talk about "covenant." In fact, covenant theology stresses this story of God working out his promise to send a Redeemer (SC 20). There are two big things that I hope you noticed about this story. First, the story has a basic *continuity*. There is unity to this story of redemption. As we mentioned earlier, it is divided up into two phases—whether you call them promise and fulfillment, or old covenant and new covenant, or law and grace—but it is still one continuous story about this one great thing that God is doing.

And this is a place where Presbyterians often part company with other evangelicals, many of whom have been trained in a system of understanding the Bible called *dispensationalism*. Dispensationalism stresses the *discontinuity* between the two phases of the story of redemption. Focusing on two peoples of God, dispensationalists hold that the Old Testament was about God dealing with Israel and the New Testament is about God dealing with the church. These two peoples are distinct, dispensationalists claim, and have two different stories. Israel is God's *earthly* people, and most of the Old Testament promises are physical promises that will be "literally" fulfilled in time and space. The church is God's *heavenly* people, and they are taken to heaven ("raptured") before God brings his wrath to bear on the world for seven years in a period called the tribulation. After the church leaves the scene, God turns his attention back to Israel; purified by the tribulation, Israel will enjoy the direct rule of Jesus Christ, whom they finally recognize as the Messiah, for a thousand years. At the end of that time, God brings the story to a close by defeating and judging all his enemies and ushering in eternal existence.

As you can see, dispensationalism emphases *two* people, *two* stories, *two* destinies for God's people(s). Presbyterians' covenant theology, on the other hand, speaks about *one* people, *one* story, and *one* destiny for God's people. Dispensationalism stresses discontinuity; covenant theology, continuity. Sometimes, though, Presbyterians may overstress continuity. There are those who argue, for example, that the continuity between the Old and New Testaments means that the civil laws of ancient Israel should be applied to governments today, or that the representation of children in the Passover meal means that small children should come to the Lord's Supper without a prior profession of faith. The Presbyterian tradition has tended to see these claims as overextensions of continuity. After all, there are basic differences between the old and new covenants, wrought by Jesus' death and resurrection. As one theologian wryly noted, we know there *are* basic differences between the old and new covenants because, for one thing, we don't sacrifice bulls and goats anymore. Still, the thing to remember here is that God is telling *one story* in Scripture, the story of his redeeming activity for the sake of his people.

## God's Covenant Is an Irrevocable Promise

The second thing I hope you noticed in this survey of the history of redemption is that this story about God's covenant is all about God's promise to provide a Redeemer for his people. At the beginning of human history, after Adam's fall, there was a promise about a Seed that would come to crush all of God's enemies (Gen. 3:15). This promise developed through Noah to Abraham to the point that God told Abraham that through his Seed all the families of the earth would be blessed (Gen. 12:2–3). The promise continued to be revealed progressively as the story unfolded: the Seed would be a prophet, priest, and king; the Seed would redeem his people from slavery; the Seed would rule over his people perfectly; the Seed would intercede for his people as the priests interceded for Israel. In the writings of the kings of Israel and Judah, particularly in David and Solomon, the promised Seed was shown forth as one who would personify the wisdom of God

(Prov. 8), as one who would be forsaken by God and pierced for the iniquities of men and women (Ps. 22), and as one who would not see corruption (Ps. 16:10).

This Redeemer, this Seed, whom God's gospel sets forward and about whom God's covenant story tells us, is Jesus (Gal. 3:16). He has come to accomplish his work as "the only Mediator of the covenant of grace" (LC 36). Jesus as God's Mediator was (and is) God: hence, he sustains and keeps "the human nature from sinking under the infinite wrath of God, and the power of death; give[s] worth and efficacy to his sufferings, obedience, and intercession; and to satisfy God's justice, procure his favor, purchase a peculiar people, give his Spirit to them, conquer all their enemies, and bring them to everlasting salvation" (LC 38). Jesus as God's Mediator was (and is) also man (1 Tim. 2:5); hence, he advances "our nature, perform[s] obedience to the law, suffer[s] and make[s] intercession for us in our nature, has a fellow feeling of our infirmities; that we might receive the adoption of sons, and have comfort and access with boldness unto the throne of grace" (LC 39). As the God-man, God's Mediator for God's people, Jesus reconciles God and man and provides the proper works of each nature to God for us and to be relied on by us for our salvation.

And God's promise, which the covenant holds forth to us, is nothing less than Jesus himself. He is the special benefit that we receive as those whom God has chosen and for whom God is working out this story of redemption: "The members of the invisible church by Christ enjoy union and communion with him in grace and glory" (LC 65). This union with Christ, effected by the work of God's Spirit and by faith in Christ, joins us to Christ as our head and husband "spiritually and mystically, yet really and inseparably" (LC 66). We enjoy genuine common union with God in Christ by the Spirit. Thus, while we may love the benefits of Christ's work on the cross, promised to us by God, yet what we long for and what we receive by faith is *Jesus himself*. One of my favorite hymns puts it this way:

> The sands of time are sinking,
> the dawn of heaven breaks,

the summer morn I've sighed for,
    the fair sweet morn awakes;
dark, dark hath been the midnight,
    but day spring is at hand,
and glory, glory dwelleth
    in Emmanuel's land.

The King there in his beauty
    without a veil is seen;
it were a well-spent journey
    though sev'n deaths lay between;
the Lamb with his fair army
    doth on Mount Zion stand,
and glory, glory dwelleth
    in Emmanuel's land.

O Christ, he is the fountain,
    the deep sweet well of love!
The streams on earth I've tasted
    more deep I'll drink above;
there to an ocean fullness
    his mercy doth expand,
and glory, glory dwelleth
    in Emmanuel's land.

The bride eyes not her garment,
    but her dear bridegroom's face;
I will not gaze at glory,
    but on my King of grace:
not at the crown he gifteth,
    but on his pierced hand;
the Lamb is all the glory
    of Emmanuel's land.[3]

God's covenant is his promise of Christ extended to his people, and this promise is the same in the Old Testament as it is in the New. In the Old Testament, this promise was exhibited in "promises, prophe-

62

cies, sacrifices, circumcision, the Passover, and other types and ordinances." These things "were for that time sufficient to build up the elect in faith in the promised Messiah" (LC 34). In other words, the object of the faith of the Old Testament saints, though different in details, was the same as our own—God's promised Redeemer. Jesus pointed this out to the Pharisees. Once, he told them, "If you believed Moses, you would believe me; for he wrote of me. But if you do not believe his writings, how will you believe my words" (John 5:46–47). Later, Jesus claimed that "your father Abraham rejoiced that he would see my day. He saw it and was glad" (John 8:56). There are not two ways of salvation—one by the law, the other by faith. There has always been only *one* way of salvation—faith in Jesus, God's Redeemer. The difference is that the Old Testament believers looked *forward* to the Redeemer, relying on God's promise, seeing it dimly and from afar (Heb. 11:13–16); we look *back* to Jesus Christ, the one revealed as fulfilling God's promises about his chosen Redeemer (Heb. 12:1–2).

## GOD'S COVENANT SEEKS THE ESTABLISHMENT OF HIS KINGDOM

God's promise about a Redeemer is also tied to the establishment of God's kingdom. You cannot help but notice this as you read through the Gospels, particularly Matthew. Over and again, it is plain that the gospel that Jesus came to preach was the good news of God's kingdom. For example, Mark records that "after John was arrested, Jesus came into Galilee, proclaiming the gospel of God, and saying, 'The time is fulfilled, and the kingdom of God is at hand; repent and believe in the gospel' " (Mark 1:14–15). This kingdom that Jesus was talking about was both a *reign* and a *realm*. On the one hand, the kingdom that Jesus came to proclaim had everything to do with the establishment of his reign. Actually, it might be more accurate to say that with the coming of the kingdom of God, God's reign in Jesus Christ was being made manifest to the entire world. After all, we have noted previously how God is already King, sovereign over all his creatures and all their actions. All creation lives and moves and has its being according to the plan and desires of God. Further, the people of Israel knew from the very beginning that God was their King, even when they wanted an earthly ruler (1 Sam. 8; 10:17–19). What is new in Jesus is that God's reign is being made manifest to the entire world, a world that has been in rebellion against God.

This reign was not established in a typical way, through the conquering power of military might. As Jesus told Pilate, "My kingdom is not of this world. If my kingdom were of this world, my servants would have been fighting, that I might not be delivered over to the Jews. But my kingdom is not from the world" (John 18:36). As a result, God's reign is not necessarily tied to the advance of geo-political entities. Rather, God's reign is intimately connected to the work of his Spirit in bringing women and men into right relationship with him: "Unless one is born again he cannot see the kingdom of God" (John 3:3). And this right relationship is established by the cross and resurrection, which secured the redemption by which God's people might enter into relationship with him and come under his reign.

Yet God's reign was not what Jesus' first followers expected. They believed that, when God's reign was established, the Day of the Lord would come, bringing final judgment, especially upon the Romans, and salvation for God's people, Israel. After that Day of the Lord, the followers of God's Messiah would serve as vice-regents of God's reign over a reestablished Israel, purified from idolatry and regathered from exile. As a matter of fact, Jesus tells the disciples that this reign is quite different from their expectations. Instead, good and evil will grow up side by side—children of the kingdom and children of the Evil One—until a future, final judgment (Matt. 13:24–30, 36–43). Likewise, Jesus notes that God's reign will start out quite small, with only twelve disciples and some other followers, but it would expand throughout the entire world (Matt. 13:31–33). Those who recognize God's reign will understand how valuable it is, but it will be hidden to many, requiring searching and inquiry (Matt. 13:44–46). And yet, though it may seem that evil will be allowed to exist forever, God will bring judgment to bear at the end of the age (Matt. 13:47–49).

Presbyterian theologians like to express this tension by saying that God's reign is *already* inaugurated but is *not yet* consummated. That is, God's reign in Jesus Christ is being manifested throughout the world, and this began when his reign was inaugurated with his crucifixion, resurrection, and ascension. Because Jesus has been exalted at the right hand of God, he is *already* "holding session" at the Father's right hand and is making all his enemies his footstool (Acts 2:33–36). And yet, as the writer of Hebrews recognized, "at present, we do *not yet* see everything in subjection to him" (Heb. 2:8). God's reign is being extended throughout the world as men and women are being called under God's reign by Word and Spirit. This is how the story of redemption is playing out in our own day; in places that we as North Americans cannot see, particularly in Asia, Africa, and Central and South America, God is manifesting his reign in the transformation of lives. And when the story is complete, Jesus will return to judge the world in justice and truth. His reign will be fully realized in time and space, in the new heavens and new earth (Isa. 66:22–23; Rev. 21–22).

This suggests that the kingdom of God is not only a reign, but is also a *realm*. And the realm in which God's reign is being manifested is the earth itself. Jesus said quite plainly in his interpretation of the parable of the weeds, "The field is the world" (Matt. 13:38). Elsewhere, the Lord teaches that the promised inheritance for believers is the entire earth (Matt. 5:5). In addition, in Romans 8, Paul indicates that God's redemption has cosmic implications:

> For the creation waits with eager longing for the revealing of the sons of God. For the creation was subjected to futility, not willingly, but because of him who subjected it, in hope that the creation itself will be set free from its bondage to decay and obtain the freedom of the glory of the children of God. For we know that the whole creation has been groaning together in the pains of childbirth until now. (Rom. 8:19–22)

God intends for his people to inherit the earth in its full development as a City (Heb. 11:13–16), completely renovated by the judgment and mercy of God.

Until that final manifestation of God's reign on earth, which we do *not yet* see, his reign is *already* present and made most obvious in the church. As God's people submit to God's reign in his worship and government, they make his reign manifest. In fact, unbelievers should be able to look at the church for a sneak peak of what God's reign looks like: under God's reign, men and women love one another, submitting to one another under the rule of God's Word; under God's reign, men and women worship God, being led by the Spirit in the renewal of our communion with God; under God's reign, his people serve one another, laughing and crying together as we wander as pilgrims together through this wilderness on our way to the City of God. While there are other ways in which God's reign is made manifest in our lives individually—as we work in our vocations, engage in the arts, and raise our families—his reign is most obviously manifest when we come together as the church and his will is done on earth as it is in heaven (Matt. 6:10). And God's will in heaven is that his people worship him, adoring him as the King who alone is worthy of our best endeavors (Rev. 4–5).

## »Questions for Thought and Review

1. In what ways have you noticed the overuse of the word *covenant*? What are some other good theological words that get overused within the Christian community so that they lose their meaning?
2. Based on your reading in this chapter, if you were to come up with a one-sentence definition of the word *covenant*, what would it be?
3. How does understanding covenant as story help you in reading the Bible? By what other master narratives do we live our lives (e.g., the American story)? Do these stories come into conflict with the biblical story that owns us? If so, how?
4. What are some themes of the covenant story in the Old Testament? How do these themes find fulfillment in Jesus?

66

5. What are some implications of believing that the redemptive story demonstrates a basic continuity? What are some of the temptations that arise from the over-extension of continuity? Is Scripture "sufficient" for every detail of our lives?
6. What do you think about the claim that the promise which God's covenant makes is his promise of Jesus Christ extended to his people? How does that help us understand that salvation was the same in the Old Testament as it is in the New Testament?
7. In what ways does connecting God's promise and story with God's reign help us in thinking through the relationship between the Old and New Testaments?
8. How should thinking about God's kingdom impact one's Christian life?

### »For Further Reading

Clowney, Edmund P. *The Unfolding Mystery: Discovering Christ in the Old Testament*. Phillipsburg, N.J.: Presbyterian and Reformed, 1989.

Ridderbos, Hermann. *The Coming of the Kingdom*. Philadelphia: Presbyterian and Reformed, 1962.

Robertson, O. Palmer. *The Christ of the Covenants*. Phillipsburg, N.J.: Presbyterian and Reformed, 1980.

Vos, Geerhardus. *Biblical Theology: Old and New Testaments*. Carlisle, Pa.: Banner of Truth, 1994.

———. *The Teaching of Jesus concerning the Kingdom of God and the Church*. Nutley, N.J.: Presbyterian and Reformed, 1972.

Williams, Michael. *Far as the Curse Is Found: The Covenant Story of Redemption*. Phillipsburg, N.J.: P&R, 2005.

# CHAPTER 4

# What in the World Is the Church?

WE HAVE NOTICED HOW GOD'S STORY tells us about the unfolding of his reign in the world and how this reign will be most manifested in this time between times in the church. This body called church has had a difficult time over the past thirty years or so. Part of the reason for this is generational. Baby Boomers led a general rebellion against institutions in the 1960s, fearful of the power that these entities had over the lives and choices that people make. The idea was that, if we could be free to make our own choices, women and men might be able to bring about a revolution that would maximize freedom and usher in an era of good feelings and peace. Obviously, that vision was utopian, and the erstwhile rebels found that institutions were still necessary to organize human beings and effect change in the world. But this recognition has not led that generation to embrace institutional churches. Instead, the past thirty years has seen a massive hemorrhaging in old-line Protestant denominations and the rise of nondenominational churches. Churches that have downplayed distinctive beliefs or practices have grown rapidly, while those which have affirmed particularity in any form have generally grown very slowly, if at all. This trend has caused some to refer to this period in which we live as a "post-denominational age."

Not only do we live in an apparently post-denominational age, but it also sometimes appears to be a "post-church" age. With postmodern approaches to spirituality, some have increasingly come to doubt whether or not they even need to bother going to church. After all, if spirituality is simply my own personal connection to God or the "transcendent being," then the church can be a messy and seemingly unnecessary complication. Others have been all too willing to "worship" God in nature or rest or family time rather than to worship and serve him in this organism and institution called the church. We will discuss the importance of the church and its means of grace for Reformed spirituality (or Presbyterian piety) in the appropriate place. But it should be obvious that the dismissive attitude just described is a long way from the thinking that Presbyterians historically have had regarding the church.

In fact, Presbyterians confess that outside of the church "there is no ordinary possibility of salvation" (WCF 25.2). This affirms that God has given to the church "the ministry, oracles, and ordinances of God, for the gathering and perfecting of the saints, in this life, to the end of the world" (WCF 25.3). In other words, everything that is necessary for communion with God in Christ is found in Christ's church. And so, if we desire salvation—which is nothing less than glorifying God and enjoying him throughout all eternity—then we must desire Christ's church. The songwriter Derek Webb has put this well:

> 'Cause I haven't come for only you
> But for my people to pursue
> And you cannot care for me with no regard for her
> If you love me you will love the church.[1]

Far from having a dismissive attitude toward the church, Presbyterians have long believed that the church is at the center of God's purposes for the world.

## What Is the Church?

The Bible speaks about the church in a number of different ways. Perhaps you are familiar with descriptions of the church as the "bride of Christ" or the "body of Christ." Others may refer to the church as Christ's new community; still others may think about the church as "the household of God." What I would like to suggest are several historic ways that the church has described itself, drawing upon biblical images and themes. Theologian and teacher Edmund Clowney, in his book *The Church*, helpfully pulls together a great deal of this material in a single place for our reflection and mediation.[2]

*The church can be described in Trinitarian terms.* That is, the church can be described first of all as "the people of God." God the Father has called us to be "a chosen race, a royal priesthood, a holy nation, a people for his own possession" for the purpose of declaring "the excellencies of him who called you out of darkness into his marvelous light." Once we were not a people, "but now you are God's people" (1 Peter 2:9–10). The church is also the "body of Christ." In response to the fractious division in the church at Corinth, the apostle Paul suggests the image of the body of Christ as a means for describing the unity and diversity that characterizes the church: "For just as the body is one and has many members, and all the members of the body, though many, are one body, so it is with Christ. For in one Spirit we were all baptized into one body—Jews or Greeks, slaves or free—and all were made to drink of one Spirit" (1 Cor. 12:12–13). "The fellowship of the Spirit" is a third descriptor for the church. God's purpose for the church is to be filled with "the fullness of him who fills all in all." This filling is the work of the Holy Spirit, who is given to the church as a guarantee of God's good promises and as the giver of wisdom and revelation in the knowledge of God (Eph. 1:7–23). And so, the church can be described as God's people, Christ's body, and the Spirit's fellowship, expressing the fact that we are people who march under the banner of the triune God.

*The church can also be described in terms of the gospel.* By this, I mean that the church can be described in the language of the Nicene Creed: "We believe in one holy catholic and apostolic church." This is the kind of church that is formed by the gospel of Jesus Christ. For example, we believe that the church is "one." By that, we mean several things. The church shares one message—that sinners are justified by faith alone in Christ alone. This was why Paul was extremely frustrated in Galatia with the reaction of the "pillars" of the church. Peter and Barnabas should have understood that the common message that Jews and Gentiles believed to become part of Christ's church relativized old covenant dietary laws, circumcision, and feast days. Jews and Gentiles are alike declared right with God by faith alone in Christ alone; no other requirement or practice from the law as a deed that must be done can be added (Gal. 2:11–21). Moreover, the church also enjoys a common union with Jesus Christ. Jesus, in his farewell prayer, prays for his new community:

> I do not ask for these only, but also for those who will believe in me through their word, that they may all be one, just as you, Father, are in me, and I in you, that they also may be in us, so that the world may believe that you have sent me. The glory that you have given me I have given to them, that they may be one even as we are one, I in them and you in me, that they may become perfectly one, so that the world may know that you have sent me and loved them as you loved me. (John 17:20–23)

This essential unity for which Jesus prays arises from the union that we have with Christ and that Christ has with his Father. The church's unity is also expressed in its common baptism (Eph. 4:4–6). The unity of the Spirit is demonstrated in the fact that all those who belong to the church have shared in a baptism in water in the name of the Father, the Son, and the Holy Spirit.

Not only is the church "one," but the church is also "apostolic." This does not mean, as some Christians claim, that there is a succession of church leaders who can trace the lineage of their ordinations all the way back to the apostles themselves. Rather, it means that there is a succession of apostolic *teaching* down to the current day, the result of the preservation of the original apostolic message in Holy Scripture. In fact, the church is "built on the foundation of the apostles and prophets, Christ himself being the cornerstone, in whom the whole structure, being joined together, grows into a holy temple in the Lord"

(Eph. 2:21). This apostolic message is to be communicated to "faithful men who will be able to teach others also" (2 Tim. 2:2). This is the way by which the apostolic mission will be passed on from generation to generation. It is also the way by which the apostolic commission will be accomplished: "Go therefore and make disciples of all nations, baptizing them in the name of the Father and of the Son and of the Holy Spirit, teaching them to observe all that I have commanded you" (Matt. 28:19–20). The church continues to be apostolic as it continues to preach the apostles' message, further their mission, and fulfill their commission.

The gospel also creates a church that is "holy." It fills the church with "saints" (1 Cor. 1:2)—literally, those who are called to be "set apart ones," holy ones. As the church's members are conformed to the image of Jesus Christ, they put off their sinful ways ("the passions of your former ignorance") and put on the ways of holiness (1 Peter 1:14–16).

This united church, preaching the apostolic message and purifying itself by the gospel in order to live holily, will also expand beyond a particular nationality or people group—it will be truly universal or "catholic." That is what our common baptism teaches us: "There is neither Jew nor Greek, there is neither slave nor free, there is neither male nor female, for you are all one in Christ Jesus" (Gal. 3:26–29). Breaking down racial or cultural barriers, the church expands to every region of the world with the good news of salvation in Jesus Christ.

*Furthermore, the church can be described in terms of its "marks."* This way of talking about the church is rooted in the Reformation concern to distinguish the "true" from the "false" church. In order to do so, Presbyterians have talked about what marks out a true church and makes it obvious to a watching world. Our confession, for example, notes the fact that "particular churches, which are members [of the universal church], are more or less pure, according as the doctrine of the gospel is taught and embraced, ordinances administered, and public worship performed more or less purely in them" (WCF 25.4). These "marks" of the church were articulated in a similar fashion by

John Calvin, when he claimed that "wherever we see the Word of God purely preached and heard, and the sacraments administered according to Christ's institution, there, it is not to be doubted, a church of God exists" (Calvin, *Inst.*, 4.1.9). Having a basic idea of the essentials that mark out the church is helpful as we seek to understand the boundaries of our common union with other Christian churches. Where the Word is preached and heard, and where the sacraments are administered according to Scripture, we recognize other churches, and we recognize them to be part of Christ's universal church.

*Next, the church can be described in terms of space or location.* In other words, we can talk about the church locally as well as the church universal. You probably are most familiar with the fact that the church is local. Many of the letters in the New Testament appear to be written to congregations who worshipped in "house" churches. For example, the apostle Paul urged the church at Rome to "greet Prisca and Aquila, my fellow workers in Christ Jesus, who risked their necks for my life, to whom not only I give thanks but all the churches of the Gentiles give thanks as well. Greet also the church in their house" (Rom. 16:3–5; cf. 1 Cor. 16:19). In a similar fashion, Paul addressed Philemon, greeting both him and "the church in your house" (Philem. 2; see also Col. 4:15). Other times, the word church is applied to "regional" churches, suggesting that there is both a local and a broader geographical view of the church. After Paul was converted and ceased persecuting Christians, "the church throughout all Judea and Galilee and Samaria had peace and was being built up. And walking in the fear of the Lord and in the comfort of the Holy Spirit, it multiplied" (Acts 9:31). Likewise, the apostle wrote the letter to the Galatians to be circulated among "the churches of Galatia." Paul saw these churches as having a concern for and influence over the Christians in a given geographical region (Gal. 1:2; see also Col. 4:16).

*Moreover, the church can be described in terms of its character.* We can think about the church has an organism. The Bible, for example, uses a number of relational metaphors to speak of the church. The church is a "body" (1 Cor. 12:27; Eph. 4:12–16; Col. 1:18), a "bride" (Eph. 5:22–33), a "flock" (1 Peter 5:1–5), and a "household" (1 Tim. 3:5, 15). Each of these images is deeply organic; they suggest growth, increased stature, loving union, nourishing and cherishing, and committed care and concern. We learn from this that the mechanical imagery of the modern world can only be applied to the church with great difficulty. Rather, the church is something to be nurtured and loved; it has its basis in relationship, in friendship. Yet, thinking about the church as an organism does not exclude considering the church as an organization. The Bible also speaks of the church as being "built on the foundation of the apostles and prophets, Christ Jesus himself being the cornerstone, in whom the whole structure, being joined together, grows into a holy temple in the Lord. In him you also are being built together into a dwelling place for God by the Spirit" (Eph. 2:20–22). The idea of building upon a foundation suggests a certain degree of organization—something that is inevitable in any human society. In fact, the apostle Paul said that he wrote what we call the pastoral epistles in order that we might "know how one ought to behave in the household of God, which is the church of the living of God, a pillar and buttress of truth" (1 Tim. 3:15). And so, the structure provided in these epistles is necessary for the church to work according to the divine design. The organizational structure of the church is not something alien to and imposed on its organic nature; rather, organization is necessary in order to ensure that the organic life of the church will occur and flourish.

## THE CHURCH "VISIBLE" AND "INVISIBLE"

The final description of the church that we need to consider is the one that is most familiar to those who know something about Presbyterianism: the church can be described from the perspectives of both earth and heaven. We typically think about this in terms of the "visible" and the "invisible" church. In recent times, this terminology has come under increasing scrutiny within conservative Presbyterian circles. For example, John Murray, the great theologian at Westminster Seminary, once argued that

> "the church" in the New Testament never appears as an invisible entity and therefore may never be defined in terms of invisibility. That is why . . . the advisability of the use of the actual term "invisible" has been questioned. It is a term that is liable to be loaded with the misconceptions inherent in the concept "invisible church," and tends to support the abuses inherent thereto.[3]

While Murray and others have had laudable concerns about the way some believers misuse the idea of the "invisible church" to excuse sloppy living or to avoid uniting with very real and visible congregations, these concerns do not disqualify this way of talking about the church. In fact, I would go so far as to suggest that, even if we did do away with this description, we would have to develop some sort of similar substitute.

First, it is important that we understand how these terms are used in Presbyterian confessions of faith. We confess that "the catholic or universal church, which is invisible, consists of the whole number of the elect, that have been, are, or shall be gathered into one, under Christ the Head thereof; and is the spouse, the body, the fullness of him that filleth all in all" (WCF 25.1). Notice that what the confession is speaking of here is a universal church that can only be viewed in its entirety by God himself. In other words, God alone can see the true church whole. God alone sees all those throughout time and space whom he has chosen and united to Christ by his Spirit. Neither human eye nor any visible institution can encompass all of God's elect; the true church is literally invisible to us and will remain so until the end of the age. Indeed, Calvin speaks of the church as it "is actually in God's presence, into which no persons are received but those who are children of God by grace of adoption and true members of Christ by sanctification of the Holy Spirit" (Calvin, *Inst.*, 4.1.7).

We also confess that "the visible church, which is also catholic or universal under the gospel (not confined to one nation, as before

under the law), consists of all those throughout the world that profess the true religion; and of their children" (WCF 25.2). This is the
human perspective, the church that we can see. This church is also
"universal" in that it is not confined to any one nation. Instead, as
one historian has noted, Christianity represents the only truly
"world" religion, because it is spread throughout the world and has
representation in virtually every nation. This church, which we can
see in every community, is made up of all those who profess Christ
as well as their children. In this visible church, we have "mingled
many hypocrites who have nothing of Christ but the name and outward appearance" (Calvin, *Inst.*, 4.1.7) as well as those who love
Jesus with all their hearts.

There are very specific historical reasons why Presbyterian and
Reformed believers think about the church in these terms. During
the years leading up to the Reformation, the Roman Catholic Church
argued that all those who are in good standing with the visible
church—i.e., with the Roman Church—were in good standing with
God. Rome merged the visible church with the church that God
alone can see so that the two were identified. Erasing the distinction
between the church as God sees it and the church as we see it resulted
in a culture-religion that led to formalism, superstition, and the loss
of vital biblical Christianity. On the other end of the spectrum were
the sixteenth-century Anabaptists. They believed that they could
gain God's insight into who was truly regenerate and, hence, who
was truly part of the church as God sees it. The Anabaptists sought
to identify this universal, "invisible" church with the visible church;
their program was to "purify" the membership of the visible church
so that it matched that of the church that God alone can see—this,
of course, was the ideal of a "regenerate church membership." In
response to this, Reformers such as Calvin argued that Christians
should have "a certain charitable judgment" toward those who, "by
confession of faith, by example of life, and by partaking of the sacraments, profess the same God and Christ with us" (Calvin, *Inst.*,
4.1.8). Hence, our assurance of others' regeneration is not necessary.
On the other hand, in order to make room for the reality that our

76

knowledge of others' faith and standing with God does not match God's own knowledge of such things, the Reformers also spoke of a universal church that is invisible to us.

And this points us to what, I think, are important biblical and theological reasons for holding on to this visible/invisible distinction as a valid and necessary way of describing the church. The apostle Paul, in explaining that the promises of God to Israel did not fail, argued that "not all who are descended from Israel belong to Israel, and not all are children of Abraham because they are offspring, but 'Through Isaac shall your offspring be named.' This means that it is not the children of the flesh who are the children of God, but the children of the promise are counted as offspring" (Rom. 9:6–8). Paul here suggests that not everyone who belonged to Israel *visibly*—in terms of ethnicity, circumcision, sacrifice, or other duties—necessarily belonged to the "true" Israel—those chosen by God to be his children of promise.

If we consider this matter in terms of the diagram below, we can see that "visible" Israel included all the adults and children who belonged to Israel—"to them belong the adoption, the glory, the covenants, the giving of the law, the worship, and the promises" (Rom. 9:4). But we know from what Paul says that not everyone who

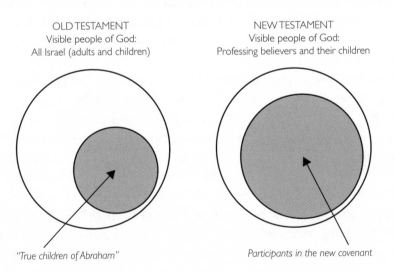

OLD TESTAMENT
Visible people of God:
All Israel (adults and children)

NEW TESTAMENT
Visible people of God:
Professing believers and their children

*"True children of Abraham"*

*Participants in the new covenant*

belonged to visible Israel was given the grace to look through the entire old covenant system, see the Redeemer of God's chosen people, believe in him, and be justified by God. Only some within Israel received this grace. Hence, within the visible Old Testament people of God, there was a "remnant" who were the "true children of Abraham" to whom God's promises came and for whom they were fulfilled.

In the New Testament, the situation is similar. The visible people of God in Christ's church are those who have made professions of faith in Jesus Christ, who have been baptized, and who participate in the Lord's Supper; included in this visible people of God are the children of such believers. Still, we know that not everyone in this number is part of the true people of God, those who truly participate in the new covenant, who receive the Spirit of God, a new heart, and all of Christ's benefits, as well as Christ himself. There are hypocrites in this number, as well as those who will at some point depart from the faith (2 Tim. 4:10; Heb. 6:4–6; 1 John 2:19). As we confess, "the purest churches under heaven are subject both to mixture and error" (WCF 25.5), and part of that error is represented in people who name Christ's name but may in some way be hypocritical or even heretical. By recognizing that the church we see does not match up to the church as God sees it, we have a workable explanation for the problem of apostasy as well as an understanding of how God's promise relates to those who identify with the visible church. As the Westminster Larger Catechism teaches us, "All that hear the gospel, and live in the visible church, are not saved; but they only who are true members of the church invisible" by God's electing grace and genuine faith in Jesus Christ (LC 61).

## WHO ARE "MEMBERS" OF THE CHURCH?

Another value of the distinction between the visible church and the invisible church is that it enables us to gain a better grip on who are members of the visible church. Our Larger Catechism teaches us that "the visible church is a society made up of all such as in all ages and places of the world do profess the true religion, and of their children" (LC 62). On one level, this statement seems obvious. Go into any worship service in virtually any church of any denomination and you will find parents worshipping God together with their children. In fact, many people who have been away from church for a time, usually beginning during their college years, are motivated to return to the fold by the birth of their children. There is something instinctive within us that recognizes that children should be brought up in the presence of God, that God desires for us to worship him as entire households.

In addition, there is a solid theological rationale for seeing our children as members of the visible church. For God's goal in human history is to redeem a people for his own possession and for his own glory (Ex. 19:5–6; 1 Peter 2:9–10). This is God's unchangeable purpose that progresses throughout biblical history in a movement from promise to fulfillment. God set about accomplishing his purpose of redeeming a people by starting with a household—Adam and his progeny (Gen. 3:15). Holy Scripture continually stresses the importance of households following the Lord (e.g., Josh. 24:15). The preeminent example of this is the story of Abraham, who was called out of pagan darkness, given glorious promises about a Seed and a Land, and then was given a sacramental sign to seal God's promises to him and his household (Gen. 12, 15, 17). Again and again, God makes special promises to heads of households about their children (see, e.g., Isa. 49:25; 54:13; 60:9). When we move to the New Testament, God's redemptive program remains the same: "For the promise is for you and for your children and for all who are far off, everyone whom the Lord our God calls to himself" (Acts 2:39). This is why the apostles, in addition to recognizing children of believers as set apart federally by virtue of their relationship to parents who are professing Christians, so often speak of those same children as having responsibilities to their parents that are rooted in their relationship to the visible church (Eph. 6:1–3; 1 Cor. 7:14). All of this suggests that children of professing believers are members of the visible church.

For this reason, children of believers rightly receive the sign of initiation that marks them as belonging to the visible church—baptism. We will look more closely at sacraments in the next chapter, but it is important to point out here that Presbyterians need to refine our terminology somewhat when it comes to this issue. We should be speaking about "household baptisms" rather than "infant baptisms." We baptize the children of professing believers because God has given parents as household heads many strong promises that indicate that he cares for our children and suggest that he works primarily through such households. In addition, God gave his Old Testament sign of circumcision to Abraham's entire household—in Old Testament terms, defined as sons and male slaves—as a rite of initiation into God's visible people (Gen. 17:22–27). Because Abraham believed in God, his entire household was circumcised, including Ishmael, who was not the promised child. In the same way, because you as a household head believe, your entire household is viewed by God as set apart—as holy (1 Cor. 7:14)—and should receive the sign of initiation into God's visible people. This sign seals to you and to your children God's promise to care for your family (Acts 16:15, 33–34).

Those who are members of the visible church, whether professing adult or covenant child, receive certain privileges. For example, we enjoy "being under God's special care and government." Our spiritual lives are "protected and preserved in all ages, not withstanding the opposition of all enemies" (LC 63). Further, as members of the visible church we receive a number of important benefits—we enjoy the communion of the saints, the ordinary means of salvation, and, particularly, the continual free offer of the gospel of grace through the preached Word of God. Each week, as we and our children hear the gospel preached, the promises of God are rehearsed to us again and again.

It is for these reasons that we are called by God to love the church. As members of Christ's visible church, we are given glorious privileges, but even more, we enjoy the presence of God himself in worship, we hear the gospel of Christ proclaimed, and we know the fellowship of the Spirit in the bond of peace. We learn to sing with all the saints:

The church shall never perish!
    Her dear Lord to defend,
to guide, sustain, and cherish,
    is with her to the end;
though there be those that hate her,
    and false sons in her pale,
against or foe or traitor
    she ever shall prevail.

For she on earth hath union
    with God the Three in One,
and mystic sweet communion
    with those whose rest is won:
O happy ones and holy!
    Lord, give us grace that we,
like them, the meek and lowly,
    on high may dwell with thee.[4]

## »Questions for Thought and Review

1. What are some of the reasons that you have heard your friends or family give for not going to church, or for going to a nondenominational church? Do you agree that we live in a "post-church" age?

2. What do you think the Westminster Confession of Faith meant when it confessed that outside the church "there is no ordinary possibility of salvation" (WCF 25.2)? Does this suggest a higher view of the church than is common today? Do you agree with the Confession's claim?

3. How do we reconcile the claim that "we believe in one holy, catholic, and apostolic church" with the fact that the Christian church is divided into hundreds (perhaps thousands) of denominational groupings?

4. Have you ever met someone who believed in "apostolic succession"? What did they mean by that term: were they talking about

(Episcopal) ordination or true (Baptist) churches? What do we mean when we say that we believe in the "apostolic" church?

5. In some Reformed traditions, discipline is added as a third "mark" of the church. Why should discipline be included as a mark of the true church? Why should it not be included?

6. Some people criticize the Confession's understanding of a universal church "which is invisible to us," by mocking the possibility of having an invisible church with invisible members feasting on an invisible sacrament. How does this caricature represent a radical misunderstanding of the confessional and biblical point?

7. Many evangelicals believe in the ideal of a "regenerate church membership." How would you discuss this point with a friend who believes in this ideal, in order to demonstrate that this represents a confusion of the church we see with the church that God alone can know?

8. What are some of the ramifications that follow from the belief that children of believing parents are members of the visible church? Does this belief make the argument for "household baptisms" easier to sustain?

## »For Further Reading

Clowney, Edmund P. *The Church.* Downers Grove, Ill.: InterVarsity Press, 1995.

Habig, Brian, and Les Newsome. *The Enduring Community: Embracing the Priority of the Church.* Jackson, Miss.: Reformed University Press, 2003.

# CHAPTER 5

# Sacraments:
# Signs and Seals of God's Grace

FOR MANY PEOPLE with backgrounds in broader evangelicalism, Presbyterian beliefs about the sacraments of baptism and the Lord's Supper are perhaps the greatest intellectual hurdles to overcome. When you say the word "sacrament," these brothers and sisters immediately think about the Roman Catholic Church, which structures its entire religious life around seven sacraments that provide "grace" for individuals from birth to death. Or perhaps these friends have come to Christ through more formal church backgrounds, joined evangelical churches, and been convinced that they needed to be "rebaptized"; they may have been told that their having been baptized as infants was not legitimate because the action was not preceded by a profession of faith. Through the influence of "common-sense" readings of Scripture and a general reluctance to believe that sacraments can serve as means of grace in any sense, many brothers and sisters struggle with the Presbyterian understanding of how baptism and the Lord's Supper operate as true means of grace in the Christian life.

You may be aware that the Roman Catholic Church holds that there are seven sacraments: in addition to baptism and the Lord's Supper, they include confirmation, penance, marriage, ordination (or Holy Orders), and last rites (or extreme unction). Presbyterians, following the Reformers, have not seen these other pastoral actions as "sacraments" for a couple of reasons. First, sacraments of the New Testament are directly established by Jesus himself. Both baptism and the Lord's Supper have that character (Matt. 28:19–20; 1 Cor. 11:23). Second, these New Testament sacraments directly represent Christ and his benefits. While these other pastoral rites may be important life-markers, only baptism and the Supper point us to the death, burial, and resurrection of Jesus and the benefits that he offers. As a result, Presbyterians hold that "there be only two sacraments ordained by Christ our Lord in the gospel; that is to say, Baptism and the Supper of the Lord" (WCF 27.4).

## What Is a Sacrament?

Presbyterians, along with many other believers who think sacramentally, would say that sacraments are "holy signs and seals of the covenant of grace" (WCF 27.1). In other words, a sacrament pictures or *signs* God's promises. In biblical usage, a "sign" is like a big road sign with an arrow pointing you to Jesus Christ. This is how the word is used in John's Gospel: "This, the first of his signs, Jesus did at Cana in Galilee, and manifested his glory" (John 2:11). The sign was meant to point the disciples (and John's readers) to Jesus as God's promised Messiah. The same is true with sacraments—they direct us to the one who is the savior of our souls.

A sacrament also *seals* God's promise. In older times, documents would bear a mark from the author of the letter or treaty that sealed the material contained in it and vouched for its authenticity and authority. In our day, we often talk about people or organizations giving their "seal of approval" for certain actions or products, such as, for example, the "Good Housekeeping Seal of Approval"; when you see that seal, you know that Good Housekeeping has tested the product in question and approved it. Or, to change the image, sports memorabilia often comes with a "seal of authenticity" to let buyers know that the autograph is real and true. In other words, a seal gives you confidence that the product (or the letter or document) it seals is what it purports to be. In the same way, a sacrament seals God's promises and gives you confidence that his promises can be trusted. As the Westminster Confession of Faith puts it, sacraments "confirm our interest in him" (WCF 27.1). They give us assurance or confidence as they confirm our interest in God and his promises.

Sacraments also do something else. They "put a visible difference between those that belong unto the Church and the rest of the world" (WCF 27.1). They mark believers as different from unbelievers, as being on a different team, if you will. That is why I like to say that baptism is like a jersey that marks us as part of the baptized team. It identifies us and our children as members of the visible church, those who have been baptized and who profess faith in the triune God. In a similar fashion, the Lord's Supper marks off those who have made a good profession in Jesus Christ from the rest of the world that has not. It serves as a picture of those who will participate in the final "marriage supper of the Lamb" (Rev. 19:6–11), those who will be part of the new heavens and new earth.

How do sacraments *do* these things? We must be clear that there is no power in the sacrament itself that causes God's grace to come to an individual; that is, a sacrament in and of itself has no power to confirm a person's interest in God or "to engage him to the service of God in Christ" (WCF 27.1, 3). Instead, the sacraments serve as signs of a spiritual reality, namely, Christ and his benefits. And there is a "sacramental union"—a "spiritual relation"—between the sign and the spiritual reality. That's why when we distribute the Lord's Supper, the minister will often say, "This is the body of Christ. Take and eat." Presbyterians don't believe that the bread in the Lord's Supper is actually transformed into Christ's body; nor do we believe that Christ's body is somehow "in, with, or under" the bread. Rather, we believe that there is a spiritual relationship between Christ's ascended and glorified body and the bread by which we are enabled, by God's grace and his Spirit, to feed upon Christ's presence and receive his benefits. It is because of this sacramental union between the sign and the thing signified that "the names and effects of the one are attributed to the other" (WCF 27.2).

In thinking about how sacraments "work," it is important to distinguish the validity of a sacrament from its efficacy. A sacrament is *valid*—that is, we have warrant for a sacrament—because it is based on God's command and promise, contained in the words of institution. But a sacrament is *efficacious*—it "works," if you will—because the Spirit applies Christ and his benefits to the individual who responds in faith to the promise.

And so, with baptism, we could say that the *validity* of the sacrament of baptism—for professing adults as well as for their children—is rooted in God's promise. In baptism, God promises certain benefits—"his ingrafting into Christ, of his regeneration, of remission of sins"—that obligates the individual "to walk in newness of life" (WCF 28.1). The promise is valid because *God* promises it, not because the individual testifies to some new spiritual reality in himself. However, the *efficacy* of baptism is tied to the choosing purposes of God, the work of the Holy Spirit, and the individual's response of faith. The grace that baptism signs and seals—that baptism exhibits and confers (WCF 28.6)—is not tied to the moment of administration, nor is it given to everyone to whom baptism is administered (WCF 28.5). Instead, grace is given by the Holy Spirit to those whom God the King has chosen "in his appointed time" (WCF 28.6).

This distinction between the validity and the efficacy of a sacrament is important; because many evangelicals fail to recognize this distinction, they misunderstand what happens in baptism and the Lord's Supper. For example, those who reject infant baptism do so because they presume that baptism is only valid *when* it is efficacious. That is, they believe that the only truly "biblical" baptism is one in which the individual by his or her own profession of faith at the moment of administration receives the grace offered in baptism. Ironically, others who have a very high view of infant baptism often make the same mistake. They believe that something must "happen" at the moment of baptism, and so they argue that a child's faith is awakened at baptism in order that the child may grasp the promise of God's Word and so receive grace. Or, they presume that the child is already regenerate and thus baptize based on the assumption that God's grace is already at work

86

in the child's life. But both of these approaches confuse the sacrament's validity with its efficacy. A baptism is valid when it proclaims the promise of God by means of an ordained minister using water and the biblical, Trinitarian formula. It is efficacious—it confers grace—when God's Spirit creates faith in the individual so that he or she grasps God's promise by faith and thus fulfills the meaning of the sign. This conferral of grace may or may not happen at the moment when the baptism itself takes place—in some cases, it may occur immediately; in others, years later; in some, it may not occur at all.

One other thing to consider when we think about sacraments is that there were sacraments in the Old Testament as well as in the New Testament. The Old Testament sacraments were circumcision and Passover, while the New Testament sacraments are baptism and the Lord's Supper. Presbyterians believe that, "in regard of the spiritual things thereby signified and exhibited," the sacraments of both the Old and New Testaments pointed to the same things (WCF 27.5). That is, circumcision and the Passover both pointed to God's promise of Christ and his benefits; baptism and the Supper do as well. This continuity in terms of the substance of the things signified is significant—it means that there are not two stories, two religions, in the Bible, but one story and one "religion" in which God demands the worship of his people and they respond to him in faith. But the discontinuity is noteworthy as well—the forms, the terms of admittance, and the rules and regulations were all changed. That means we cannot simply draw a straight line between circumcision and baptism or between Passover and the Supper; rather, we must be sensitive to the way the risen Christ transforms these signs and seals. There are connections between the Old and New Testament sacraments (Col. 2:11–12; 1 Cor. 5:7; 10:1–4; 11:23–28), but there are differences as well. It is important to bear these similarities and differences in mind.

## BAPTISM: ENTRANCE INTO GOD'S VISIBLE PEOPLE

Though some may believe that Presbyterians' understanding of baptism is somewhat complex, it actually is rooted in the larger story of what God is doing in this world through his people. The sign of baptism is rooted in God's larger unchanging purpose in human history. From the very beginning, God has been redeeming a people for his own possession and for his own glory. While God certainly calls individuals to himself, he has, from the very beginning, especially emphasized the relationship of professing believers and their households, and their place within his larger and unchanging purpose of redemption. Thus, redemptive history began with Adam and his household; with Abel and Cain and their households; and particularly, with Abraham and his household.

God made a covenant with Abraham, promising "to be God to you and to your offspring after you" (Gen. 17:7). In order to seal that promise, God gave Abraham a sign—circumcision—which was to be administered to Abraham and to all the males in his household. This sign was a promise, a community marker that always went with Jewish males as a reminder that God had promised to be their God. Circumcision also served as the initiatory rite into the body of those who professed to be God's people. The content of the promise that God made to Abraham—"to be God to you and your offspring after you"— remained the same throughout the Old Testament. Each father was charged with instructing his household in the meaning of circumcision—the need to have one's heart circumcised by God, the need to claim the covenant promises by faith in the coming Redeemer of God's elect, and to repent of sins (Deut. 10:16; 30:6).

In the New Testament, the apostle Peter makes plain that the *content* of God's promises has not changed—God promises to be a God to believers and their households (Acts 2:38–39). What changed was the *form* and *subjects* of God's promise: in the Old Testament, circumcision was applied to *all males* in the household; in the New Testament, baptism was applied to *all who professed faith* in the Redeemer of God's people, as well as their households. For example, in Acts 16, Lydia and the Philippian jailer, both of whom are heads of households, believe in Jesus and their entire households are baptized. The reason such household baptisms are appropriate is that the "household logic" that was operative in the Old Testament is still operational in the New.

The children of New Testament believers—in the first century and now— are set apart ("holy") in God's sight because we as household heads profess faith in Christ (1 Cor. 7:14); as a result, it is right to extend to our children the sign that they belong to God's visible people. This sign seals God's promise to our children, reminds our children of God's promise, and marks them off from the world as belonging to God.

Just as Old Testament believers were called to instruct their children in the meaning and importance of their covenant sign of circumcision, in this New Testament era, we, as household heads, are called to instruct our children in the meaning and importance of their baptism, to urge them to embrace God's promise in Jesus Christ by repenting of their sins and professing faith in him, and to improve their baptism at every opportunity (LC 167). And God's work of redemption is extended when his purpose in our households is fulfilled—when our children leave their father's house to establish their own households, where they in turn baptize and instruct their own children, urging them to repentance and faith in Jesus Christ (to whom the signs point), and dedicating themselves to raising godly offspring for God's glory.

This understanding of baptism is grounded in a particular understanding of the church as a visible people. As we saw in the previous chapter, Presbyterians believe that the visible church is made up of professing believers and their children. In other words, the ideal of a "regenerate church membership" is unbiblical because it makes too direct a connection between the visible people of God and the body of those whom God has chosen from the beginning to the end of time. Those who are responsible for admitting people to the Lord's Supper have no way of ascertaining who is regenerate and who is not. All we have are individuals' professions of faith. Certainly, elders do their best to investigate those professions of faith to ensure that they are credible and sincere. And, in a judgment of Christian charity, we do believe that these professions of faith are genuine and represent true spiritual reality. Still, that is a long way from saying that the membership of the visible church is to be restricted to those whom we deem to be truly elect and genuinely regenerate. Only God can make judgment calls of this magnitude. But, once we shift our view of who makes up the visible church, our understanding of baptism as a sign of initiation into the visible church shifts as well. Suddenly, baptism is no longer *our* act of testifying that we are regenerate and following Jesus in obedience; rather, it is *God's* act of initiating us into his visible people. It follows from this that baptism is properly administered to those who make professions of faith, as well as to their children, because God's promise is offered "for you and for your children" (Acts 2:39).

## THE LORD'S SUPPER: STRENGTH FOR THE JOURNEY

Most people who go to church know what the Supper is, even when they call it something different, such as "the breaking of the bread," "communion," or "the Eucharist." The name "Lord's Supper" comes from 1 Corinthians 11:20, and the heart of the ritual is common among all Christians: "the Lord's Supper is a sacrament, wherein, by giving and receiving bread and wine, according to Christ's appointment, his death is showed forth" (SC 96). Typically, the mechanics of the Supper involve ordained ministers who

> set apart the bread and wine from common use, by the word of institution, thanksgiving and prayer; to take and break the bread, and to give both the bread and the wine to the communicants; who are, by the same appointment, to take and eat the bread, and to drink the wine, in thankful remembrance that the body of Christ was broken and given, and his blood shed, for them. (LC 169)

While the validity of the sacrament is fairly easy to establish from Scripture, its efficacy is much more difficult to understand. In fact, at one point the Westminster Confession describes the Supper as a "holy mystery" (WCF 29.8). And because how the Supper "works" is a mystery, there have been numerous disagreements about what *happens* in the Supper. Presbyterian confessional documents attempt to deal with a number of "mistaken" views while at the same time setting forth our understanding of what happens in this meal. Sometimes, the qualifications and caveats in the Standards are so confusing that it is hard to understand what is at stake or even what Presbyterians are trying to say. But if we are patient, I think we can derive a basic understanding of what happens in this holy mystery called the Lord's Supper. It is important to understand that Reformation debates over the Supper had everything to do with where Christ's ascended body is and how believers "feed" upon that ascended body. We will have more to say about this as we go along.

Notice first that the confessional documents are very careful to tell us what does *not* happen in the Supper: the bread and the wine do not actually and substantially *become* Christ's body and blood. The belief that they do, a doctrine called transubstantiation, is held by Roman Catholics. They believe that, in the act of consecration by the priest (when he says in Latin, "this is my body"), the bread, which is lifted up in the sight of the congregation for their adoration, actually and really becomes the substance of Christ's body. The Westminster Confession spares no language in rejecting this position: this doctrine "is repugnant, not to Scripture alone, but even to common sense, and reason; [and it] overthroweth the nature of the sacrament, and hath been and is the cause of manifold superstitions; yea, of gross idolatries" (WCF 29.6). Presbyterians believe that when the bread and wine are consecrated by God through a minister's prayer, "they still remain truly and only bread and wine, as they were before" (WCF 29.5). We also do not believe, as Roman Catholics do, that the Lord's Supper provides an opportunity for Christ to be offered up to his Father once again in a real propitiation for sins. This "popish sacrifice of the mass (as they call it) is most abominably injurious to Christ's one, only sacrifice, the alone propitiation for all the sins of His elect" (WCF 29.2).

Furthermore, Presbyterians do not believe that Christ's body is somehow "in, with, or under the bread and wine" (WCF 29.7). This describes the Lutheran view, which is based on a belief that Christ's resurrected and ascended body is "ubiquitous" (that is, everywhere at the same time). The result of the Lutheran view is that, when an individual partakes of the bread in the Supper, the bread itself is not

Christ's body, but is united to Christ's physical body which surrounds it. Presbyterians do not believe that Christ's ascended body works in this way. Rather, we believe that Christ's resurrected body has ascended to heaven where he sits at the Father's right hand (Acts 2:33). Therefore, his body is not present everywhere at the same time to surround the bread and wine at the Supper in all the churches where it may be taking place.

What, then, *do* Presbyterians believe happens in the Lord's Supper? How do believers feed upon the body and blood of Christ? The Confession takes great pains to stress that we do not feed on Christ "corporally or carnally," but "spiritually" and yet "really and indeed" (WCF 29.7). Perhaps you've read the somewhat tortured section of the Confession in 29.7:

> Worthy receivers, outwardly partaking of the visible elements, in this sacrament, do then also, inwardly by faith, really and indeed, yet not carnally and corporally but spiritually, receive, and feed upon, Christ crucified, and all benefits of His death: the body and blood of Christ being then, not corporally or carnally, in, with, or under the bread and wine; yet, as really, but spiritually, present to the faith of believers in that ordinance, as the elements themselves are to their outward senses.

Did you catch what the Confession is trying to say here? It says two important things: first, worthy receivers of the Supper receive and feed upon Christ crucified and all benefits of his death; and second, in the Supper the body and blood of Christ are as surely present to the faith of believers as the elements themselves are to their outward senses. How do these two things happen? Not corporally or carnally, but *spiritually*. In a way that we cannot fully grasp intellectually, when we outwardly eat and drink the visible elements, we are inwardly feeding on Christ's body and blood by faith. There is no change or transformation in the elements, no surrounding of the bread and wine with Christ's body. And yet, really and indeed, we feed on Christ's body and blood spiritually. John Calvin, the great sixteenth-century Reformed pastor and theologian, believed that in the Supper the Holy

Spirit works to lift our hearts and minds to heaven, where Christ is seated, so that we might feed spiritually (that is, by means of the Spirit) on his presence (*Inst.*, 4.17.18). Yet Calvin was also careful to point out that our feeding upon Christ is a mystery that is felt more than explained, because words themselves are inadequate to describe what is transacted in the Lord's Supper (*Inst.*, 4.17.7).

The upshot of all this is that in the Lord's Supper, we "receive and apply unto ourselves Christ crucified and all the benefits of his death" by faith (LC 170). The benefits that we receive are consequential to our living the Christian life well. We believe that in this meal we gain what is vital for "our spiritual nourishment and growth in grace," including the confirmation of our union and communion with Christ, the renewal of our thankfulness to God and our commitment to belong to him, and the engagement of our mutual love and fellowship with one another (LC 168).

In order to receive these spiritual benefits, however, we must prepare ourselves before we come to the Lord's Supper in at least two ways. First, drawing upon Paul's injunction in 1 Corinthians 11:28, Presbyterians have long urged one another to examine themselves before they come to the Lord's Table, seeking to ascertain "their being in Christ; their sins and wants; the truth and measure of their knowledge, faith, repentance, love to God and the brethren, charity to all men, forgiving those that have done them wrong; their desires after Christ; and their new obedience" (LC 171). Second, we must seek to renew the exercise of all of our spiritual graces. As we consider and examine ourselves, we should meditate on the truths of God's Word and on his great grace and forgiveness for those who fail in their spiritual duties. We also need to pray fervently, seeking God's mercy and grace for our sins and failures and asking that he meet us in the Lord's Supper to grant us his strengthening and nourishing grace.

During the Supper, we are called to wait upon God in the sacrament, observing diligently what is going on: the minister's explanation of the sacrament, the words of institution, the invitation to the Supper, the prayer of consecration for the elements, the breaking of bread and pouring of wine, and the distribution of the elements. In the midst of these actions, we should seek to discern Christ's body, believing that, in the bread and in the wine, Christ's crucified body and blood are spiritually present to our faith and that, in these elements, Christ and all his benefits are given to us by that faith. In thus discerning Christ's body, we are stirred up to judge ourselves and sorrow for our sin, to hunger and thirst after Christ, to feed upon him and receive of his fullness, trusting in his merits, rejoicing in his love and giving thanks for his grace, and to renew our covenant with God and with other church members (LC 174). In many ways, the Lord's Supper is the renewal of the solemn covenant between God and ourselves—we are forsaking our sin, resting on Christ and his merits for acceptance with God, and renewing our obedience to God and his Word in gratitude for his mercy. In response, God grants us all of Christ's benefits—but more importantly, he grants us Christ himself.

After the Supper, we should take some time to consider how we participated in the meal. If we found spiritual comfort and renewal, then we should bless God for his mercy, beg him for the continuance of this gracious renewal, watch against relapses into sin, and fulfill our spiritual duties. If we did not find that comfort and renewal, then we should think back to how we prepared ourselves beforehand and how we carried ourselves during the Supper. If we were prepared for the Supper and sought God's presence in the meal, then we wait for the spiritual benefit that God will grant in his good time. But if we did not prepare well, or if we did not use the meal well, then we should be humbled and seek God's presence more fervently and diligently the next time we have opportunity to participate in the Lord's Supper (LC 175).

Presbyterians historically have taken the Lord's Supper very seriously, perhaps more seriously than other evangelicals. That seriousness is reflected in the Presbyterian practice of "fencing the table." In the eighteenth century, Scots and American Presbyterians were examined by their ruling elders concerning their faith in Jesus Christ and their current spiritual condition; if they were deemed to be "worthy professors," these hardy souls were given "communion tokens" that would admit them to a place at the Lord's Table. In contemporary practice, Presbyterian ministers invite to the Supper those have made a profession of faith in a particular congregation and have been admitted to the table by either the local church session or some other authorized church leadership. We also warn those who have not made a profession of faith or who are living in unrepentant sin not to come to the table, so that they will not "eat and drink judgment to themselves" (SC 97; 1 Cor. 11:27–32; BCO 58-4). In this way, Presbyterians have tried to preserve the purity of the Lord's Table.

This seriousness is also demonstrated in the way in which we deal with our children in approaching the table. Perhaps the best way of getting at this point is to think through the similarities and differences between baptism and the Lord's Supper. The similarities are somewhat obvious (LC 176). We believe that God is the author of both baptism and the Lord's Supper; they are both God's idea and have his warrant. The focus of both is Christ and his benefits. Both are seals of the same covenant, the same promises. Each is to be administered by ordained ministers of the gospel and by none other. And each is to be continued in the church until the end of the age. Some of the differences between the two are obvious as well, or at least they should be (LC 177). Baptism happens, or should happen, only once in a person's life; the Lord's Supper is administered often. Baptism uses water; the Supper uses bread and wine.

But other differences are more important. The Catechism says that baptism is a "sign and seal of our regeneration and ingrafting into Christ," a grace that is conferred in God's appointed time and that evidences itself in a full-hearted turn to Christ as Savior and Lord (LC 165). The Lord's Supper, on the other hand, is received by those who have already begun the journey of faith, "to confirm our continuance and growth" in Jesus Christ (LC 177). Or, we could put it this way: baptism *initiates* our children into the visible people of God, into the "church people," and into the care of the church and the benefits that membership in that community brings. But the Lord's Supper has a different focus; it serves to *confirm* our faith and assure our hearts that, as surely as we partake of bread and wine, so surely did Christ die for our sins.

Thus, Presbyterians believe that baptism is rightly administered "even to infants," as we have just seen. Because our children belong to our households of faith, they should belong in a visible way to *the* household of faith; and baptism initiates them into God's visible people. However, we believe that the Supper is to be administered "only to such as are of years and ability to examine themselves." The emphasis here is not upon *adult-only communion* but on *professing believers-only communion*. Our catechism presumes that infants or toddlers cannot examine themselves of their "being in Christ" (LC 172); that is, they cannot recognize their sinfulness and turn to faith to Jesus Christ. When they come "of years and ability to examine themselves" (LC 177), if they make a credible profession of faith in Jesus, then the local church's session has the opportunity—and the responsibility—to admit them to the Lord's Table (BCO 57-2). As a result, Presbyterians typically do not admit to the table children who have not made a credible profession of faith; not because they are children, but because acknowledged faith in Jesus Christ is necessary for a worthy reception of the Supper.

## »Questions for Thought and Review

1. Think about your religious upbringing prior to encountering Presbyterianism. As you consider Presbyterian beliefs about the sacraments, how does your prior religious life cause you to react to this chapter?
2. Reflect on how this chapter described the way in which sacraments sign, seal, and mark. Are these helpful descriptions of what sacraments do? What are some other pictures or analogies for speaking about what sacraments do?
3. How do sacraments "work"? What do we mean when we talk about a "sacramental union" between the sign and the spirituality reality? Who is the "spiritual reality" communicated by the sacrament?

96

4. What do you think about the distinction between the validity and the efficacy of a sacrament? How does this distinction clarify the way you may have thought about baptism in the past?
5. How does the "household logic" of the Bible, in both the Old and New Testaments, provide a strong rationale for household (hence, infant) baptism?
6. How does the shift away from the ideal of "regenerate church membership" shift the focus of baptism?
7. What do Presbyterians believe happens in the Lord's Supper? How do we feed spiritually upon Christ and all his benefits?
8. What does this meal provide for our Christian lives? In order to receive these benefits, how should we prepare to receive the Lord's Supper?
9. What are some similarities and differences between baptism and the Lord's Supper? How does seeing baptism as initiation and the Supper as confirmation clarify some of the differences in relation to our children?

## »For Further Reading

Booth, Robert R. *Children of Promise: The Biblical Case for Infant Baptism.* Phillipsburg, N.J.: P&R, 1995.
Bruce, Robert. *The Mystery of the Lord's Supper.* Edited by T. F. Torrance. London: James Clarke, 1958.
Gerrish, B. A. *Grace and Gratitude: The Eucharistic Theology of John Calvin.* Minneapolis, Minn.: Fortress, 1993.
Old, Hughes O. *The Shaping of the Reformed Baptismal Rite in the Sixteenth Century.* Grand Rapids, Mich.: Eerdmans, 1992.
*Report of the Ad-Interim Committee to Study the Question of Paedocommunion.* This 1986 PCA position paper on paedocommunion can be found on the Internet: http://www.pcahistory.org/pca/index.html.
Riggs, John W. *Baptism in the Reformed Tradition: A Historical and Practical Theology.* Louisville, Ky.: Westminster John Knox, 2002.
Vander Zee, Leonard J. *Christ, Baptism, and the Lord's Supper: Recovering the Sacraments for Evangelical Worship.* Downers Grove, Ill.: InterVarsity Press, 2004.

# PART TWO

# ≫*Presbyterian Practices*

CHAPTER **6**

# A Heart Aflame:
# Presbyterian and Reformed Piety

PERHAPS YOU ARE WONDERING why "piety" represents the first set of Presbyterian practices that we are going to consider. Perhaps you are wondering what piety is, period. Those are good questions to ask. We don't use the word *piety* very much today. Nowadays, the word *spirituality* is used far more often. This latter term originated from Roman Catholic sources during the seventeenth century, but has since become the dominant term for describing how people approach religious things. Pop culture figures as diverse as Madonna, Bruce Springsteen, and Oprah Winfrey talk about spirituality as a means of connecting with some "higher power," religious truth, or even themselves. Because of the prevalence of the word, some people speak about "Reformed spirituality" as a means for understanding how Presbyterian believers enjoy communion with God. However, as scholar Hughes Oliphant Old noted, "Calvinists have usually preferred the term *piety* to the term *spirituality*."[1] Part of the reason for this is that piety (from the Latin word *pietas*, literally meaning "dutifulness" or "fidelity") often communicates "reverence joined with love of God which the knowledge of his benefits induces" (Calvin, *Inst.*, 1.2.1). But piety also stands for a whole realm of practices that shape our reverence and love for God. Practices such as worship, prayer, singing, and service help form and guide the way our reverence and love for God express themselves. These practices also remind us of Christ's benefits granted to us through faith in him; they thus become a means for inducing piety. Because piety points us both to the spiritual graces and to the practices needed to inculcate those graces, we will be talking about Reformed piety, instead of spirituality, in this chapter.

From what we have just said, it may be obvious that Reformed piety is nothing less than how Presbyterians believe that the Christian life should be lived. Perhaps less obvious is the fact that the Westminster Standards themselves provide excellent guidance on what Reformed piety is and what it should look like. All too often, we have allowed ourselves to think that the Standards are simply doctrinal statements meant to ensure the maintenance of orthodoxy; aside from that purpose, they have little use. On the contrary, the Standards, in the way that they reflect the teaching of Holy Scripture, serve as a wonderful norm and guide for the Christian life. Therefore, in this chapter, I want to use these documents to guide our thoughts about Reformed piety. In particular, I want us to see that the Standards argue that the very basis of the Christian life is our union with Christ. All the benefits of salvation are found in Christ, and these benefits become ours as we are united to Christ by Spirit-wrought faith. By starting with our union with Jesus, we understand that we are justified and sanctified, not by any works that we can do, but through our union with him as effected by faith. From this root, we desire to see spiritual fruits manifested in our lives. God provides a number of practices that serve as means for spiritual nourishment to help us grow in grace. In fact, if we do not use these "means of grace," we will soon find our spiritual growth stunted or misshapen; in addition, we will not experience the assurance that God offers us as we use these practices.

By using the Presbyterian confessional standards to spell out what Reformed piety is, I also hope to make another point. Much of what passes for the evangelical understanding of the Christian life separates knowledge *about* God (doctrine) from knowing God personally (life). What Presbyterians (and other Reformed believers) have always understood is that the Christian life is a *way of life* that is based on doctrine; or, to put it another way, our practices are based squarely on our beliefs. Throughout Presbyterian and Reformed history—whether it was sixteenth-century theologian John Calvin writing his *Institutes* as a manual of piety, nineteenth-century theologian Charles Hodge spelling out the basics of the Christian life in his *The Way of Life*, or twentieth-century theologian J. I. Packer leading people through a well-wrought discussion of the attributes of God in his *Knowing God*—we have always stressed that the means for "experiencing God" in our lives is through a proper understanding of who God is, who we are, and what Christ has done for and in us. Indeed, I hope you will notice how the beliefs about which we have already thought impact the way in which we relate to God. Presbyterian beliefs about God's sovereignty and kingdom, the priority of grace, the covenant of grace, and the nature of the church and its sacraments all profoundly shape the way we enjoy communion with God.

In sum, only as we embrace *orthodoxy* (healthy doctrine) can we demonstrate *orthopraxy* (healthy practice). The rule of doctrine can and should be the rule of faith, practice, and prayer.

### THE ROOT OF REFORMED PIETY: UNION WITH CHRIST

Though there is not a separate heading in the Westminster Confession for union with Christ, the language of union and communion with Christ can be found throughout our Presbyterian confessional documents. We believe that those whom God the King has chosen to save "are spiritually and mystically, yet really and inseparably joined to Christ as their head and husband" (LC 66). Notice how the language here is similar to that which we found in the sections of the Standards dealing with the Lord's Supper. The writers of the Standards were trying hard to guard against one particular error while affirming a vital biblical truth. The error they sought to avoid was any sense that believers are "in any wise partakers of the substance of his Godhead" (WCF 26.3). Drawing from the language of 2 Peter 1:4, Eastern Orthodoxy teaches the doctrine of "theosis," the idea that, by participating in the Trinitarian communion by union with Christ, believers are divinized. But the Confession plainly proclaims that there is no sense in which believers so participate in the divine that they are united to God's own substance and thus are made divine themselves.

Rather, this union with Christ is spiritual or mystical, as the apostle Paul makes clear in 1 Corinthians 6:17: "He who is joined with the Lord becomes one spirit with him." The picture most often used to depict this union with Christ is marriage. The Catechism draws upon this image by referring to Ephesians 5. Christ is our head and husband, we are his bride: "For the husband is the head of the wife even as Christ is the head of the church, his body, and is himself its Savior" (Eph. 5:23). Indeed, in biblical thought, we are "members of [Christ's] body" (Eph. 5:30; cf. 1 Cor. 12:27); our connection with Christ as our head is that close. We are his body and we are filled with "the fullness of him who fills all in all" (Eph. 1:23). Hence, we are united to Christ singly as individuals and corporately as the church (WCF 25.1).

It is because of our union with Christ as our head that God imputes Christ's righteousness to us and sees us as holy in his sight. The Larger Catechism teaches us that "the communion in grace which the members of the invisible church have with Christ is their partaking of the virtue of his mediation, in their justification, adoption, sanctification, and whatever else, in this life, manifests their union with him" (LC 69). God views us as having been crucified with Christ, buried with him, raised in newness of life, adopted as his children, and seated in the heavenly places in Christ (Rom. 6:1–4; Gal. 2:20; Eph. 1:3–14; Col. 3:1–4). Hence, we have a new status with God—namely, the status of being right with God, which is granted to us by virtue of our union with Christ. Indeed, our very persons are "accepted through Christ"; likewise, our good works are not accepted because of any merit in themselves, but rather "are accepted in him" (WCF 16.6). Not only this, but our union with Christ is "inseparable" (LC 79); this means that those who are united to Christ will be preserved in grace and will persevere to the end.

This union with Christ does more than simply confer a new status with God (amazing enough in itself!); it also means that we have intimate communion with him, a communion that is the fruit of this union and that is the restoration of what our first parents experienced in their original created state before the fall (WCF 4.2, 6.2). But we must understand that our communion with God is always through our Mediator, Jesus Christ. Indeed, we believe that we "have no access into his presence without a mediator" (LC 181; WCF 21.2). Thus, just as we receive the benefits of redemption through "the virtue of his mediation," so we enjoy communion with God through his mediation—it is communion with God through Jesus by his Spirit. By virtue of our union with Christ, we have "communion in glory" with Christ in this life, which includes enjoying "the sense of God's love, peace of conscience, joy in the Holy Ghost, and hope of glory" (LC 83). Moreover, after we die, we have communion in glory with Christ which results in our souls being made perfect in holiness and welcomed into the highest heavens while we await the resurrection of our bodies and the consummation of God's reign at the end of the age (LC 86). These benefits are ours through our union with Jesus.

One last thing we need to recognize here is that our union and communion with Christ is also the basis for our union and communion with other believers, both those in our local congregation and those in the church at large (WCF 29.1). Because we are united individually with Jesus by Spirit-wrought faith in him, we enjoy communion "in each other's gifts and graces, and are obliged to the performance of such duties, public and private, as do conduce to their mutual good, both in the inward and outward man" (WCF 26.1). This is why it is so distressing to us when fellow church members withdraw from our worship and fellowship (Heb. 10:25) or when there is a breakdown of love and trust among believers (1 Cor. 3:3–9). Division of this sort fractures our common union and calls into question our claim to be united to Christ (Eph. 4:1–4).

## THE PRACTICES OF REFORMED PIETY: MEANS OF GRACE

By using the means of grace, we enjoy communion with God and have assurance that we are united to Christ. We are taught that the way in which Christ communicates the benefits of his mediation—

104

which are ours through union with him—"are all his ordinances; especially, the word, sacraments, and prayer" (LC 154). That is to say, the means of our spiritual growth, the very engine of Presbyterian piety, is worship. And at the heart of Presbyterian worship, and hence, of our piety, is the reading and preaching of God's Word. We confess that God's Spirit makes "the reading, but especially the preaching of the word, an effectual means of convincing and converting sinners, and of building them up in holiness and comfort, through faith, unto salvation" (SC 89). The preached Word does this in many ways: by enlightening our minds, by convincing and humbling us as it drives us out of ourselves, by pointing us to Jesus Christ, by conforming us to his image, by strengthening us in times of temptation, by granting grace and strength to war against our corruptions and to be conformed to his will, and by "establishing our hearts in holiness and comfort" (LC 155). Clearly, the preaching of God's Word accomplishes much in the way of our salvation and in preparing us for the world to come. It is no accident that at key points in John Bunyan's classic *The Pilgrim's Progress*, the traveler, Christian, turned aside to hear the preaching of God's Word, whether at the Interpreter's House or from the shepherds on the Delectable Mountains. Likewise, in order to progress in our communion with God, we must turn aside regularly to the preaching of the Word of God, which is an effectual means of our salvation.

Part of the process of hearing God's Word preached week by week is preparing our hearts to receive that Word through prayer. As the Word is preached, we are to be diligent in listening, not allowing ourselves to become distracted, but focusing our hearts on what Christ is saying through the minister of his Word. The Scriptures also call us to examine what we hear preached, comparing it with the rest of the Scriptures to ascertain whether this is truly God's Word. As we discern that it is, we then "receive the truth with faith, love, meekness, and readiness of mind, as the Word of God." We meditate on it and hide it in our hearts. And above all, we seek to "bring forth the fruit of it in our lives" (LC 160). In this way, the preaching of God's Word will be a means of God's grace to us—a means whereby we put off our sin and live in conformity with God's will as expressed in his Word.

The sacraments of baptism and the Lord's Supper are also used by God to teach us reverence and love of him and to remind us especially of our union with Christ. Baptism serves as "a sign and seal of ingrafting into himself" (LC 165). Hence, as the answer to Larger Catechism question 167 makes clear, every time we see a baptism, we are reminded of "the privileges and benefits conferred and sealed thereby" including being baptized by the Spirit into union with Christ and his body. Yet there are also other ways in which baptism serves as a means of grace, not only at the time we receive it, but throughout our lives, and "especially in the time of temptation." We improve, or use, our baptisms by giving thoughtful consideration to what baptism means, and especially to our own sinfulness, the inward filthiness that the Spirit comes to wash away. We also use our baptisms well when we turn to the gospel, growing up into assurance of pardon of sin and "all other blessings sealed to us in that sacrament." One of the great blessings sealed to us in baptism is our "drawing strength from the death and resurrection of Christ." We were baptized into him, into his death and resurrection, by the Spirit (Rom. 6:1–4; 1 Cor. 12:12–13). Because of this, we have power "for the mortification of sin, and quickening of grace." Finally, we use or improve our baptism by endeavoring to live holy lives by faith in Christ as we walk in brotherly love with one another, recognizing that we have been "baptized by the same Spirit into one body."

In a similar fashion, the Lord's Supper serves as God's "bond and pledge" of our "union and communion with him" (LC 168; WCF 29.1). As we feed upon the presence of Christ, the Supper is a pledge or seal to us, reminding us that we belong to him and that we enjoy communion with him. Indeed, the very visibility of these signs serves to comfort us, for we are prone to forget or to doubt that Christ died for us and cherishes us *in particular*. The Heidelberg Catechism, the doctrinal standard for Dutch Reformed churches, is very helpful here. In answering the question about how the Lord's Supper reminds us and assures us that we share in Christ's sacrifice for sin upon the cross, the catechism teaches that we have a promise that accompanies the Supper:

First, as surely as I see with my eyes the bread of the Lord broken for me and the cup given to me, so surely his body was offered and broken for me and his blood poured out for me on the cross. Second, as surely as I receive from the hand of one who serves, and taste with my mouth the bread and cup of the Lord, given me as sure signs of Christ's body and blood, so surely he nourishes and refreshes my soul for eternal life with his crucified body and poured-out blood. (Heidelberg Catechism, Q 75)

And so, in the Lord's Supper, we gain assurance, confidence, and boldness in our faith, trusting in the promise of grace found in the meal and resting in that gospel grace for our salvation. Both the Lord's Supper and baptism remind us of our union with Christ and our communion with him.

A third means that God uses to transform us and make us more like him is prayer. In fact, we could say that this is a "special part" of worship and Presbyterian piety (WCF 21.3). And yet, for many believers, this is the most difficult aspect of living in communion with God. Perhaps part of the difficulty is our tendency to make prayer more difficult or more "sanctified" than it need be. As Presbyterians, we believe that "prayer is an offering up of our desires unto God." To be sure, there are qualifications to this—our prayers are offered in the name of Christ and with the help of the Spirit, confession of sin, and thankful acknowledgment of God's mercy (LC 178). Likewise, we are not to pray for the dead, for those "of whom it may be known that they have sinned the sin unto death," or for "anything unlawful" (WCF 21.4; LC 184). Still, these are qualifications to the main point, which is decidedly straightforward and nonmystical—prayer is offering up our desires to God.

That being said, the real issue for most of us is not the content of our prayers, but the way in which we pray. And it is how we pray that provides the means of our transformation through the work of God's grace. We are called upon to pray with a full apprehension that God is our King and with an intense realization that we are sinners who would be totally and completely lost without the initiative of God's grace. Further, as we pray, recognizing who it is that we are addressing and who we are as we address him, our prayers are filled with gratitude to the God and King who saved us; we offer them with understanding, with wholehearted belief in and fervent sincerity toward him, with love and determined perseverance. Finally, we offer our desires up to God with a humble submission to his will, recognizing that he is the King who governs all his creatures and all their actions in accordance with his perfect will. Thus, in offering up our weighty desires to God, we offer up *ourselves* to him as well, so that we might know what is good, acceptable, and perfect in God's sight (LC 185; Rom. 12:1–2).

Presbyterians believe that "God is to be worshipped everywhere, in spirit and truth; as, in private families daily, and in secret, each one by himself; so, more solemnly in the public assemblies" (WCF 21.6). These three spheres of private, family, and corporate worship are mutually reinforcing; we are called upon to pray, read Scripture, and sing praises on our own, in our families, and as a church body. Although not everyone is equipped for the public reading and preaching of God's Word, it is the case that "all sorts of people are bound to read it apart by themselves, and with their families" (LC 156). And this is why the Reformed tradition has been the leader in Bible translation—because we have long believed that one of the most important means of spiritual growth is reading God's Word. We believe that every believer has a "right unto, and interest in the Scriptures" and are commanded to "read and search them" in the fear of God. As a result, Presbyterians have a mandate to translate Holy Scripture out of the original Greek and Hebrew and into common languages for people groups all around the world (WCF 1.8; LC 156). Notice, however, that the rationale for Bible translation is not only so that people might read the Bible apart by themselves; rather, they are also called to read the Bible together as families. The PCA Book of Church Order promotes family worship, which consists in prayer, Bible reading, and singing praises to God, as a necessary and vital part of instructing our families "in the principles of our holy religion" (BCO 63-3, 4). As a result, when our churches gather together for corporate worship on the Lord's Day, they are gathering not simply as disparate individuals, but as worshipping households who have worshipped together all week long as families.

While these are the particular means to which our confessional standards point for spiritual growth and communion with God, our Presbyterian and Reformed forefathers made use of other means as well. For example, our confession talks about "religious oaths, vows, solemn fastings and thanksgivings" which could be corporate, familial, or individual times of communion with God (WCF 21.5). But a major part of our worship in every sphere, and hence a major part of our piety, is the singing of praises to God. Church historian Hughes Oliphant Old observed that "any kind of Protestant spirituality is going to be a singing spirituality."[2] Thus, singing the Psalms as well as hymns and other spiritual songs is an important means for enjoying communion with God. On one level, singing psalms, hymns, and spiritual songs represents a type of prayer. In medieval monasteries, the office of daily prayer which centered on the Psalter was entirely sung; in the same way, when we sing to God—whether with hymns and new songs, or with psalm settings such as those represented by the *Trinity Psalter*—we engage in a form of prayer, offering up our desires to God through the mediation of Jesus Christ. One of the reasons that many congregations used to sing the "amen" at the end of hymns was that it represented the proper affirmation of and conclusion to the musical prayer that the people of God had just finished singing.

All of these practices connected with worship mean that Presbyterians have viewed Sabbath-keeping, or the observance of Sunday as the Lord's Day, as an important part of our piety. Sadly, however, Reformed believers have all too often approached Sunday in a legalistic manner, prescribing what must be done on that day and proscribing other things as violations of God's command to keep the Sabbath. Such a focus on the do's and don'ts of the day obscures the fact that God granted us the Lord's Day as a "means of blessing to us," not as a curse (LC 120). It is meant to be a day of rejoicing in the resurrection of Jesus Christ and in the new creation that has been brought about through him. We are called to "make it our delight," to use the entire day for resting from our weekday work and for feasting in God's presence (LC 117; WCF 21.7–8).

But how do we do this? First of all, we are called to remember the Lord's Day *in advance* in order to set it apart as different and special for the Lord's use. As we remember the day, we recognize how "very ready" we are "to forget it" because it restrains us from our lawful work and because there is so much that happens from week to week. In addition, the devil is very active to take our minds off the upcoming Sunday (LC 121). And we must confess that sometimes we are simply "weary" of the regularity of the Lord's Day (LC 119). By remembering the day in advance, we are then "more free and fit" to spend the day in re-creation, in being made new by worshipping God in Word and Spirit, and by deeds of mercy and fellowship with the saints (LC 117). As we offer a portion of the week to God's service, we testify that all of our time belongs to him. And we have the opportunity to engage in the communion between God and his people that occurs uniquely in corporate worship.

Presbyterian piety is concerned not only with our communion with God and the saints in corporate worship, but also with the very practical matter of service toward one another. Our communion with each other commits us to "such spiritual services as tend to their mutual edification" (WCF 26.2). This communion that we share as believers in Christ is epitomized in the church office of deacon; the PCA Book of Church Order explicitly states that "it expresses also the communion of saints, especially in their helping one another in time of need" (BCO 9-1). In other words, if someone wants to see what our communion with one another looks like, he should be able to watch the church's deacons and follow their example. But even if a church doesn't have deacons, or perhaps has poor deacons, each of us still has a basic responsibility as a believer united to Christ and to others to express our communion toward each other in deeds of love and mercy.

And so, our financial support of the church's work is not simply a means for paying the salaries of the ministerial staff, funding local and global evangelization projects, or supporting theological education. It is also a means for providing benevolent assistance to those within

110

and outside the family of faith (Gal. 6:6, 10). As believers, we are to be involved in deeds of mercy within our own congregations, certainly; but also, and more particularly, we are to work with our poorer congregations—often located in urban areas—to assist in bringing transformation and hope to our cities. Following the pattern of the apostle Paul in gathering together collections for the believers in Jerusalem who were experiencing terrible famine, local churches and entire presbyteries should seek to provide financial, material, and spiritual assistance for our sisters and brothers in need (2 Cor. 8, 9). As we work together in this way, we will express our common union with Jesus and strengthen our bonds to one another in the gospel of grace, which transcends race, gender, and class distinctions.

## THE GOAL OF REFORMED PIETY: GRATEFUL GROWTH IN GRACE

Presbyterians have often confessed that the Christian life is a journey. Whether drawing upon the classic imagery of Bunyan's *The Pilgrim's Progress* or the biblical imagery of endurance in a marathon race (Heb. 12:1–2), we have long recognized that, as a pilgrim people, we are on a journey home and we have not yet arrived. In terms of the goal of our piety—that reverence and love of God which brings about our spiritual transformation—we do not look for perfection in this life. We believe that there still abides in every part of each believer some "remnants of corruption," which bring about "a continual and irreconcilable war" between our remaining sinfulness and the indwelling Spirit (WCF 13.2). Therefore, the goal of our piety is not a perfect or even "moment by moment" sinlessness, but rather long-term growth in grace, progress in communion with God, and a "practice of true holiness" (WCF 13.1). Our great hope for our growth in grace is "the continual supply of strength from the sanctifying Spirit of Christ" (WCF 13.3). Any progress that we make in the Christian life is due solely to the sovereign work of God's Spirit, motivated by God's amazing grace and rooted in God's glorious gospel. And the practices of piety that we have considered take our focus away from ourselves and our striving for God and plant us firmly in the gospel itself. In corporate, family, and private worship, we read and hear God's Word, which confronts us with our sin and points us to the rich stores of grace in Jesus Christ. In prayer, as we offer our desires to God through Jesus' mediation, we acknowledge our remaining inability to please God in our own strength, and we plead God's grace through our union with Jesus' blood and righteousness, begging that God will hear our desires. In addition, the Spirit helps us as we pray "by working and quickening in our hearts . . . those apprehensions, affections and graces" necessary for genuine communion with God (LC 182). As we participate in the sacraments, meditating on our sinfulness and Christ's work on the cross on our behalf, God's grace meets us and we feed on the presence of Christ. We are strengthened in our journey, encouraged by the gospel to continue putting to death sin by the Spirit and the Word. We move from worship to the service of others, and we are confronted with the ravages of sin in the lives of others; we confront that sin with the gospel in word and deed, bringing financial and personal resources to bear on the human tragedies in our communities.

In each of these practices, the gospel meets us. We are shown time and again our own sinfulness, and "all the miseries spiritual, temporal, and eternal" that our sinfulness brings to us and our world (WCF 6.6). But we are also brought repeatedly to believe in Jesus Christ: in our union with him; in the declaration of the right standing we have with God through his counting of Jesus' standing as our own; and in the promise of God's continuing transformation of us until our deaths, which will bring about the "communion in Christ's glory" promised to us in the gospel. Over and over we come to believe that

> Not the labors of my hands
>      can fulfill thy law's demands;
> could my zeal no respite know,
>      could my tears forever flow,
> all for sin could not atone;
>      thou must save, and thou alone.
>
> Nothing in my hand I bring,
>      simply to thy cross I cling;

112

naked, come to thee for dress;
    helpless, look to thee for grace;
foul, I to the Fountain fly;
    wash me, Savior, or I die.[3]

And as we confess that this gospel of God's amazing grace is all we need, we grow in our communion with God and gain more fully "assurance of God's love, peace of conscience, joy in the Holy Ghost, increase of grace, and perseverance therein to the end" (SC 36).

Presbyterians and other Reformed Christians believe that we demonstrate our growth in grace by an all-encompassing thankfulness to God, which flavors every area of our lives. Once again, the Heidelberg Catechism helps us here. It is well known that the three sections of this catechism, which outline the Christian experience, are guilt, grace, and gratitude; and the catechism correctly claims that "we do good because Christ by his Spirit is also renewing us to be like himself, so that in all our living we may show that we are thankful to God for all he has done for us, and so that he may be praised through us" (Heidelberg Catechism, 86). In a similar fashion, our own confessional standards maintain that "good works, done in obedience to God's commandments, are the fruits and evidences of a true and lively faith: and by them believers manifest their thankfulness" (WCF 16.2). This gratitude is founded upon our union with Jesus, in which we recognize our profound sinfulness and the glorious grace of God our King, who by his Spirit drew us to Christ, transformed our wills, and granted us faith to believe in him. And so, all the practices of our piety, rooted in this union, teach us continually that we should be thankful to God, magnifying his grace in praise:

Creation, life, salvation too,
    and all things else both good and true,
come from and through our God always,
    and fill our hearts with grateful praise.
Come, lift your voice to heaven's high throne,
    and glory give to God alone![4]

1. What are the advantages or disadvantages of using the word *piety* instead of the more common word *spirituality* to describe one's religious practices? When you think about the word *piety*, what images come into your mind?

2. Have you ever considered that the Westminster Standards are documents about piety? How does that change or contradict the view of them that you may previously have held?

3. In the past, have you known folks who allowed their concern for correct doctrine to overwhelm their consideration for healthy Christian living? What was the problem? What should have been the solution?

4. While most Protestant denominations have made the sermon central to their worship, the sermon is commonly viewed more as a means of information than of transformation. How can you better improve the way you receive and use each Sunday's sermon so that it might be a means of increasing your reverence and love for God?

5. In times of temptation, do you "improve" your baptism by recalling the promises that God has made to you in it?

6. Can you recall a time when you sensed the Lord's presence and assuring comfort as you participated in the Lord's Supper?

7. How might a revised understanding of prayer as the "offering up of our desires to God" make a more continual attitude of prayer possible?

8. With the stress on worship, do you think that Presbyterian piety might be too inwardly focused? How does the stress upon stewardship and service help to balance our piety?

9. How does the belief that the Christian life is a journey rooted firmly in God's gospel of grace comfort you when you sometimes fail in your struggle against sin? How do the means of grace serve as an encouragement in this journey?

10. Consider for a moment what a continual sense of gratitude to God would do for the way in which you approach the Chris-

114

tian life. How does an overwhelming sense of gratitude to God change your attitude in your work? Your worship? Your ministry to others?

## »For Further Reading

Bennett, Arthur, ed., *The Valley of Vision: A Collection of Puritan Prayers and Devotions*. Carlisle, Pa.: Banner of Truth, 1975.

Chapell, Bryan. *Holiness by Grace*. Wheaton, Ill.: Crossway, 2002.

Hambrick-Stowe, Charles. *The Practice of Piety: Puritan Devotional Disciplines in Seventeenth-Century New England*. Chapel Hill: University of North Carolina Press, 1982.

Hodge, Charles. *The Way of Life*. 1841. Reprint, Carlisle, Pa.: Banner of Truth, 1959.

Johnson, Terry. *The Family Worship Book: A Resource Book for Family Devotions*. Fearn, Scotland: Christian Focus, 2000.

Ryken, Philip Graham. *What Is a True Calvinist?* Phillipsburg, N.J.: P&R, 2003.

———, ed. *The Communion of Saints: Living in Fellowship with the People of God*. Phillipsburg, N.J.: P&R, 2002.

# CHAPTER 7

# Gospel-Driven Presbyterian Worship

IT IS NO SECRET that the single most divisive issue in most congregations today—whether Presbyterian or some other denomination—is worship style. The situation has degenerated to the point that writing books about the "worship wars" has become a minor industry. Within Presbyterianism recently, a number of books have been published urging us to worship in spirit and truth or with reverence and awe, books that represent contrasting views and emphases. Others have urged a more liturgical approach, drawing from the same streams of thought that inform modern liturgical renewal in the high church traditions. Still others desire worship services crafted to reach the unchurched by being relevant specifically to them. Following all of this literature is a confusing process; no doubt visiting various Presbyterian churches, with their different styles of worship, can be confusing as well.

It is safe to say that some of the conflict with regard to this issue is generational—children of the 1960s and 1970s generally desire worship in the cultural styles and forms of their own generation, while those from previous generations tend to want to hold on to "traditional" worship. Ironically, as two generations now follow the "baby boom" generation, the "contemporary" worship that is championed in many suburban churches populated by fifty-somethings now seems as "traditional" as the worship against which the Boomers originally rebelled. Also ironically, the children and grandchildren of Boomers, raised on contemporary Christian music, evidence a much greater interest and concern for the ancient traditions of Christian worship while melding these forms with contemporary music styles. And so, the boundary lines between "traditional" and "contemporary/ innovative" worship may be as generational as they are ideological. Finding out what is central and what is ephemeral is vital for understanding what it means to worship God.

Presbyterians historically have thought quite a bit about what worship is. Some scholars have even argued that the sixteenth-century Reformation was more a reform of worship than of doctrine. Although this reformation of worship is part of the Presbyterian legacy, there has been a tendency to make sacrosanct the style of worship derived from the Reformation era or the golden age of hymnody or mid-nineteenth-century Anglo-America revivalism. When there are deviations, people get nervous. Whether they are on the "contemporary" or "liturgical" sides of the worship fence, people tend to view expressions of worship that are different from their own as silly, trendy, strange, or simply divisive. Certainly, as we will see shortly, Scripture does give us a pattern for how we are to worship God. The correctness of our worship ought, therefore, to be judged by its adherence to scriptural patterns and norms. And yet, I would suggest (along with a growing number of other Presbyterian pastors, teachers, and worship leaders) that gospel-driven, biblical and Reformed worship transcends style and yet at the same time is able to be expressed in local churches through a variety of valid worship expressions.[1]

I would suggest also that, in the midst of this dizzying diversity that typifies conservative Presbyterian worship, there are common, gospel-driven, biblical principles that hold our worship together—whether we are part of a traditional, middle class, rural congregation; a multinational, multiracial, urban congregation; or a nontraditional, contemporary, suburban congregation. Even more, I would claim that there is a basic continuity between contemporary Presbyterian worship practices and principles and those of the Christian tradition throughout the ages. At the center of Presbyterian and Reformed worship are several things: the Word and sacrament; a movement from the world to God and back to the world to live for God's glory; and a recognition of the formative importance of worship as we are called to believe the gospel week by week. With all that seems new, different, strange, and maybe even divisive in our worship, the core continues to bear great similarity to the worship of the first-century Christians; it is shaped by the same biblical principles and forged in the same practices.

## WORSHIP IS REGULATED BY GOD'S WORD

Obviously, when it comes to worship, Presbyterians share broad areas of commonality with other evangelicals. For example, all evangelicals believe that worship is shaped by our fellowship with the Trinity. God the Father calls us into his presence; receives our worship as mediated by his Son; and quickens, transforms, and saves his worshippers by the Spirit: all evangelicals believe this, even when they might not be able to articulate it well. Also, most evangelicals hold that, even though it is desirable to make use of the wide range of giftedness among the members of a congregation, some sort of recognized leadership is necessary—even required—during the church's worship services. Whether it is the pastoral staff or the elders or the deacon board, someone is responsible for the oversight of worship. In addition, various elements are common to most evangelical worship services—the reading and proclamation of Scripture, singing praises, baptism and the Lord's Supper, and prayers. Thus, we have to admit up front that the basic elements of most Presbyterian worship services share a great deal with other evangelical worship services. And this, I would say, is a good thing—it is a real expression of the unity of the saints across the Christian tradition, a true demonstration that people who take Scripture and worship seriously will arrive at similar basics regardless of denominational differences.

That being said, Presbyterians have long distinguished themselves from most other Protestants by thinking quite seriously about how Scripture regulates corporate worship. And, not surprisingly, this is exactly where the disagreements within Presbyterianism have centered: does Scripture regulate how we are to worship? And if so,

118

how does it? Historically, Presbyterians have held to "the regulative principle of worship," which was defined in the Westminster Confession as follows: "The acceptable way of worshipping the true God is instituted by himself, and so limited by his own revealed will, that he may not be worshipped according to the imaginations and devices of men, or the suggestions of Satan, under any visible representation, or any other way not prescribed in the holy Scripture" (WCF 21.1).

Presbyterians typically root the regulative principle in the second commandment. For example, the Larger Catechism summarizes the position exhaustively in both positive and negative ways. Positively, we are required by the second commandment to practice

> the receiving, observing, and keeping pure and entire, all such religious worship and ordinances as God hath instituted in his Word; particularly prayer and thanksgiving in the name of Christ; the reading, preaching, and hearing of the Word; the administration and receiving of the sacraments; church government and discipline; the ministry and maintenance thereof; religious fasting; swearing by the name of God, and vowing unto him: as also the disapproving, detesting, opposing, all false worship; and, according to each one's place and calling, removing it, and all monuments of idolatry. (LC 108)

Negatively, we are urged to put off

> *all devising, counseling, commanding, using and any wise approving, any religious worship not instituted by God himself;* tolerating a false religion; the making any representation of God, of all or of any of the three persons, either inwardly in our mind, or outwardly in any kind of image or likeness of any creature whatsoever; all worshipping of it, or God in it or by it; the making of any representation of feigned deities, and all worship of them, or service belonging to them; all superstitious devices, corrupting the worship of God, adding to it, or taking from it, whether invented and taken up of ourselves, or received by tradition from others, though under the title of antiquity, custom, devotion, good intent, or any other pretence whatsoever; simony; sacrilege; all neglect,

contempt, hindering, and opposing the worship and ordinances which God hath appointed (LC 109; emphasis added).

While this seems long-winded, what is key in this understanding of the second commandment is the belief that worship is regulated and limited by God and his Word. Also important in shaping the Presbyterian view of worship has been Leviticus 10, in which Nadab and Abihu, the priestly sons of Aaron, were struck down for offering "strange fire" to the Lord; that is, worshipping him in a way other than that which he had prescribed. At the seventeenth-century Westminster Assembly, which produced our confession and catechisms, Puritan Jeremiah Burroughs preached a series of sermons on "gospel worship" from this text, cementing the relationship between the regulative principle and the failure of the two brothers to observe it.

To summarize, then: the regulative principle claims that God has instituted "the acceptable way" of worship, that God has limited worship by his own revealed will, and that human beings are not to worship in any way not prescribed in Scripture. The popular way of putting this is that Christians are to worship God only as he has commanded, and whatever God has not commanded for worship in Scripture is forbidden. In recent days, this understanding has been challenged by some who desire to redefine the regulative principle to claim that Scripture norms every activity of life, or who believe that the Westminster Confession goes beyond the principles of other Reformers, becoming legalistic as it establishes the supremacy of Scripture in matters of faith and worship. Still, it is the case that Presbyterians historically have claimed that God's Word serves to regulate our worship in such a way that our worship is based on what is revealed in Scripture. If we deviate from the scriptural pattern, we worship in a way that is unacceptable to God.

That being said, it is not always plain how we should apply this "regulative principle": "there are some circumstances concerning the worship of God, and government of the Church, common to human actions and societies, which are to be ordered by the light of nature, and Christian prudence, according to the general rules of the Word,

120

which are always to be observed" (WCF 1.6). Typically, this conces-
sion has led Presbyterians to talk about the *elements* of church government and worship, which are mandated by Scripture, and the *circumstances*, which are not biblically regulated and are free to be
ordered according to human insight and common sense. Elements of
worship are things such as the reading and preaching of Scripture; the
administration of the sacraments of baptism and the Lord's Supper;
the presentation of offerings; the singing of psalms and hymns; and,
sometimes, the taking of oaths (BCO 47-9). Circumstances of worship are things that are necessary for an element to be done. Thus, for
example, an element of worship is the singing of psalms and hymns,
but a circumstance could be that this singing is accompanied by an
accordion and a banjo. Again, an element in worship is that the reading and preaching of God's Word should occur on the Lord's Day; a
circumstance is that it should happen at ten thirty on Sunday morning instead of two o'clock on Sunday afternoon.

In addition, the regulative principle means that the church may not
introduce into worship new elements that are not contained in Scripture. In this way, the church's power is strictly limited. For example,
we confess that "the acceptable way of worshipping the true God is
instituted by himself, and so *limited by his own revealed will*, that he
may not be worshipped according to the imaginations and devices of
men, or the suggestions of Satan, under any visible representation, or
*any other way not prescribed in the Holy Scripture*" (WCF 21.1;
emphasis added). And so, the church may not make the burning of
incense before a statue of Jesus part of the worship service because
there is no place in Scripture where this action is commanded. Only
what God has commanded in Scripture is to be done.

The Westminster Confession claims that worship is to be directed
by Scripture alone in order to preserve the liberty of believers' consciences (WCF 20.2). Our consciences are only safe when they are
under the lordship of Jesus Christ as directed by his Word and Spirit.
Though the church's power to introduce new elements of worship,
government, or doctrine is limited by God's Word, this does not
mean that every "new way" of doing worship is necessarily out of

bounds. We must be careful to discern what is an *essential element* commanded by God's Word and what is a *circumstantial means* for accomplishing the element. And above all, as we think about this, we must not forsake one biblical principle—love for our brothers and sisters in Christ—in order to preserve another—liberty of conscience. Rather, we must all commit ourselves to search the Scriptures carefully and to submit ourselves to the lordship of Christ as he speaks by his Spirit through Holy Scripture, trusting that, as we all mature in our faith, we will eventually come to the same views (WCF 1.10; Phil. 3:15–16).

I believe that this understanding of worship as being regulated by Scripture makes Presbyterian worship a little different. We *are* typically reticent to introduce innovations into our worship services. In most Presbyterian churches, plays or movies are not used on Sunday morning as replacements for the preaching of the Word and the administration of the Supper. The move to incorporate audio-visual elements into sermons, or various liturgical movements and positions into worship services, also generally raises questions among Presbyterians. Instead, Presbyterian, gospel-driven worship is guided and saturated by Scripture. The result is that the singing, preaching, praying, and sacraments are, as we like to say, "full of Bible."

## WORSHIP IS COVENANT RENEWAL

We have already noticed that Presbyterians use the word "covenant" quite a bit. It comes up again here in our discussion of worship because, at its very heart, worship is covenantal. That means many things, but at the minimum it means that worship involves a two-way movement between God and his people. Think about what a covenant entails. Earlier we said that a covenant is a sovereign administration of grace and promise. God the King, as an example of his undeserved favor, extends certain promises to his people, summed up in the great promise, "I will be your God and you shall be my people" (Ex. 6:7; Jer. 30:22; 2 Cor. 6:16–18; 1 Peter 2:9). While these promises were made by God unilaterally, they were conditioned on people responding by faith. And God's covenant people evidenced that they had seized these promises by faith as they lived in conformity to God's Word and worshipped him alone as the true God. So, while God is the one who initiates his covenant, this administration or relationship entails mutuality as well. God moves toward his people in gracious promise and his people respond to him by faith, which results in practices of love.

Taking this understanding and applying it to worship, we can see how our belief that worship is covenantal would mean that in worship there is a two-way movement between God and his people. Some people have even suggested that in worship there is a dialogue between God and his church. God is the one who makes the first move toward us by calling us to worship, and we respond by invoking his presence in our midst. And the rest of worship is a movement back and forth between God and his beloved people, a movement in which God meets us in Word and sacrament and we respond to his presence with prayers and praises.

Perhaps you have noticed a certain ebb and flow to many Presbyterian worship services:

- God calls us into his presence by his Word and Spirit.
- *We enter God's holy presence, are convicted of sin, and confess our sins to him.*
- God responds by his Word with an assurance of his pardon.
- *In prayers and songs, we praise our God for calling us into his presence and forgiving our sins.*
- God speaks to us by his Word in the reading and preaching of Scripture, as well as through his visible signs of baptism and the Lord's Supper.
- *We respond to God in thanksgiving with praise and offerings.*
- God sends us away with his blessing (or benediction).
- *We move back into the world for loving service, assured that we are God's people.*

The structure of the worship service—call to worship, invocation, confession of sin, assurance of pardon, reading and preaching God's Word, administration of the sacraments, giving of offerings, and benediction—help to form us as God's covenant people. We recognize that we are engaged with God's holy presence in his appointed worship to which we have been called by him. Liturgical action—whether in a "traditional" or a "contemporary" service—shapes us through a dialogue with God's presence, a dialogue which he initiated. The result is spiritual transformation, for, as Hughes Oliphant Old puts it well, "Worship is the workshop where we are transformed into his image."[2] Worship is that workshop because God condescends to meet with us, make promises to us, keep those promises, and transform us for Jesus' sake.

This idea that worship is covenantal means not only that there is a dialogue going on between God and his people. It also speaks to the fact that, during worship, the covenant between God and his people is being renewed. Each week we are called into God's presence and God reminds us of his promises by his Word and Spirit. Likewise, through the central elements of worship, we renew our faith in the promises of God and receive assurance and confirmation that we belong to him. The central acts of this renewal are Word and sacrament. In the preaching of God's Word, God declares to us his promises: to save those who come to him through faith in Jesus Christ, to view those united to Christ as right with God and holy in his sight, and to continue the work of transformation into the image of Christ until the final day. And if we are prone to doubt God's Word, he has granted us the Lord's Supper as a visible sign to confirm those promises to us and strengthen our confidence in them. We respond in faith to these two gracious acts of God, seizing his promises made in the spoken and visible words and assuring our hearts by them. We then go from God's presence in worship back out into the world to live our lives, reveling in the grace shown to us by God in Word and sacrament and serving others with our loving words and deeds.

## WORSHIP IS AT THE HEART OF OUR COMMUNION WITH CHRIST

It should follow from this that worship serves our communion with Christ by re-presenting the gospel in such a way as to glorify God and

124

to sanctify his people. Here is an amazing accommodation by God to our weakness and frailty. He knows that we are a people who are prone to wander and forget the benefits he offers us. He comes to us constantly urging us to remember:

> Take care lest you forget the Lord your God by not keeping his commandments and his statutes, which I command you today, lest, when you have eaten and are full and have built good houses and live in them, and when your herds and flocks multiply and your silver and gold is multiplied and all that you have is multiplied, then your heart be lifted up, and you forget the Lord your God, who brought you out of the land of Egypt, out of the house of slavery, who led you through the great and terrifying wilderness, with its fiery serpents and scorpions and thirsty ground where there was no water, who brought you water out of the flinty rock, who fed you in the wilderness with manna that your fathers did not know, that he might humble you and test you, to do you good in the end. Beware lest you say in your heart, "My power and the might of my hand have gotten me this wealth." You shall remember the Lord your God, for it is he who gives you power to get wealth, that he may confirm his covenant that he swore to your fathers, as it is this day. (Deut. 8:11–18)

The old covenant people of God had experienced God's redemption in the exodus, his sustaining of them in the "great and terrifying wilderness," provision of manna in that same wilderness, and his fulfillment of his covenant promises of land and plenty. And yet, what did God warn the people against? An arrogant and ignorant forgetting that ascribed their good to their own power rather than to God's promised provision. So what did God do for the people? Through Moses, God reminded them; in the book of Deuteronomy, he re-presented the entire story of redemption, along with exhortations to remember his promises in faith and to respond to them in faithfulness.

Importantly, the same thing happens for us as the people of God on this side of the cross. God comes to us in Word and sacrament and re-presents, reminds, and recalls to us the story of redemption. God's call summons us to worship and reminds us of his effectual calling in our lives. We confess our sin to God, which recalls our first sense of conviction as well as our continuing need for repentance. God speaks a word of assurance and teaches us that our only hope, from the first steps of faith to the last, is to cling to the gospel by faith alone in Christ's finished work alone. We sing praises to God's name, echoing our rejoicing in the salvation that God brought to us from the first moment of faith. God speaks his Word to us in preaching and in the sacramental meal, and he instructs us in the Christian life and the continuing application of the gospel. Finally, God proclaims his good word to us in the benediction, commissioning us to be his witnesses in our Jerusalems, Samarias, and the ends of our earth. The very movement of worship re-presents the gospel to us and recalls for us the hour we first believed.

Even more specifically, in the Word and sacrament, the Christ-centeredness and gospel-centeredness of our faith is stressed for us. In the preached Word, each text drives us to take hold of Jesus Christ by faith, relying on him alone for our justification and sanctification. And in the Lord's Supper, we have a "perpetual remembrance of the sacrifice of himself in his death" as well as "the sealing all benefits therefore unto true believers" (WCF 29.1). The heart of the gospel—"while we were still sinners, Christ died for us" (Rom. 5:8)—is represented to us in the breaking of bread and the pouring out of wine. In receiving those elements, we are taught that we must receive Christ by faith as he is offered in the gospel of the cross. And in receiving Christ, we are granted the fullness of his benefits, including our adoption as children of God (John 1:12).

This continual preaching and re-presenting of the gospel results in a deepening of our communion with God and in our further sanctification as God's people. As we saw in the chapter on piety, at the heart of our reverence of God and love for him is corporate worship. As we together delight in God through the means of grace—preaching, sacraments, prayers—we are set apart more and more by the Holy Spirit's activity in our hearts and lives: sin is confronted, repentance is made, the gospel is proclaimed, faith is renewed, hope is strengthened, love is kindled, and service is envisioned. We must remember that holiness is not something that qualifies us *to* worship; rather, holiness is the *result* of an engagement with the Holy God by the Spirit through the Son. And so, the Trinitarian shape of worship serves not only to lead us to glorify and enjoy the triune God, but also serves to lead us in the paths of greater conformity to him. Worship stands at the heart of our communion with God because, fundamentally, it entails the week-by-week re-presentation of the gospel of God's grace in Jesus Christ. That, by the way, is why many theologians and pastors in the Reformed tradition have urged a weekly observance of the Lord's Supper. We are such weak creatures that we not only require the hearing of God's Word with our ears, but also need to see it in picture form and experience it tangibly. Just as young children are enabled to grasp complex stories such as Walter Scott's *Ivanhoe* through the *Great Illustrated Classics* series, so we as God's children are able to grasp the complex story of redemption through the illustration of the Lord's Supper.

## WHAT ABOUT WORSHIP MUSIC?

Certainly, this is not everything that could be said about worship. My goal here has been merely to stress the characteristics of Presbyterian worship that all conservative Presbyterian churches have in common. Obviously, one shared characteristic is *not* musical style.

The church has not given its best thought to the problem of how to discuss reasonably issues related to musical style and the incarnation of the gospel in particular places, spaces, and times. In an essay for the book *The Conviction of Things Not Seen*, John Witvliet, director of the Calvin Institute of Christian Worship, offered six helpful questions for discerning the criteria for music used in Christian worship:

- Do we have the imagination and resolve to speak and make music in a way that both celebrates and limits the role of music as a conduit for experiencing God?

- Do we have the imagination and persistence to develop and play music that enables and enacts the primary actions of Christian worship?
- Do we have the imagination and persistence to make music that truly serves the gathered congregation, rather than the music, composer, or marketing company that promotes it?
- Do we have the persistence and imagination to develop and then practice a rich understanding of "aesthetic virtue"?
- Do we have a sufficiently complex understanding of the relationship between worship, music, and culture to account for how worship is at once transcultural, contextual, countercultural, and cross-cultural?
- Do we have the imagination and persistence to overcome deep divisions in the Christian church along the lines of socioeconomic class?[3]

While these questions won't necessarily provoke the kinds of conversations that conservative Presbyterians need to have about worship music, they do transcend the typical "contemporary" versus "traditional" division often found in our circles, and it is helpful to consider them in relation to the major points raised in this chapter.

First, think about how these questions intersect with the thought that worship is regulated by God's Word. If that principle is true, then even our worship music must serve the "primary actions of Christian worship" which we find in Holy Scripture. That being said, Scripture also judges our musical expressions and provides us an opportunity to bring these expressions under the lordship of Christ. For example, if the only type of worship music that we embrace is that associated with Euro-American high culture or Anglo-American popular culture, then perhaps we must ask ourselves if we have fully understood the Bible's vision of a multicultural worship of God by people from every tribe, language, and people group. A more profound grasp of this vision would help us to better express our union and communion with saints around the world and across the political and national boundaries created by the pretended lords of this earth (Rev. 4–5, 7).

Next, consider how worship as covenant renewal impacts worship music style. If worship is the renewal of God's covenant with his people, which again transcends class, race, or gender boundaries, then this should be reflected in our worship music. It follows, then, that the simplicity of worship music and styles found in many rural and urban congregations should be as valued as the extravagant, "professional" worship music and styles found in large suburban mega-congregations.

Finally, believing that worship stands at the heart of our communion with Christ provides room for considering music style. But it is not music alone that is at the heart of that communion—which makes Witvliet's first question so vital. In his explanation of this question, Witvliet writes:

> Can we safely take the next step and believe that music generates an experience of *God*? By no means. That places far too much power in music itself. Music is not God, nor is music an automatic tool for generating God's presence. . . . Music is an instrument by which the Holy Spirit draws us to God, a tool by which we enact our relationship with God. It is not a magical medium for conjuring up God's presence.[4]

Music, as represented in the aspects of singing hymns, psalms, and spiritual songs, is one element that is not absolutely necessary to corporate worship in the same way that the prayers or the reading and preaching of the Scriptures are. That is why Presbyterians confess that the means of grace are reading and preaching Scripture, receiving the sacrament, and making prayers; singing psalms and hymns has typically been seen as *a way of praying*, not as a discrete element of worship in itself. Therefore, questions about and arguments over musical expression and style stand in a subservient position to the broader principles of worship that we have been examining here. And that is why I believe that the contention with which I started this chapter is true: gospel-driven, biblical, and Reformed worship transcends style; it can be expressed in a variety of local churches through a variety of valid expressions.

At the end of the day, we must believe that corporate worship is the God-ordained means of delighting in and enjoying God as his covenant people. Whether we sing Bach or rock is relatively unimportant compared to the much greater need that we have to hear God speak to us by his Word, to recall God's promises made to us in Christ, to be reminded of the gospel in Word and sacrament, and to be transformed by the Spirit using his Word in our lives. And so, at our best, as we are called into God's presence to worship him, we sing:

> Thou lovely Source of true delight,
> Whom I unseen adore;
> Unveil Thy beauties to my sight,
> That I might love Thee more.
>
> Thy glory o'er creation shines;
> But in Thy sacred Word,
> I read in fairer, brighter lines,
> My bleeding, dying Lord.
>
> 'Tis here, whene'er my comforts droop,
> And sins and sorrows rise,
> Thy love with cheering beams of hope,
> My fainting heart supplies.
>
> But ah! Too soon the pleasing scene
> Is clouded o'er with pain;
> My gloomy fears rise dark between,
> And I again complain.
>
> Jesus, my Lord, my Life, my Light,
> O, come with blissful ray;
> Break radiant through the shades of night,
> And chase my fears away.
>
> Then shall my soul with rapture trace
> The wonders of Thy love;
> But the full glories of Thy face
> Are only known above.[5]

130

## »Questions for Thought and Review

1. Have you ever been in a church that has experienced a major conflict over worship style? How devastating was it to the witness and testimony of the church?

2. Does the regulative principle of worship limit the way in which we actually worship? What is something that you wish you could do in worship that is prohibited by the regulative principle? Have you ever thought about Leviticus 10 in relationship to contemporary discussions over worship?

3. How does the distinction between elements and circumstances assist in mediating disagreements over worship within the church? In your church, have you noticed any circumstances of worship that have been wrongly elevated to the status of a biblical element?

4. Think about liberty of conscience as it relates to worship. How can churches use this idea to bind believers' consciences in an unbiblical way in worship? How can individuals use this idea as an objection in an unbiblical fashion in order to stymie worship of which they do not approve?

5. If you have your church's order of worship at hand, look at how the service is structured. Do you notice a two-way movement from God to his people and back to God? If not, what does your church's worship structure suggest about the congregation's view of God, human beings, and salvation?

6. What does renewal of your faith look like as you worship God? Is it an internal sense of strengthening? Is it a conscious claiming of God's promises made in Jesus? What is it?

7. Recall one period in your life when you forgot God even though you may have always "worshipped" him. Contrast that time with another time when you felt very close to God in worship. What were the differences? Did you return back to the first principles of the gospel again?

8. What do you make of the six questions posed by John Witvliet? In a discussion time, take up each of those questions

and consider how they might affect your understanding or your church's approach to worship music style.

## »For Further Reading

Frame, John M. *Worship in Spirit and Truth*. Phillipsburg, N.J.: P&R, 1996.

Gore, R. J., Jr. *Covenantal Worship: Reconsidering the Puritan Regulative Principle*. Phillipsburg, N.J.: P&R, 2002.

Hart, D. G., and John R. Muether. *With Reverence and Awe: Returning to the Basics of Reformed Worship*. Phillipsburg, N.J.: P&R, 2002.

Old, Hughes Oliphant. *Worship: Reformed according to Scripture*. Rev. ed. Louisville, Ky.: Westminster John Knox, 2002.

Ryken, Philip Graham, Derek W. H. Thomas, and J. Ligon Duncan, III, eds. *Give Praise to God: A Vision for Reforming Worship*. Phillipsburg, N.J.: P&R, 2003.

Witvliet, John D. "Beyond Style: Rethinking the Role of Music in Worship." In *The Conviction of Things Not Seen: Worship and Ministry in the 21st Century*. Edited by Todd E. Johnson, 67–81. Grand Rapids, Mich.: Brazos, 2002.

———. *Worship Seeking Understanding: Windows into Christian Practice*. Grand Rapids, Mich.: Baker, 2003.

# CHAPTER 8

# "Decently and in Order": Presbyterian Church Government

ONE OF THE GREAT MYSTERIES for those coming from baptistic churches into Presbyterianism is how Presbyterian polity (or church government) works. Some come from backgrounds where church government means lengthy congregational business meetings in which the church's membership votes on everything from who the next pastor will be to whether the Sunday school department is authorized to spend fifty dollars for Vacation Bible School. Others attended churches in which the congregational meeting is held each Wednesday at a prayer meeting and new or departing members are voted on with varying degrees of indifference. Still others come from "elder-led" churches in which the elders serve as coordinators of various ministry areas, but leave most of the actual "ruling" of the church to the professional staff. Needless to say, when these people join a Presbyterian church, the way we do things might seem a little strange.

One of the oddest things to new Presbyterians is our Book of Church Order (BCO). For example, the PCA's BCO is a loose-leaf binder full of pages divided into sixty-three chapters, not to mention an entirely separate section containing the "rules for Assembly operation," a manual that guides the work for our annual General Assembly. All of these rules and regulations seem odd to those from churches who believe that the Spirit and the Bible, with a healthy dose of Robert's *Rules of Order* and common sense, are all that is necessary to govern Christ's church. And yet, other people come to appreciate the fact that all elders in the PCA take ordination vows in which they "approve the form and discipline of the Presbyterian Church in America, in conformity with the general principles of biblical polity" (BCO 24-5). Because we all agree to use the same rules, we are able to ensure that discipline and order are fairly consistent throughout the denomination. Likewise, there are no surprises in our church order—all communicant members and officers have access to the BCO, are able to take advantage of its provisions, and are liable to its process of discipline. This propensity for order in the church has led some to claim that Presbyterians' favorite verse is "all things should be done decently and in order" (1 Cor. 14:40).

Yet even those who greatly appreciate Presbyterians' regular way of governing Christ's church may fail to recognize the important biblical and confessional principles that support these practices. In particular, most contemporary Presbyterians have probably never thought about the nature of "church power" (or church authority) and its source. But for our Presbyterian and Reformed forefathers, this was a vitally important issue that separated Presbyterians from other church groups—independent Congregationalists and Baptists; Lutherans, Anglicans, and Methodists; and Roman Catholics. A large part of Presbyterian identity is shaped by what we believe about church power: what it is, where it comes from, how it is to be exercised, and who is to exercise it. Thus, it would be helpful for conservative Presbyterians, especially those in the PCA, to understand a little bit more about our own church, its courts, and agencies in order to support more fully the work of our branch of Christ's church.

In an earlier chapter, we considered what Presbyterians believe about the nature and marks of the church. There, we saw that Presbyterians believe that the word *church* is used biblically in three different senses—as referring to a local congregation, a regional grouping of churches, or the church universal. We also sought to establish that the Presbyterian belief in the "connectional" nature of the church is biblical; even churches of the Southern Baptist Convention, for example, find the need to associate together for the purpose of missions, evangelism, and theological education through their local, state, and national associations and conventions and through their "cooperative program." The reason for this is quite simple—churches are not and cannot actually be "independent and autonomous," as some like to claim. Rather, by virtue of our shared union with Christ, local churches that share the same faith and practice cannot help but unite together to further the work of God's rule in this world. In other words, even "independent and autonomous" churches that work together for ministry demonstrate the basic biblical truth of Presbyterianism, whether they want to admit it or not. In fact, even the very notion of a "denomination"—especially a denomination made up of supposedly "independent and autonomous" churches—suggests that no local church exists in a truly independent and autonomous state. We have already established, then, that the nature of the church is "Presbyterian." Therefore, this chapter will focus more directly on how our Presbyterian churches exercise their authority in the continuing life of the body of Christ.

## THE NATURE OF CHURCH POWER: SPIRITUAL

Churches err in two directions when considering the issue of the ecclesiastical (church) power or authority. On the one hand, some claim that the church's authority is such that to hear the voice of the church on a particular topic or issue is to hear the voice of Christ himself. Thus, in this view, no one may dissent from the church's decisions or actions. The Roman Catholic Church, for example, with its belief in the authority of the pope, his magisterium (the teaching office of the church, represented in its bishops as led by the pope), and its declaration of papal infallibility, makes the word of the church the final word in all matters of faith and practice. On the other hand, many evangelicals claim that the church has no real authority at all, no legitimate power. For these people, the church is a voluntary association in which individual Christians, governed by Christ's Spirit, agree to participate in a body of believers for the purpose of mutual encouragement and edification. The church as an institution has no real power, save what is agreed upon by the members themselves. In fact, many churches do not even receive "members" and view themselves as service organizations that provide ministry services to those who choose to attend. If these churches were to declare their doctrine definitively or attempt to bring discipline against someone, the individual in question could simply declare the church's authority to do so null and void. The person would then leave that congregation, go to a different congregation, and be received into the new church's fellowship with no further ramifications.

Both of these views of church power contain a kernel of truth. It is undoubtedly true, as those who hold the former view claim, that the church has some measure of power to declare what Christ has said in his Word about doctrine, ordinances, and discipline. The church also has the authority to require the obedience of its members to the extent that its declarations agree with God's Word. Yet, as those who hold the latter view claim, it is also true that believers submit themselves voluntarily to the government and oversight of the church. Furthermore, church members have the right to disagree with and appeal the church's declarations or decisions if they believe that the church's representatives have erred in doctrine or discipline. But both of these positions also contain a great deal of error as well. In order to think clearly about the nature of the church's authority, we need to back up a bit and think about why the church has authority in the first place, in what sphere that authority is meant to operate, and how that authority is different from other types of God-ordained authority.

By the very nature of the case, two characteristics are necessary for the work of every society or organization, no matter what it is: *officers* and *laws*. Officers are required to represent the group and to do the work of the organization. No society can function properly if every member takes direct control of its activity; the proverb about "all chiefs and no Indians" teaches that every group must have those who lead and those who follow. Likewise, laws are necessary in order to guide the group in its work. Whether it is a charter granted by the state, an employee handbook, or a law code, rules and regulations provide reference points for the society to accomplish its task. In addition, these

136

laws or rules provide warrant or authorization for the group. Now, the notion that every society must have officers and laws leads to this observation—officers and laws have to do with authority, with power. After all, what is the point of being a ruler if you cannot rule? What is the point of having laws if they do not empower one to action? In short, any collection of people that comes together for some purpose implies a general "power" or "authority" for that purpose.

Clearly, if this is true for societies in general, then it is also true for that particular society called church. The church as a society of those who believe in Jesus Christ has the power or authority to carry out its tasks. To be sure, the sphere in which the church exercises its power is limited by the very nature of its mission, which is to seek the salvation of men and women. This entails a movement in an individual from love for sin to a love for God—a movement that is spiritual at its core. And because the church's mission is spiritual, its means must be spiritual as well. This involves persuasion, not coercion; the preaching of the Word, not the use of the sword. Therefore, we can say that the church's sphere of authority is spiritual because its mission and means are spiritual.

More specifically, the church exercises its spiritual power or authority in three ways. First, the church has authority to *declare its doctrine*; that is, the church has the authority to say that it believes certain things to be true and other things to be not true, based on its understanding of the Bible. The church has the right and responsibility to witness to the gospel in the face of persecution. And when times of apostasy come, the church has the power—and the responsibility—to identify deviant doctrine and to witness against it. Second, the church also has the power to *order its worship, administer its sacraments, and govern its affairs*. For example, the church has the authority to perform the biblical elements of worship, to administer the sacraments of baptism and the Lord's Supper, to determine when its worship services will be and where they will be held. In line with biblical rules, the church may decide what it will require of those whom it admits to the ministerial office. It may determine the process for calling larger meetings of the church beyond that of the individual local congregation. Finally, the church has the power—and the responsibility—to *discipline its members*. It has the authority to call erring members back from patterns of sinfulness using the biblical means of admonition, censure, and excommunication. It also has the power to restore these members to good standing by the removal of censure through the absolution of God's gospel. This is often called "the power of the keys of the kingdom" (WCF 30.2, 4; cf. Matt. 16:19; 18:17–18).

Because the church's power is exclusively spiritual, it is not to be confused with the power granted to the state, nor is the state to usurp the power of the church. The state, with power delegated to it by God, exercises authority in temporal matters and wields coercive power on God's behalf (Rom. 13:1–7). The state has the power to tax, wage war, defend its citizenry, and punish lawbreakers (WCF 23.1). The church has none of these powers, nor may it use the state's power to accomplish its spiritual mission. In fact, Jesus himself explicitly distinguished the state from the church (Matt. 22:21), marked off the power that civil rulers had from that which the church's rulers had (Matt. 20:20–28), and declared that the church's authority was of a different kind altogether from that of the state, because God's rule is not of this world (John 18:36–37). Because of this distinction between the power of the church and the power of the state, Presbyterians have long confessed that the church is "to handle, or conclude nothing, but that which is ecclesiastical" and is "not to intermeddle with civil affairs, which concern the commonwealth" (WCF 31.4). The church's commitment not to involve itself in temporal affairs is a recognition that the church's sphere, power, mission, and nature are spiritual in nature and are different from those of the state.

## THE SOURCE OF CHURCH POWER: JESUS CHRIST

The source of the church's power lies neither in itself as an institution nor in the combination of individuals within it who themselves possess spiritual power. Rather, the church's authority comes directly to it from the Lord Jesus Christ. As the resurrected One, in Matthew 28, Jesus declares that "all authority in heaven and on earth has been

138

given to me." He is the one who has all authority, all power; he is Lord over all and is seated at God's right hand. Out of this declaration of authority, Jesus commissions his followers to "go therefore and make disciples of all nations." He grants them this power for the purpose of making more followers of Christ (based on a confession of faith in him) and to gather them together into the new community that he is forming (cf. Matt. 16:18–19). The means for making disciples are baptism and instruction: "baptizing them in the name of the Father and of the Son and of the Holy Spirit, teaching them to observe all that I have commanded you." And the promise attached to this grant of authority is the continuing presence of Jesus until the end of the age (Matt. 28:16–20). Thus, Jesus' followers are granted power by Jesus himself—power to gather disciples, administer sacraments, and teach his Word authoritatively (WCF 30.1).

All of this teaches us that Jesus himself is the only head of the church (Eph. 1:22–23). He stands as its Lord, its ultimate ruler, its King. As one classic writer on the church put it:

> Within the province of the Church, the Lord Jesus Christ is the only Teacher, Lawgiver, and Judge. If doctrine is taught, it is taught because he has revealed; if ordinances are administered, they are administered in his name, and because they are his; if government is established and exercised, it is through his appointment and authority; if saving grace is dispensed, it is dispensed through the virtue and power of his Spirit; if a blessing is communicated, it is because he blesses.[1]

The church has access to God only through Jesus for "there is no other head of the Church but the Lord Jesus Christ" (WCF 25.6). Therefore, Christ alone can bind our consciences and require submission, because he alone is Lord. As disciples of Jesus, we are "free from the doctrines and commandments of men, which are, in anything, contrary to His Word; or beside it, in matters of faith or worship" (WCF 20.2). Jesus as head of the church is the source of its authority, and he alone can bind the conscience by his Word.

## THE LAWS AND LIMITS OF CHURCH POWER: THE WORD OF GOD

Based on what has already been said, you can probably guess what
the law might be that regulates the church's use of the power granted
to it by Christ: the will of Christ himself as expressed in Holy Scripture. To be sure, the Bible does not contain a Book of Church Order
(or a Confession of Faith, catechisms, or a directory of public worship, for that matter). However, this does not mean that the church is
left without any direction when it comes to knowing how Christ would
want the church to be ordered. After all, Paul told Timothy that he
wrote the pastoral letters so that "you may know how one ought to
behave in the household of God, which is the church of the living God,
a pillar and buttress of truth" (1 Tim. 3:15). Certainly, there are many
particular rules and laws laid down in Scripture that teach about how
the church's government, worship, and doctrine are to be ordered.
Not only that, but there are also examples throughout Scripture that
are normative for understanding how we are to exercise the church's
authority. And when there are not explicit precepts and examples,
there are enough general principles—whether they are "expressly set
down in Scripture, or by good and necessary consequence may be
deduced from Scripture"—to discern what God would have us do
(WCF 1.6).

The distinction that we made earlier between the elements and the
circumstances of worship also comes into play when thinking about
church government. There are some biblically defined elements of
church government that no church can exist without: ordained leadership, order of discipline, administration of worship. But there are
some circumstances to that government which are open to the light
of nature and good old common sense. For example, an element of
Presbyterian church government is that elders should gather region-
ally in presbyteries to conduct the work of Christ's church; but a circumstance is that the presbytery meets three times a year in alternat-
ing locations. In the matter of church discipline, an element is that
discipline follows certain procedures of investigation and judgment
outlined in texts such as Matthew 18; but a circumstance is the set of

"DECENTLY AND IN ORDER"

rules in BCO 32-3 regarding the way a prosecutor in a discipline case is appointed. One is a matter of biblical revelation; the other a matter of church procedure that a church has the right to declare, but which does not have the weight of Scripture.

The issue here again is the liberty of Christian conscience. Christ alone is King of his church; he alone has authority to bind our consciences by his Word. No one else may intervene in this way unless he can demonstrate that "thus says the Lord." And so, Christ's Word provides both the warrant and the limit to the church's power over God's people.

## THOSE ENTRUSTED WITH CHURCH POWER: OFFICERS

In his office of King, Jesus calls out of the world a people for himself and gives them "officers, laws, and censures, by which he visibly governs them" (LC 45). In fact, the apostle Paul teaches us that the resurrected and ascended Christ received "gifts" to give to his church, which are "the apostles, the prophets, the evangelists, the pastors and teachers, to equip the saints for the work of ministry, for building up the body of Christ" (Eph. 4:7–12). Through these officers, whom Christ the King gives to his church as a gift, and through his Word, which he gives as its law, Christ visibly governs his church.

Yet this does not mean that church officers have this authority in distinction from the church as a whole. As the PCA BCO aptly puts it: "The power which Christ has committed to his church vests in the whole body, the rulers and those ruled, constituting it a spiritual commonwealth. This power, as exercised by the people, extends to the choice of those officers whom He has appointed in his church" (BCO 3-1). In other words, Christ has entrusted authority to his church as a whole so that each member might enjoy its benefits and submit to its authority. But Christ has entrusted power more particularly to those believers within his church who are officers that they might administer and exercise that power on behalf of the rest. As one writer put it, "[Church power] belongs equally and by Divine warrant to both; but under different characters, suited to the different places each party occupies in the Christian Church."[2] Further, church officers do not exercise this power on their own initiative. All church power is granted to officers through the call of Jesus Christ, which comes by the consent of the church. That is why local congregations nominate, call, and elect their own officers, both elders and deacons; no body is to be ruled by officers whom they do not choose for themselves (Acts 6:1–6; 14:23).

Even in the grant of power by Christ through his church, officers are not then freed to do whatever they wish. Power to order the church's worship is exercised by officers "severally" (or individually) only because they have been commissioned by the church for the exercise of that authority. As a result, the authority to preach the gospel and administer the sacraments comes through a call issued by a local church and by powers granted by a presbytery. No one takes it upon himself to preach or administer the sacraments without proper authorization from a presbytery or without invitation from a session. Power of "jurisdiction" (the right and power to interpret and apply the law) is exercised by officers jointly as church courts. Thus, no elder has the right to bring judgment in a discipline case as an individual; only as a group of elders, whether in a local church "session," in a geographical presbytery, or in the General Assembly of the church, can such power be exercised. Moreover, no single elder has a right to declare doctrine authoritatively that is different from what the church has already declared it believes to be the teaching of the Bible. Rather, elders who have disagreements with the church's confessional standards submit their views to the judgment of a session or presbytery, which then decides whether or not to allow those "exceptions" to the church's doctrine (BCO 3-2, 21-4). In the end, whether this church power is exercised individually or jointly, it has divine sanction only when it is in conformity with the Word of God, which norms and limits all use of the church's authority.

In Presbyterian churches, we have two sets of officers, one which represents oversight and the other service in the body of Christ. The office of oversight is called "elder"; the Greek word for elder is where

142

we get our word *presbyter*, and hence the denominational name Presbyterian. Elders have oversight over the church's doctrine, morals, and discipline. They "exercise government and discipline, and take oversight not only of the spiritual interests of the particular church, but also the Church generally when called thereunto" (BCO 8-3). Elders have a number of duties, which include visiting people in their homes, caring for the sick, instructing the ignorant, comforting the mourner, nurturing the church's children, setting a spiritual example for the church, evangelizing the unconverted, and praying with and for people.

Within this class of officers, there are two orders (1 Tim. 5:17). *Ruling elders* are specifically entrusted with the administration of order and discipline in a particular church; in addition, they are called upon to "cultivate zealously their own aptness to teach the Bible and should improve every opportunity of doing so" (BCO 8-9). *Teaching elders* are those who, in addition to having the responsibility of ruling in the church, also have the added functions of feeding the flock by reading, explaining, and preaching the Word of God and administering the sacraments (BCO 8-5). Teaching elders are sometimes called ministers of the Word. But teaching elders and ruling elders are two orders within the same class of officers; thus, both orders have "the same authority and eligibility to office in the courts of the Church" (BCO 8-9). In addition, teaching elders are not elders (or ministers) because they *teach*, but they teach because they are *elders*. That is, the right of ministers to preach within Christ's church is due to the fact that they have the office of elder, not because they have been called as the preacher. Within Presbyterian churches, there is no special priestly class that has special powers or authority; rather, the office of oversight is elder (1 Tim. 3:1–7; Titus 1:5–9).

The office of service within the church is called "deacon." In Acts 6, the apostles, as elders of Christ's church, are doing both the ministries of oversight and service. Because the task of service is taking them away from their task of oversight, they appoint those who would serve God's people, allowing the elders to focus on the ministry of the Word and prayer. And so, from the very beginning, the office of deacon is "one of sympathy and service" (BCO 9-1). It is also an office that operated under the oversight and through the delegation of authority by the elders (BCO 9-2). And finally, spiritual men are chosen from within the body and are ordained to the office by the laying on of hands (BCO 17, 24).

The deacon's responsibilities of stewardship and service include ministering to those in need, the sick, the friendless, and any in distress. Deacons also seek "to develop the grace of liberality in the members of the church," devising means for collecting the gifts of the people and for distributing the benevolences of the church (BCO 9-2). In addition, they have oversight of the church's property, seeking to maintain it properly. Notice how vital these things are for effective church ministry—only in deeds of mercy to the lost and needy will the word of God's mercy take on its fullest complexion; only in deeds of liberality and benevolence can the communion of the saints be realized; only as the church shows itself to be a good steward of material things can others trust it to be a good steward of the mysteries of God. Hence, a well-ordered diaconal ministry is vital for the church's proclamation of the gospel of God's grace.

## THE CONNECTIONAL NATURE OF THE CHURCH

We have already made mention of the fact that elders never exercise power on their own initiative; even when they are acting individually (or "severally"), they do so with warrant from some church court which has authorized them. These church courts, made up of "presbyters" or elders, are church sessions, presbyteries, and the General Assembly. A *church session* consists of teaching and ruling elders of a local congregation who have been called by Christ through the election of God's people to exercise oversight in that congregation. A *presbytery* consists of "all the teaching elders and churches within its bounds that have been accepted by the presbytery." When the presbytery meets as a court, it comprises all the teaching elders and ruling elders as elected by the session to represent the church (BCO 13-1). The *General Assembly*, the highest court of the church, represents in one body all the churches of the denomination (BCO 14-1). When elders gather together as a church court, they have power to declare in their ministry only what God has already said in his Word in the areas of doctrine, order, and discipline. However, they do not have power to bind the conscience in ways that contradict God's Word, nor do they have authority to compel obedience by using the state's power or coercive means.

In thinking about these church courts and how they relate to one another, there is a very important principle to keep in mind, a principle which, in my opinion, represents the heart of the Presbyterian system: *in Presbyterianism, the parts are in the whole and the whole is in the parts.* A number of important corollaries come from this principle. One is that all of the courts of the church are essentially equal in power. A lower court (e.g., a local church session), which represents a "part" of the church, has all the power necessary to declare ministerially what God's Word says in areas of doctrine, order, and discipline, because it stands as a court representing the whole church. In a similar way, the highest court (the General Assembly), which represents the "whole" church, has no more power than a local church session to declare doctrine, order, and discipline, except in ways that the church has already decided beforehand. That is why our Book of Church Order says, "All Church courts are one in nature, constituted of the same elements, possessed inherently of the same kinds of rights and powers, and differing only as the Constitution [of the church] may provide" (BCO 11-3).

A second corollary from this principle is sometimes called "review and control" (BCO 11-4). Each higher court has responsibility for the actions of the lower court. This is most clearly represented in the fact that the minutes and records of lower courts are reviewed by higher courts: session minutes are reviewed and approved by presbyteries; presbytery records are reviewed and approved by the General Assembly; and General Assembly minutes are reviewed by the entire church. Another way in which this is represented is in the fact that presbyteries are responsible for the church's work in a given locale and are charged to care for the health of all of the churches in an area. When a particular church experiences tensions between the pastor and other elders, presbytery will appoint a committee to review the situation and work out a solution. This principle also plays out with the church's agencies—presbyteries appoint commissioners to General Assembly to serve on committees to review the work of the church's agencies, ensuring that the larger work is controlled by representatives of the entire body. Review and control demonstrates the mutual submission of the parts of the church to the whole and the whole to its parts (BCO 40).

This principle also means that the parts have the right of appeal to the whole. If a minority believe that a court has acted contrary to Scripture or to the church's order, that minority has the right to bring the court's action to the notice of the whole church. Sometimes this is represented by a reference, sometimes by an appeal, and sometimes by a complaint. In each of these actions, a specific request is made of the higher court by a minority in a lower court. A *reference* is a request by a lower court to a higher one seeking advice or other action on a matter before the lower court (BCO 41-1). When a court's action goes against a church member, he or she has the privilege of *appeal* to a higher court, which will hear and rule on the grounds of the appeal (BCO 42-1). And when a court makes a decision or action that appears to a communing member to go against the Bible's teaching or against the church's constitution, that member has the right of *complaint* to that court (BCO 43-1, 2). Each of these actions is a means of testifying that Jesus Christ alone is Lord of the conscience, that church courts do make mistakes and err, and that the parts are in the whole and the whole in the parts.

A final corollary from this principle is sometimes called the "connectional" principle: each part of the church has a responsibility to other parts and to the whole. Local churches give benevolence funds to support the common work of the church in missions, church planting, and theological education. If local churches do not support the work of the whole church, opting rather to go their own way in missions, Christian education, or theological education, then the whole church suffers. Likewise, one local church does not plant a daughter church without the authorization of the presbytery; one reason for this is to ensure that new churches are planted in such a way as not to harm the ministry of another church in near proximity (BCO 5-8). Again, the point here is that each part of the church has a responsibility to the care for the whole. Another example of our connectional nature is the fact that doctrinal errors or moral lapses in one part of the church affect the entire church. In cases where a presbytery is unwilling to deal with significant doctrinal or moral deviancy, two other presbyteries might request the General Assembly to assume "original jurisdiction" of the case in order that the matter might be handled for the good of the whole church (BCO 34-1). We are not allowed simply to close our eyes to doctrinal or moral problems going on in one of our presbyteries; rather, each part of the church has a responsibility to the church as a whole to deal with such situations appropriately.

In the PCA, we also demonstrate our connectedness through our ten national agencies and permanent committees:

- the Administrative Committee (which is the office of the denomination's Stated Clerk),
- Christian Education and Publication (CE&P),
- Covenant College,
- Covenant Theological Seminary,
- PCA Retirement and Benefits, Inc.,
- Mission to North America (MNA),
- Mission to the World (MTW),
- PCA Foundation,
- Ridge Haven Conference Center,
- Reformed University Ministries (RUM).

One way to think of the work of these agencies and committees would be that the whole church has a responsibility to care for the education and spiritual well-being of covenant children from childhood to college (CE&P, Covenant College, RUM), as well as for the denomination's aged and retired ministers (Retirement and Benefits). We also have a responsibility to train ministers of the Word (Covenant

Seminary) and encourage laymen and women in their faith (Ridge Haven). We are called to make disciples in every nation as well as to care for our own "Jerusalem and Samaria" in planting churches (MTW and MNA). And we must be good stewards of those material blessings God has given us so that we might use them well for the kingdom (PCA Foundation).

We cannot do any of these tasks alone; we must band together with other parts of the church to accomplish them for the whole church. Furthermore, we have no power or authority to accomplish these tasks alone; as we cooperate as Christ's church, we truly care for our covenant children, our future and retired ministers, our laypeople, the lost around the world, and the financial benefits that God grants— and we do this together. As we demonstrate to a watching world that we are Christ's church, then it will be true that "the gates of hell shall not prevail against it" (Matt. 16:18). May all of this be to the glory of Christ the King and for the expansion of his kingdom.

## »Questions for Thought and Review

1. Think about your church background: did your church recognize that it had the power to order doctrine, worship, government, and discipline? How did it use its power?
2. What are some ramifications that result from the Presbyterian belief that the church's mission, sphere, and power are spiritual? Does that necessarily exclude caring for people's physical or material well-being for spiritual ends?
3. Does the church have any right to appeal to the state to use its power wisely? If so, when and how should the church do this (see WCF 31.4)?
4. What are some practical ways to express the truth that Jesus Christ "is alone Lord of the conscience" while still maintaining the "peace, purity, and unity" of the church?

5. What do you think about the fact that church officers do not exercise power on their own, but only as authorized to do so? Is there a certain amount of protection offered to believers in the truth that elders exercise discipline jointly as a session or presbytery?

6. What are some of the implications of the statement, "teaching elders are not elders because they teach, but they teach because they are elders"? How can viewing both the teaching elders (pastors) and ruling elders as *elders* resolve some tensions that may result between these two orders of office?

7. Why do you think a well-ordered diaconal ministry is necessary for the church's proclamation of the gospel? How does your answer help to answer question 2 above?

8. How does the principle of "the part is in the whole and the whole is in the parts" express the unity of the church while still respecting differences within it?

9. Have you ever had dealings with the PCA agencies or committees? How have those experiences shaped your view of the work of the whole church?

## »*For Further Reading*

Bannerman, James. *The Church of Christ*, 2 vols. 1869. Reprint, Carlisle, Pa.: Banner of Truth, 1960.

Dickson, David. *The Elder and His Work*. Edited by Philip G. Ryken and George McFarland. Phillipsburg, N.J.: P&R, 2004.

Hall, David W., and Joseph H. Hall, eds. *Paradigms in Polity*. Grand Rapids, Mich.: Eerdmans, 1994.

Hodge, Charles. *Church Polity*. 1879. Reprint, Westminster Discount Books, 2002.

Witherow, Thomas. *The Apostolic Church—Which Is It?* Reprint, Glasgow: Free Presbyterian Publications, 1967.

The PCA maintains a useful Web site at www.pcanet.org. There you will find links to each of the committees and agencies maintained by the General Assembly.

# PART THREE

# »*Presbyterian Stories*

CHAPTER **9**

# The Glorious Reformation: Calvin, Knox, and the Beginnings of Presbyterianism

WHEN WE TALK ABOUT Presbyterian stories, we must start over five hundred years ago with the Reformation. Recent scholars have questioned whether the Reformation (roughly the period between 1500 and 1550) really was as cataclysmic as most Protestants have come to believe that it was. These historians have argued that the periods directly preceding and succeeding the Reformation were actually more significant and effected more profound and lasting social change than the Reformation itself. The older view of the Reformation as a series of events that marked a new era characterized by new beginnings has been replaced by a model that views the period as part of a larger process of social transformation that began modifying and changing the medieval synthesis as far back as the fourteenth century.

Perhaps a good way to challenge this developing consensus is to think about what European life would have looked like if the Reformation had never happened. What would the church and the people's religious practices have looked like? What would have characterized society and its culture? What would the future have held for countries that, in reality, did embrace the Reformation, and countries that had not yet been born? Several things could be said here. First, if the Reformation had never happened, it seems very likely that the Roman

152

Catholic Church would have become completely secularized and largely irrelevant to European life by the end of the seventeenth century. In actuality, the corruption of the Roman church, with its divided papacy in the fourteenth century and its corrupt papacy in the fifteenth and early sixteenth centuries, led to the rise of several "forerunners of the Reformation," as they have commonly been called. John Huss and John Wycliffe gave voice to the growing social and spiritual anxiety of the laity. While the Roman church did respond to these radical voices by initiating a series of internal reforms, these efforts were not enough to soothe the consciences of the people. The result was the Reformational explosion, fueled by Luther's recovery of the biblical doctrine of justification by faith alone.

But consider further what the state of affairs would have been if the Reformation had never happened. Certainly, there would have been continued attempts to reform the church from within. However, as several historians have suggested, most of the avenues for internal reform had already been attempted by 1500, and with only limited success due to the sheer size and complexity of the church's bureaucracy. Thus, it is entirely conceivable that without the Reformation, the church would have caved in on itself and rendered itself irrelevant. Though this might have come about even before the seventeenth century, certainly by that time, a corrupted church, unwilling to bear reform and unable to be reformed, would no longer have commanded the respect and attention of European society. The Enlightenment age, with its exaltation of reason over revelation and the "superstitions" of the age, would have ignored the church and its claims. In particular, the challenge of Thomas Hobbes and his *Leviathan*, which argued for a thoroughgoing materialism and a utilitarian political rule with total allegiance given to the state, would have been unanswerable—for centuries, the church had pursued that same strategy as popes maximized their profits and pleasures under the banner of "might makes right." Any protest lodged by the church against Enlightenment thought would have been met with a scoff and a shrug. Without the Reformation, Europe would have been a thoroughly secular society by the end of the seventeenth century.

Again, if the Reformation had never happened, the rising capital-
ists of Europe would have led the secularization process with disas-
trous results for the continent's political and moral situation. The
period of the Reformation coincided with the growth of a new European middle class, connected to the rise of capitalism, who united with
the Reformers to topple oppressive popes and priests, and eventually,
in the seventeenth century, monarchs as well. This was particularly
the case in John Calvin's Geneva. At precisely the time when the city
of Geneva achieved independence and was implementing Calvin's
reforms, it was transitioning from an older style of capitalism to a
more modern form. After a period of economic recession from 1535
to 1540, the city-state experienced a twenty-year period of growth
that coincided with the decision to invite Calvin to return to the city
in order to reinaugurate and further the Reformation there. To be sure,
it is difficult to argue that the Reformation caused the rise of capitalism in Geneva, or elsewhere. Yet it appears to be without question
that the Reformation did much to make sixteenth-century capitalism
more compassionate.

The chief example of this was the social welfare movement that
Calvin promoted in Geneva. The outpouring of benevolence, directed
through the churches into a central "general hospital" for the care
of the poor and sick, helped to soften the increasing displacement
caused by population growth, war, plague, and famine. The "hospital" employed deacons directly in the disbursement of funds and in
caring for the poor and sick, creating a "hospital" movement throughout Reformed countries. Eventually, these hospitals devoted themselves to caring for the sick alone, but they were part of Calvin's vision
of word and deed ministry in Geneva. Care for the suffering was also
part of Calvin's rationale for encouraging the development of wealth.
Riches were not to be spent on oneself in luxurious wastefulness, but
to be distributed for the furtherance of God's kingdom. In order to
encourage this, the city-state of Geneva organized general collections,
either to meet a crisis or to aid refugees within its borders. By caring
for the poor compassionately, Calvin's Geneva restrained some of the
selfishness inherent in the capitalist economic system.

Now imagine if there were no Reformation Geneva, or, indeed, any relevant church to check, channel, and challenge capitalist aspirations. The scenes of eighteenth-century France or nineteenth-century England, with marked divisions between elites and the poor; boiling ferment on the streets ready to explode at any moment in revolution; and the ever-ready possibility of a Napoleon or a Bismarck to unite the nations under his nationalistic banner—all of these would have been present much earlier, without the charitable and compassionate works that Protestantism offered in Germany or England. The figures that would have emerged in a world without Protestantism would have looked much more like Mussolini, Stalin, or Kim Jong-Il—amoral dictators seeking to unite the populace in a pagan devotion to the state, financed by a rising upper class that received special favors.

One last thing to think about along this line is this: if the Reformation had never happened, then the gospel of free grace would have been overshadowed by the unreformed ritual and malformed theology of the Roman Catholic Church. Early in the church's life, it had committed itself to affirming the sovereignty of God's grace and the utter depravity of humankind, even while it hedged on exactly how "predestination" worked. After the Council of Orange in 529, the church's theologians sought to give more and more freedom and responsibility to human beings. By the time the fifteenth century came to an end, there was a form of covenant theology that was summarized in the phrase, "God will not deny his grace to anyone who does what lies within him." Ultimately, in this view, salvation was communicated to those who did good works, especially being baptized, participating in the sacrament of penance, and shunning evil. Penance became a key part of the Catholic means of gaining assurance of forgiveness and pardon. This penitential system was typically quite rigorous, but provided only temporary relief with conditions attached. If the church were to provide an effective removal of guilt this side of heaven, then many of the medieval religious institutions, which relied on the income that the penitential system brought into the church, would have collapsed.

The gospel of the Reformation, which proclaimed that God's righteousness shall come to those who live by faith alone, fundamentally challenged the basis of medieval religion and piety. If salvation came by faith alone in Christ alone, and if this provided an effective removal of religious guilt and anxiety, then the forms of penance that had proved so financially profitable for the church (particularly indulgences) were not only unnecessary, but blasphemous. And yet, this Reformational discovery was actually a *recovery* of the early church's understanding of the gospel—for this justification, this righteousness, could only come by faith, which was granted by God through his sovereign grace.

If this recovery of the gospel had not occurred at that point, if the Reformation had not happened, then obviously there would be no Protestant churches. And if we went to church at all, we would still be observing the Mass, perhaps slightly revised by the 1960s Vatican II (perhaps not, since there probably would not have been a Vatican II). We would still be observing an intense penitential system, seeking forgiveness and yet resigned to never fully knowing forgiveness in this life. The church as a whole would still be as fuzzy about how someone was made right with God as it had been before the sixteenth-century Council of Trent, for without the Reformation there would not have been a Counter or Catholic Reformation or a Jesuit movement. Not only would the church have become irrelevant due to its corruption, but it would have been irrelevant preeminently due to its own doctrine. In answer to the question, what must I do to be saved? the church still would be answering, "Have you thought about lighting a votive, sponsoring a mass, or making a pilgrimage?" The sheer fact that millions of Protestant Christians throughout the past five hundred years have known peace with God, having been justified by faith alone, demonstrates that the Reformation was a vitally important reality, one which transformed individuals, households, cities, and nation-states.

Out of this Reformation period that fundamentally transformed social, political, economic, and religious structures, Presbyterianism came into being. And while we cannot touch on every key point of the Presbyterian story between 1500 and 1706, when Presbyterians organized officially in the United States, there are at least three historical figures and events that have decisively shaped the Presbyterian story.

## JOHN CALVIN AND THE SWISS REFORMATION

Broadly speaking Presbyterianism—as a set of beliefs and practices—originated with John Calvin. Undoubtedly, he is the looming historical figure with whom Presbyterian historians and theologians must wrestle; his thought continues to inform, inspire, provoke, and challenge current Presbyterian theology, worship, and ethics. While Presbyterian ministers are required to subscribe to the Westminster Standards—a product of a mid-seventeenth-century gathering of theologians and church politicians in England—it is not too much to claim that we all see ourselves as Calvin's heirs in one way or another.

Born in Noyon, France in 1509, Calvin went to Paris to be trained as a lawyer when he was fourteen years old. After sustaining the arts course at the College du Montaigu, he studied law at Orleans and Bourges. Sometime during his studies, he imbibed the new "humanist" emphasis upon returning to the original sources of knowledge. For law, this meant a return to Greek and Latin classical orators and intellectuals; in line with this new emphasis, Calvin published his first book as a commentary on Seneca's *De Clementia* in 1532. For religion, the humanists argued that scholars needed to return to the sources (*ad fontes*), particularly the Hebrew Old Testament and Greek New Testament; Erasmus produced his first "critical" edition of the Greek New Testament in 1516 and so fueled questions about Roman Catholic doctrine based on questionable translations found in the Latin Vulgate.

Sometime during his legal studies, Calvin became associated with the Reformation movement in the French universities. Following the outrage in response to a 1533 address delivered by the rector of the University of Paris and probably authored by Calvin himself—an address which supported the Reformation—Calvin fled to Basel in 1535 to avoid persecution. Early the following year, he published the first edition of his *Institutes of the Christian Religion*. Shortly after the *Institutes* was published, he was passing through Geneva and was convinced by William Farel to remain in that city-state in order to advance the Reformation cause. In 1537, Calvin and Farel attempted to persuade the Genevans to institute a strict form of church discipline, which centered on the use of a confession of faith and excommunication as an instrument of social control. Internal and external political pressures were brought to bear against Calvin's reforms and he was forced to leave the city in 1538.

Calvin went to Strasbourg, where he served as pastor to the French congregation and worked closely with Martin Bucer. He learned from Bucer the importance of "managing" the Reformational program in both civil and ecclesiastical affairs; he also was able to produce a second edition of his *Institutes*, which appeared in 1539. He also found time to marry Idelette de Bure in 1540. While he may have been content to remain in Strasbourg, events in Geneva led the city council to request Calvin to return to complete the Reformation there. When he returned in 1541, he was able to restructure the church offices successfully, introduce vernacular catechisms and liturgy, and develop a system of church discipline that used a "consistory" of twelve elders to hear and decide discipline cases. Calvin faced considerable opposition to his reforms and even experienced severe political setbacks in 1549, when his opponents gained control of the city council. However, his opponents overreached themselves by supporting the heretic Michael Servetus's anti-Trinitarian theology, millenarian visions, and antinomian charges against Calvin. Servetus's views were seen as politically disruptive and condemned by the city council; he was executed on charges of blasphemy in 1553. After this, Calvin's opponents were largely discredited and he was able to work in relative peace until his own death in 1564.

The crown jewel of Calvin's work was, of course, his *Institutes*. The final version of his work appeared in 1559; Calvin struggled throughout his life to arrange the book in exactly the right way, and even a cursory look at previous editions of the *Institutes* reveals his constant tinkering with structure and form. However, Calvin's theology as expressed in the *Institutes* remained fairly consistent throughout the various manifestations of the work. For one thing, the arrangement of the *Institutes* points quite clearly to the Trinitarian framework of Calvin's theology: the first three books focus on the knowledge of God the Creator, God the Redeemer in Christ, and God the Spirit's work in giving the grace of Christ. The final book considers the church and its means of grace, through which the triune God "invites us into the society of Christ and holds us therein" (Calvin, *Inst.*, 4). Earlier, in a catechism written in 1537/38 to further the Reformation within Geneva and to publish to the world what the Reformed church believed, Calvin claimed that

> when we name Father, Son, and Spirit, we are not fashioning three gods, but in the simplest unity of God and Scripture and the very experience of godliness we are showing ourselves God the Father, his Son, and Spirit. Our understanding cannot conceive of the Father without including the Son at the same time, in whom his living image shines; and the Spirit in whom his might and power are visible. Let us cleave with the total concentration of our mind upon the one God; yet in the meantime let us contemplate the Father with his Son and Spirit.[1]

This emphasis upon the work of the Trinity—God who reveals himself as Creator and Redeemer through Christ and his Spirit—have led some to call Calvin the "theologian of the Holy Spirit." Never before in theology had the Spirit's role in the work of redemption been emphasized as it had in Calvin's thought. As the theologian I. John Hesselink has noted, "To do justice to Calvin's doctrine of the Holy Spirit one must discuss his whole theology."[2] Calvin related the Holy Spirit to every doctrine he discussed in such a way that his theology was suffused with the Spirit's activity. Hence, our belief in the authority of Scripture is rooted ultimately in the self-attestation of the Spirit and his witness to the Word in our hearts (*Inst.*, 1.7.4–5). Likewise, the Spirit forges the bond between Christ and believers in their union with him (*Inst.*, 3.1.1, 3.11.10). He calls believers effectually to Christ, renews their wills so that they might go to Christ, and grants faith so that they might believe in Christ (*Inst.*, 3.2.7). Further, the Spirit applies the redemption purchased by Christ to humankind and testifies in the hearts of the saints to the reality of Christ's forgiveness. Finally, the Spirit governs the believer's heart and guides him into all righteousness (*Inst.*, 2.3.10).

Not surprisingly for those who know something about the Reformed tradition, Calvin emphasized the profound sinfulness of humankind. Calvin argued that the biblical witness declared that humans were depraved by nature in order "to teach them that they have all been overwhelmed by an unavoidable calamity from which only God's mercy can deliver them. Because this could not be proved unless it rested upon the ruin and destruction of our nature, [the Bible] put[s] forward these testimonies which prove our nature utterly lost" (*Inst.*, 2.3.2). Because human beings cannot save themselves, God had to enter into the human situation by way of Jesus the Mediator, who came to be a perfect prophet, priest, and king for us (*Inst.*, 2.15).

We receive the salvation that Christ purchased through union with him. Calvin held that "we must understand that as long as Christ remains outside of us, and we are separated from him, all that he has suffered and done for the salvation of the human race remains useless and of no value for us. Therefore, to share with us what he has received from the Father, he had to become ours and to dwell within us" (*Inst.*, 3.1.1). This dwelling in us is the "secret" work of the Holy Spirit, who draws out our faith to Christ and effects a bond between Christ and us. Because we are "in Christ" and Christ is in us, God sees us as right with himself. We are also transformed as we live more and more in step with the indwelling Spirit of Christ, who continues to teach us what it means to live by faith.

The means that the Spirit uses to teach us how to live in step with him are the church and its means of grace. Chief among the exercises of faith is prayer. We live out our communion with God through prayer:

160

there is a communion of men with God by which, having entered the heavenly sanctuary, they appeal to him in person concerning his promises in order to experience, where necessity so demands that what they believed was not vain, although he had promised it in word alone. . . . So true is it that we dig up by prayer the treasures that were pointed out by the Lord's gospel, and which our faith has gazed upon. (*Inst.*, 3.20.2)

The preached Word and the sacraments are vital for maintaining and confirming our union and communion with God in Christ; those who do not avail themselves of these means cast doubt on their own standing with God in Christ (*Inst.*, 4.1.1). The church's structure, governed by doctors, pastors, elders, and deacons, also served as a means of strengthening grace to God's people. In particular, Calvin restored the office of elder (or church "governor" or "presbyter") to importance within the structure of the church. He believed that "governors were, I believe, elders chosen from the people, who were charged with the censure of morals and the exercise of discipline along with the bishops. . . . Each church, therefore, had from its beginning a senate, chosen from godly, grave, and holy men, which had jurisdiction over the correcting of faults" (*Inst.*, 4.3.9). Hence, the basic governing principle of Presbyterian church government derived from Calvin's recovery of the office of presbyter.

Clearly, many of the beliefs and practices that we have looked at throughout this book found their renewed origins in Calvin. While many of these things had precedence in the early church—which is why Calvin and others saw themselves as "reformers" and not "innovators"—still it is the case that Presbyterian churches throughout the world and the ages have found their inspiration and formation in the thought of the Genevan Reformer. However, it might have been possible for Presbyterianism to remain a Swiss and French effort at church renewal if it were not for a renegade Scot, who arrived in Geneva around 1553: John Knox.

## JOHN KNOX AND THE SCOTS REVOLUTION

John Knox was born in Haddington around 1513, studied at Glasgow and possibly St. Andrews, and entered into a minor religious and political role as a notary in his hometown. Sometime around 1544, he gave up these positions in order to become a private tutor. Shortly afterward, he came under the influence of George Wishart, the traveling advanceman of the Reformation in Scotland. In 1547, Knox became the preacher at St. Andrews, which ended up being a short-lived ministry due to the capture of the castle by the French. He was assigned to a galley in which he was transferred to France in 1549, but soon escaped and made his way to England, where he was made chaplain to Edward VI. In this role, Knox assisted in the revision of the Book of Common Prayer, known as the Second Prayer Book. In 1553, upon the ascension of the Catholic "Bloody" Mary Tudor as queen of England, Knox went as a preacher to Bucks but shortly afterward fled to Geneva by way of a brief stay in Frankfort, Germany.

Calvin's Geneva was a revelation to Knox: there he found Presbyterian government and discipline of the churches, moral codes enforced by the church, and order and peace in the ascendancy. Knox biographer Jasper Ridley observed, "In Geneva, Knox definitely became a Calvinist, and conceived an admiration for Calvin which he had felt for no one since Wishart."[3] What apparently appealed to Knox was the way in which Geneva actuated the Old Testament ideal of a political-religious commonwealth under the direction of God's Word. Of course, Calvin was unable to capture fully that theocratic ideal in his own time, but this vision animated Knox's own ministry upon his return to Scotland, and gave impetus to later American Puritan efforts to forge a "holy commonwealth" in New England. Ironically, much like Calvin again, Knox was forced by the pragmatic realities of politics to temper his idealism in order to move incrementally toward his ideal vision. After his death, the larger political realities swept aside many of his accomplishments, but his vision of "crown and covenant" working together under God's law remained an inspiration to his Presbyterian descendants.

During Knox's stay in Geneva, the political situation in Scotland improved so that he was able to return once again in 1555 for a brief sojourn of preaching and writing. However, persecution forced him to flee once again to Geneva, where he organized an English-speaking church. While in Geneva, in 1558, he penned his infamous *The First Blast of the Trumpet against the Monstrous Regiment of Women*, in which he mercilessly attacked Mary Tudor and Mary of Guise, asserting that governments headed by women were contrary to natural and divine law. This pamphlet appeared before the ascension of Elizabeth I to the throne in England and made him unwelcome there throughout her reign.

Knox finally returned to Scotland for good in 1559 as the leader of the Reforming Party. Early the next year, he wrote his lasting monument, the *Scots Confession* (1560), which provided a summary of his own theological perspective and helped to shape Scots Presbyterian thought until the Westminster Assembly in 1647. He also developed the *First Book of Discipline* (1560) and the *Book of Common Order* (1556–64), thus extending his influence over the entire church through its doctrine, discipline, and worship. With the return of Mary Stuart to Scotland in 1561, Knox and Mary engaged in numerous disputes over the Queen's private Masses. When Knox forced Mary from the throne in 1567, he was a strong supporter of James VI, preaching at James's coronation and wielding influence through the king's regent, the Earl of Moray. When Moray was murdered in 1570, Knox lost influence within the royal courts, and when the Scots Reformer died in 1572, Presbyterianism was still an uncertain proposition; it was not until after his death that his cause fully triumphed.

The Scots Confession serves as a good summary of the continuity that exists between John Calvin's teaching on the European continent and that of John Knox in the British Isles. Many points of commonality are obvious: the stress upon original sin, the prior claim of God to choose those who would be saved, the need for regeneration and effectual calling by the work of the Holy Spirit, the marks or notes of the church being the pure preaching of God's

Word and administration of the sacraments (Knox added ecclesiastical discipline as a third mark), the real "spiritual" presence of Christ in the sacraments. But the Scots Confession also has some other interesting features that continue to make it useful for theological reflection. Importantly, it frames many of its topics (or *loci*) in the redemptive-historical order found in Scripture. And so, since God is revealed in the first verse of Scripture, the confession begins with the triune God. It then moves to creation, especially the creation of humankind; then considers the effects of Adam's fall, along with the revelation of God's promise; and charts the continuation, increase, and preservation of the church throughout the Old Testament. The fulfillment of God's promise awaited the Incarnation of Jesus Christ, which is considered in its proper order, along with the meaning of his death, resurrection, and ascension. In addition, the pouring out of the Holy Spirit at Pentecost draws attention to the biblical teaching concerning the Spirit, the Christian life of good works, and the establishment of the true church of Jesus Christ. Framing these topics in the light of redemptive history gives the Scots Confession a more biblical-theological feel than, for example, the Westminster Confession.

Another significant feature of the Scots Confession is the way that Knox grounds God's choice of sinners in election in Jesus Christ: "That same eternal God and Father, who by grace alone chose us in his Son Christ Jesus before the foundation of the world was laid, appointed him to be our head, our brother, our pastor, and the great bishop of our souls." Knox went on to claim that

> by this most holy brotherhood whatever we have lost in Adam is restored to us again. Therefore we are not afraid to call God our Father, not so much because he has created us, which we have in common with the reprobate, as because he has given unto us his only Son to be our brother, and given us grace to acknowledge and embrace him as our only Mediator. (Scots Confession, chap. 8)

While the later Westminster Confession roots God's elective purpose back before time began in a logical sequence of abstract decrees, Knox and the Scots Confession place election in God's purpose to enter the world in Jesus.

After Knox's death in 1572, the union of crown and church was consummated in the King's Confession of 1581. Fearful that Roman Catholicism might be revived in Scotland, Knox's successor John Craig authored this brief statement of Presbyterianism. It was affirmed by the king, James Stuart, and his household; eventually, all parish clergy and graduates of Scottish universities were required to subscribe to it. The confession was reaffirmed in 1590 and 1595. Later, after the unification of Scotland and England through the Stuart royal family, Charles I attempted to establish the Book of Common Prayer, as well as an Episcopal form of church government, in 1637. In response, a number of Scots affirmed the National Covenant in 1638, which took the King's Confession as its basis and abjured the prayer book and episcopacy. Those who signed this document became known as the "Covenanters." Though they were persecuted relentlessly by Charles I and his Archbishop of Canterbury, William Laud, the Covenanters would support rapprochement with the English Parliament and eventually signed the "Solemn League and Covenant" in 1643, which pledged the two parties to seek common doctrine, worship, and church government. As part of this agreement, the Scots sent representatives to the Jerusalem Room at Westminster Abbey to join representatives from the English church in hammering out and codifying a unified Presbyterianism.

## The Westminster Assembly and the Codification of Presbyterianism

Charles I was forced to call the Long Parliament into being in 1640 when the Scottish army marched into England. One of the tasks to which the parliament turned its attention was the reform of the church. A bill to convene a synod of ministers for this purpose passed in Parliament, but failed to receive the royal assent in

1642. Parliament therefore issued an ordinance the following year that called for such an assembly. On July 1, 1643, the assembly, consisting of 151 nominated commissioners, convened at Westminster Abbey to set about reforming the church. Initially, the assembly was charged with revising the Thirty-nine Articles of the Church of England in order to remove any hints of Arminianism or Roman Catholicism. When the Solemn League and Covenant was signed by English and Scots representatives in August and September 1643, the assembly's task changed dramatically. Now it was charged to bring about "the nearest conjunction of uniformity in religion, confession of faith, form of Church government, directory for worship and catechizing."[4] The Covenant meant that the assembly would spend the majority of its time dealing with church government and worship. It was on these matters that the various national representatives who joined the proceedings had their deepest differences. While the assembly did produce a directory of worship, it was not approved by the Scots church; and though the assembly hammered out a form of Presbyterian government that was tempered by Congregationalist and Episcopalian concerns, it too was never adopted by either side because of conflicts over the jurisdiction of church courts and the nature of church censures.

The only contribution of the Westminster Assembly that had a truly lasting impact were the doctrinal standards the divines developed. The Confession of Faith took twenty-seven months to develop: it was completed on December 4, 1646, and approved by the Scots General Assembly on August 27, 1647, and the English Parliament on June 20, 1648. The Larger Catechism, based partly on Anglican bishop James Ussher's *Body of Divinity*, was mainly the work of Anthony Tuckney; in it, Tuckney attempted to restate the teaching of the Confession in a question and answer format. The Shorter Catechism was also authored by Tuckney, with assistance from John Wallis. These standards were completed in 1647 and approved by the national authorities in 1648. After the reestablishment of royal rule with the return of Charles II in 1660, one of the ironies was that the Westminster Standards were unable to preserve orthodoxy in English Presbyterianism, which became essentially Unitarian by the mid-eighteenth century. Rather, the Westminster Standards would exercise their greatest influence in Scots Presbyterian and, later, in American Presbyterian life. Likewise, the Standards would carry great influence in Congregational and Baptist life, as each denominational group produced their own lightly edited versions of the Westminster Confession and Shorter Catechism. The assembly therefore produced a confessional standard that exercised vast influence in every realm of the Presbyterian church save the one for which it was originally intended—the established church in England. The Standards continue to exercise this strong influence even today.

This was evidenced recently in the celebration of the 350th anniversary of the Westminster Standards. Conservative Presbyterians, Baptists, and Congregationalists produced multiple volumes to commemorate the occasion. Likewise, over the past decade, renewed and intensified efforts have been made to study the Standards in their original social, political, and religious contexts. In addition, we have tried in this book to take seriously Presbyterian beliefs as represented by the Standards. There may come a day when the Standards could be superseded by better summaries of Presbyterian beliefs; there may come a day when there will be genuine doctrinal advance as Presbyterians continue to study God's Word, reflect on God's triune character, and relish the wonders of grace. As renowned Presbyterian scholar and theologian J. Gresham Machen once said, "Such doctrinal advance is certainly conceivable. It is perfectly conceivable that the church should examine the particular errors of the present day and should set forth over against them, even more clearly than is done in the existing creeds, the truth that is contained in God's Word."[5] Until that day comes, however, we can be thankful for the labors of the Westminster divines and for their faithful summary of the things most surely believed by Presbyterians in their history as God's people.

## »Questions for Thought and Review

1. Have you ever considered what religious life would be like if the Reformation had never happened? What are some other differences that come to mind if you imagine the world without Protestantism?
2. In our overview of the Reformation, we studied a number of political, cultural, and social effects caused by the change in religions. What difference does being Reformed or Protestant make today? If Protestant churches ceased to exist tomorrow, what difference would it make to the social and cultural fabric?
3. How do Calvin's reflections on the Trinity differ from the way in which we often think about God? What does it mean for Christians to name the one God as Father, Son, Spirit?
4. Often, critics of Calvin see him as cold, distant, and calculating; how does the portrait of Calvin in this chapter challenge this picture (particularly the discussions of union with Christ and prayer)?
5. What do you see as strong points of Knox's Scots Confession? How might the Scots Confession serve as a guide for further reflection in contemporary confessional and theological discussions?
6. How did the union of church and state in sixteenth- and seventeenth-century Scotland and England shape the theological reflection from the period? How does the contemporary disestablishment of religion change the way we do theological confession?
7. How does the reality that the Westminster Standards were produced by a committee shape our understanding of the documents as a whole?
8. If there were to be confessional revision in the future, what form should it take? What would be some key issues that you would like to see developed or addressed in a future Reformed confession?

## »For Further Reading

Numerous studies of this period exist that would be interesting and satisfying on these topics. The following would serve as good entry points into the larger literature.

168

Benedict, Philip. *Christ's Churches Purely Reformed: A Social History of Calvinism*. New Haven: Yale University Press, 2002.

Calvin, John. *Institutes of the Christian Religion*. Translated by Ford Lewis Battles, edited by J. T. McNeill. Library of Christian Classics. Philadelphia: Westminster Press, 1960.

Duncan, J. Ligon, III, ed. *The Westminster Confession into the 21st Century*. 3 vols. Fearn, Scotland: Christian Focus, 2003–5.

Leith, John H. *Assembly at Westminster: Reformed Theology in the Making*. Richmond, Va.: John Knox, 1973.

Macleod, John. *Scottish Theology in Relation to Church History Since the Reformation*. 1948. Reprint, Greenville, S.C.: Reformed Academic Press, 1995.

McGrath, Alister. *A Life of John Calvin: A Study in the Shaping of Western Culture*. Malden, Mass.: Blackwell, 1990.

Ozment, Steven. *The Age of Reform, 1250–1550: An Intellectual and Religious History of Late Medieval and Reformation Europe*. New Haven: Yale University Press, 1980.

Paul, Robert S. *The Assembly of the Lord: Politics and Religion in the Westminster Assembly and the "Grand Debate."* Edinburgh: T & T Clark, 1985.

Torrance, Thomas F. *Scottish Theology: From John Knox to John McLeod Campbell*. Edinburgh: T & T Clark, 1996. This book makes an idiosyncratic argument throughout, but has a helpful discussion of Knox's 1560 *Scots Confession* in pages 1–49.

# CHAPTER 10

# Errand into the Wilderness: Early American Presbyterianism

SHORTLY AFTER THE WESTMINSTER ASSEMBLY completed its work, Presbyterians started showing up in the New World. Many of them were Scots and Scots-Irish who immigrated to this virgin country seeking expanded opportunities, fresh land, and freedom to worship as they believed proper. As these immigrants made America their home, they brought their Presbyterianism with them. They settled in the middle Atlantic states, particularly Pennsylvania, New Jersey, and the northern neck of Virginia. Eventually, Scots-Irish also made their way to the Shenandoah Mountains of Virginia and planted a number of Presbyterian churches that still exist today. Other English immigrants came to the areas that would eventually be known as New England and Long Island. These folks held to Presbyterian-like beliefs and practices. However, they initially practiced a congregational form of church government; they also embraced a different story about themselves and their heritage in the "Old World." Eventually, these two groups—English settlers in New England and New York, and Scots and Scots-Irish settlers in the middle Atlantic states—would come together to begin a new story together as Presbyterians in America.

## PLANTING PRESBYTERIANISM IN THE NEW WORLD

It is not exactly clear when the "first" Presbyterian church in America was founded. Rather, it appears that there were concurrent movements toward Presbyterian beliefs and practices in a number of different locations. For example, the earliest church in Long Island, Jamaica Presbyterian Church, dates at least as far back as 1672, while the First Presbyterian Church in Philadelphia was founded in 1698. Yet these churches apparently had little, if any, contact with one another. Likewise, Presbyterian churches were planted in the northern neck of Virginia as early as 1699. These Virginian churches were planted by the most important man in early American Presbyterian history, Francis Makemie (pronounced Ma-kim-ee).

Makemie was born in Ireland around 1658. After training in Glasgow, Scotland, he was ordained as a missionary by the Irish Presbytery of Laggan in 1682. He landed in America in 1683 and traveled widely throughout North Carolina, Virginia, Maryland, and New York. After spending a period of time ministering in Barbados, Makemie settled in Accomac, Virginia. From there, he managed his mercantile business, which was quite profitable, and planted churches in the area. He returned to the old country to recruit pastors for churches in Maryland in 1704–5 and to raise more funds for missionary activity in the new world.

Makemie's genius for business and organization led him to promote the formation of the first presbytery in America in 1706. He gathered together seven ministers, all Scots or Scots-Irish, in Philadelphia in March of that year. These ministers—from Maryland, Delaware, Pennsylvania, and Virginia—agreed to meet annually "to consult the most proper measures, for advancing religion and propagating Christianity, in our Various Stations, and to maintain Such a Correspondence as may conduce to the improvement of our Ministerial ability."[1] The presbytery also took to itself the function of examining and licensing ministers. With such an organization, cooperation could be effected with New England Congregationalists as well as with nascent Presbyterians in Long Island and New Jersey.

One of the more famous incidents in Makemie's career was his run-in with Lord Cornbury of New York in 1707. Early that year, Makemie was arrested by Cornbury for preaching without a license and was held in jail for three months. In June, he was acquitted when he argued in his own defense that his dissenter's license was good for preaching in New York and that the British Toleration Act allowed non-Anglican ministers to preach without molestation from the authorities. This victory was an important milestone in the developing arguments for religious freedom in the new world. Makemie left New York, went to Boston, and published there an account of his mistreatment that eventually led to Cornbury's recall to England in 1709. Makemie, though, was unable to see this political victory. The itinerant ministry, as well as the rough treatment he had received from Cornbury, undermined his health. He died in 1708, widely recognized as "the father of American Presbyterianism."

Ten years after the first presbytery meeting, Presbyterian churches had multiplied throughout the middle Atlantic states. There were now twenty-five ministers, representing a broader spectrum of origin: Welsh and English men were counted along with the Scots and Scots-Irish. In 1716, the Philadelphia Presbytery decided to create a synod that would oversee three presbyteries in Philadelphia, New Castle (Maryland and Delaware), and Long Island. Unfortunately, the Virginia churches that Makemie had planted did not survive his death, though they would eventually be revived and trace their spiritual roots back to him. Ominously for the future, the synod did not adopt a doctrinal standard at this time. Perhaps this was because the church was still relatively small, and most of the ministers had come from the Old World; each of the ministers knew where the others stood and could vouch for their doctrinal and spiritual integrity. By the middle of the next decade, however, the face-to-face relations and trust that characterized these pioneer churchmen would be replaced with a more formal type of subscription to particular doctrinal standards.

## EARLY CONFLICTS AND CHOOSING SIDES

In 1721, the Synod of Philadelphia dealt with the difficult case of Robert Cross, a minister from New Castle Presbytery. Cross was accused of committing fornication. His presbytery passed the case onto synod without investigation. The synod investigated the case and found Cross guilty, after which he admitted that he had sinned. The synod's punishment was that Cross be barred from his pulpit for four consecutive Sundays; otherwise, he was still to be pastor of his church and considered a member of his presbytery in good standing. Several members of New Castle Presbytery protested the action; one, George Gillespie, made repeated overtures to the synod to reconsider the matter. The synod refused to reconsider the Cross affair, which troubled a number of men, who believed that the matter was not simply a problem of morals, but of doctrinal aberration. This was the beginning of the "subscription controversy."

By the early 1720s, New Castle Presbytery took the lead in requiring ministerial candidates to subscribe to the Westminster Standards. Led by John Thomson, the presbyters of New Castle believed that the only way to protect the doctrinal and moral purity of the church was for ministers to declare that they claimed the Westminster Standards as their confession of faith; that is, that the Standards summarized what they believed the Bible to teach. Thomson and his allies were opposed in this understanding by Jonathan Dickinson, a minister from New Jersey.

Dickinson was one of the leading men of his age. Born in 1688 in Massachusetts, he graduated from one of the first classes at Yale College. After studying theology for two years, he was ordained to serve as pastor of the congregational church in Elizabeth, New Jersey, where he served until the end of his life. While pastor of this church, Dickinson convinced his congregation to join the Presbytery of Philadelphia in 1717. Almost immediately, he became a leading member of the presbytery. As the subscription controversy unfolded in the 1720s, Dickinson consistently argued that men's consciences ought to be bound to the Bible alone, not to any human document. By forcing ministers to subscribe to creeds, he argued, the church was casting aspersions on the sufficiency of Word and Spirit for resolving doctrinal disputes.

Dickinson and Thomson soon engaged in a major pamphlet war over the issue of subscription. Thomson refuted Dickinson's claims that subscription denigrated scriptural sufficiency. Quite the contrary; subscription was vitally important for making certain that all officers of the church read Scripture the same way and presented a common voice to the people. Because of the rapid growth of the church, Thomson pointed out, it was nearly impossible to ascertain all that should be known about potential ministers. The best way to ensure the orthodoxy of the church was by requiring subscription to a common confession. Dickinson responded by claiming that the best way to ensure orthodoxy was to investigate ministerial candidates' conversion experiences. How a minister related to God was far more important than whether or not he signed a creed, Dickinson held.

Influencing both Dickinson and Thomson were the battles over false doctrine then taking place in the Presbyterian churches of Scotland and Ireland. Conservatives in both those churches urged subscription as the best way of driving out such doctrine. These debates crossed the Atlantic and showed up in the rapidly growing Presbyterian church in America. Those from the Old World, whose origins were in the Scots and Irish Presbyterian churches, feared the same problems and proposed the same solution. By contrast, the New Englanders, who had originally been Congregationalists, were not required to subscribe to the Westminster Standards or the Saybrook Platform, the Congregationalists' version of the Westminster Confession. Subscription was viewed as an artificial remedy that missed the larger problem of spiritual infidelity.

In 1727, the New Castle Presbytery, under Thomson's leadership, sent an overture to the synod calling for official adoption of and subscription to the Westminster Standards. The overture was referred to the presbyteries, which discussed it and urged the synod to deal with the matter. When the overture came up the following year, the synod determined that it was too important a matter for a delegated assembly to handle. The presbyters decided to table the overture until 1729, and they requested that all the ministers and representative elders make an effort to attend the synod meeting.

What happened that following year was a matter of great debate long afterward; in fact, historians continue to joust about exactly what the synod did. Some claimed that, when the synod moved to adopt the Westminster Standards, it issued one "adopting act" that took effect in two stages. The "morning" act detailed what was meant by subscription, distinguished between essential and nonessential articles, and allowed for "scruples" or exceptions to the Standards. The "afternoon" act was the actual adoption of the Westminster Standards by the synod. Others held that there were two separate actions: the morning act, which only allowed one scruple for those who protested the chapter on the civil magistrate, and the afternoon act, which fully adopted the Standards "plain and simple." In whatever way the adopting act was understood, one thing was plain: it committed the Presbyterian church in America to the Westminster Standards. From this point on, there was little doubt that the doctrine summarized in those seventeenth-century documents was the doctrine these churches believed to be biblical and that they officially taught. If someone disagreed with the church's teaching, he had a disagreement with the Standards. But this adopting act would also continue to be a highly contested and disputed action. In 1730, and again in 1736, the synod attempted to clarify what it meant to do in its adopting act. The fact that subscription to the Standards has been consistently the most difficult issue faced by Presbyterians throughout their history demonstrates that the adopting act solved very little, either in 1729 or in the twenty-first century.

Another problem quickly came to the forefront. Theological subscription was one avenue by which the synod could ensure that incoming ministers were orthodox. Another avenue was through investigating the theological training that ministerial candidates received. The thinking was that, if it could be ascertained that a potential minister came from an approved university, then it was much more likely that he would be orthodox in his doctrinal views. Ultimately, this solution broke down along lines similar to those in the subscription controversy. The ministers recently removed from the Old World—from Scotland and Ulster—loved it; the ministers from New England—particularly native-born ministers and candidates, who had received their theological training by apprenticeship to other pastors—opposed it. Further, this solution became controversial because it appeared to focus upon one particular pastor and his training program: William Tennent Sr. and his "Log College."

Ironically, Tennent was probably born in Ireland, around 1673. After receiving his training at the University of Edinburgh, he eventually took orders in the Church of England. For some reason, around 1718, he emigrated to New York and was received into the Presbyterian church. After serving for several years in New York, he moved to Bucks County, Pennsylvania, where he served two churches, one in Warwick and the other in Bensalem. Tennent's log home, in Warminster on the Old York Road, served partly as a hotel, partly as a seminary for a steady stream of students whom Tennent was grooming for the ministry. He trained not only his own four sons, but also several other students who left their marks on colonial Presbyterianism, men such as Samuel and John Blair, Samuel Finley, William Robinson, John Rowland, and Charles Beatty. This contingent of "Log College men," as they were derisively called by detractors, emphasized a warm, heartfelt piety with preaching that meant to bring about the conversion of their hearers.

By 1738, the synod voted to require all ministerial candidates to have a university degree from either an Old World college or university or from one of the two New England colleges, Harvard or Yale. By that time, however, other forces were at work that intertwined the question of theological education with problems raised by the most important religious event in colonial America, the Great Awakening. Tennent's sons, particularly his oldest, Gilbert, were important allies of the itinerant Anglican minister, George Whitefield, who was touring up and down the Atlantic seaboard, drawing enormous crowds and unleashing an incredible amount of spiritual energy. From 1739 until 1742, the religious excitement raised by Whitefield swamped every American denomination—Congregationalists, Baptists, Anglicans, and particularly, Presbyterians.

The result was a major division in the Presbyterian church in 1741. The parties became known as the Old Side and the New Side. The Old Side opposed the Great Awakening, not because they disliked evangelism, but because they feared the disordering effects of itinerant ministry. As the Old Side saw it, Whitefield and Gilbert Tennent, along with a number of lesser-known awakeners, invaded churches, seized pulpits, and urged church members to leave their original congregations. The Old Side also believed that disorder was rampant in the education received by graduates of Tennent's Log College. This type of irregularity, the Old Side felt, rather than the "regular" channels of Old World education (or even, grudgingly, Harvard and Yale), would lead to the spiritual unrest of the people and ultimately to the destruction of colonial Presbyterianism. Finally, the Old Side believed that Presbyterian order was ill-served by their opponents' "loose" views of subscription. The Old Side continued to trumpet the importance of a "strict" subscription to the Standards as a means for providing order.

The New Side, on the other hand, held that the Old Side was so orderly that it missed the truly important thing in Christianity: the new birth. Influenced by an encounter with Dutch pietism, as well as with the nascent Methodist movement represented by Whitefield and John and Charles Wesley, the New Side urged that both ministers and members needed to have a personal encounter with Jesus Christ. This conversion event would be characterized by an intense sense of conviction brought about by the law, of fleeing to Christ for salvation, and of assurance brought about by the Spirit. The New Side also held that, if ministers did not have such a conversion experience, their church members were justified in leaving to start new churches. The result was predictable: scores of Presbyterian churches divided and split into New Side and Old Side factions.

The leader of the New Side was William Tennent's most accomplished son, Gilbert Tennent. Born in 1703 in County Armaugh, Ireland, Gilbert came with his parents to America in 1718. He was trained by his father and then stood for the master of arts degree at Yale College, which he received in 1725. He was licensed by Philadelphia Presbytery and eventually ended up at a pastorate in New Brunswick, New Jersey. It was there that Tennent encountered the Dutch preacher, Theodore Frelinghuysen, who urged him to consider the importance of fervent piety and immediate conversion in the new birth. Tennent began preaching the necessity of the new birth and had some measure of success within his own congregation. He also took an important leadership role in presbytery and became an ally of Whitefield during the Englishman's first American tour in 1739.

The initial turning point in Tennent's ministry was a sermon he preached in 1740 in Nottingham, Pennsylvania, on "The Dangers of an Unconverted Ministry." Tennent used the sermon to attack Old Side ministers as blind guides and "crowds of Pharisees"; to defend "private schools, or seminaries of learning, which are under the care of skillfull and experienced Christians" (such as his father's "Log College"); and to urge that only those who could testify to a conversion experience should be allowed to be ministerial candidates.[2] Not surprisingly, the Old Side was furious with this sermon, not only because of the unchristian aspersions Tennent cast on the Old Side's ministerial character, but also because he had preached that sermon as an itinerant in a pulpit that was not his own! This was the very danger against which the Old Side contended. The animosity continued to grow throughout that year, until the Old Side was able to force the New Side to withdraw into the New Brunswick Presbytery, an independent New Side presbytery that consisted of Tennent allies. Eventually, in 1745, the New Side was joined by Long Island Presbyterians to form a new Synod of New York.

The two sides co-existed uneasily in two separate synods for the next thirteen years, during which time another significant event in Presbyterian history occurred. Desirous of an officially chartered institution of higher learning, and seeing a need created by the "defection" of Harvard and Yale to the anti-revival coalition, New Side Presbyterians created the College of New Jersey in 1746. Chartered by evangelical Jonathan Belcher, governor of New Jersey, the school was first located in the manse of its president, Jonathan Dickinson, in Elizabeth, New Jersey. Unfortunately, Dickinson died almost immediately, inaugurating a pattern among the institution's leaders that continued for most of the school's early life. Another Presbyterian minister, Aaron Burr Sr., took over the school and moved it to his parsonage in Newark, New Jersey. Finally, in 1756, the school reached its final stop in Princeton, New Jersey, where a new building was erected, Nassau Hall. Burr survived through only the first year in Princeton. His father-in-law, the famous preacher and theologian Jonathan Edwards, was called to succeed him; Edwards lasted six weeks before he died in 1758. After further brief tenures by Samuel Davies and Samuel Finley, Princeton College finally gained stable leadership through the importation of the Scot, John Witherspoon.

Even though the Old Side and New Side were estranged, the work of church planting and evangelism still went on. Both sides planted churches aggressively in Virginia. The New Side established a presbytery near modern-day Richmond, Virginia, through the efforts of the powerful preacher, Samuel Davies. New Siders also successfully established a presbytery near Lexington, Virginia, through the efforts of John Blair. In the Shenandoah Valley, Old Side missionaries John Thomson and John Craig established churches among the Scots-Irish settlers. One of the oldest Presbyterian meeting houses still in continual use, the Augusta Stone Presbyterian Church, can be found in Staunton, Virginia; the building dates from around 1740. Another Old Side church that Craig established was Tinkling Spring Presbyterian Church, also near Staunton in modern-day Fishersville, Virginia.

In 1743, after the split, Gilbert Tennent moved to Philadelphia to pastor Second Presbyterian Church. The church used an interdenominational meeting house that had been erected for Whitefield; the charter explicitly allowed its use by all evangelical groups. Tennent's church was able to use the building for a few years. The church soon realized, however, that it needed its own facility. In addition, Tennent made public attacks on the Quakers, pointing out their theological inaccuracies. This ecumenical *faux pas* led to Second Church's expulsion from the building. When Whitefield upheld the trustees' decision against his friend Tennent, their relationship became estranged. In turn, Tennent began to realize that his role in the Great Awakening had caused unnecessary division. In 1749, Tennent began working for the reunion of the two sides, writing a book called

*Irenicum Ecclesiasticum; or, A humble impartial essay upon the peace of Jerusalem.* However, the wounds from the division were still too fresh for reunion to occur. In addition, the Synod of New York did not yet have the numerical strength to force compromises from the Old Side Synod of Philadelphia in any potential reunion.

In a pattern that would be replicated many times throughout Presbyterian history, a war brought the two sides back together. The Seven Years' War (also known as the French and Indian War) began in 1757, drawing the British colonies together to fight against the "barbarian" (native Americans) and the "antichrist" (Roman Catholic French). As the colonies drew closer together to cooperate against a common enemy, the two warring Presbyterian sides agreed to bury the proverbial hatchet. The Old Side accepted the New Side College of New Jersey as a Presbyterian institution; they also agreed that ministers ought to be examined for the new birth and genuine piety. The New Side conceded that confessional subscription was important and that irregular theological training ought not to be tolerated. In 1758, the two synods merged to form the Synod of Philadelphia and New York.

## Toward American Presbyterianism

Though peace had returned to the church, things continued in flux at the Presbyterian college in Princeton, New Jersey. A few months before the reunion between the New and Old Sides was consummated, the president of the college, Jonathan Edwards, died from complications due to a small pox inoculation. Edwards, the powerful theologian and defender of the Great Awakening, had been president for only six weeks before he passed away. He was a Congregationalist, but had strong affinities with and contacts among the leading Presbyterians of his time. In 1720, at the tender age of 17, he had the opportunity to preach for a Presbyterian group in New York City. And even after he became pastor of the Congregational Church in Northampton, Massachusetts, some of his closest pen-pals were Scots Presbyterians such as John Erskine, John MacLaurin, James Robe, and William McCulloch. He even confided to Erskine that

180

as to my subscribing to the substance of the Westminster Confession, there would be no difficulty: and as to the Presbyterian government, I have long been perfectly out of conceit with our unsettled, independent, confused way of church government in this land. And the Presbyterian way has ever appeared to me most agreeable to the Word of God, and the reason and nature of things.[3]

He also developed a number of friendships among New Side Presbyterians, attending the meeting of the Synod of New York in 1752. It was to these Presbyterian connections that Edwards owed his call to Princeton. In God's providence, this calling lasted only six weeks, leaving many leading historians to wonder "what if."

Princeton College trustees also wondered what to do. They turned to one of Edwards's young friends, Samuel Davies, a Virginia Presbyterian minister. He was a natural choice in some ways, because he had been so active in fundraising for the school a few years before, going on a nearly year-long tour of Great Britain and Ireland seeking financial assistance to build Nassau Hall and the president's home. Davies's election was hailed by trustees and students, but it, like his predecessor's, was short-lived. Eighteen months later, Davies was laid to rest next to Edwards on "President's Row" in the Princeton cemetery; he had died from pneumonia after being bled for a "bad cold." The trustees then elected Samuel Finley as president. A former Log College student under William Tennent Sr., Finley was pastor of a New Side church in Nottingham, Maryland (where Gilbert Tennant had preached his infamous sermon on unconverted ministers). In addition to pastoring the church, he also ran an academy which had such high educational standards that the University of Glasgow gave Finley an honorary degree in recognition of his work. But five short years later, Finley too died. Princeton College was gaining the reputation as the "Presbyterian minister's deathtrap." It took two years for college trustees to find a successor to Finley.

When they did, the choice changed the face of American Presbyterian and even American national history. John Witherspoon (1723–1794) came to America from Scotland to serve as president of the College of New Jersey in 1768. He revolutionized the school, providing the stable leadership that it had lacked since Aaron Burr Sr. died in 1757. He turned out the idealist philosophy that had reigned since Edwards's presidency, even making it convenient for Edwards's son to leave his position as tutor at the college. In its place, Witherspoon introduced American Presbyterians to the Scottish Enlightenment, a many-sided moral philosophy that is often called "Scottish Common Sense Realism." One of his earliest students, James Madison (class of 1771), imbibed Witherspoon's philosophical sentiments so well that Scots realist ideas would eventually come to undergird the United States Constitution. Witherspoon also exercised regional political leadership. At the second commencement at which he officiated, Witherspoon awarded honorary degrees to John Dickinson of Pennsylvania and John Hancock of Massachusetts, lending his influential voice to the rising protest against British colonial policies. In 1774, he joined the Somerset County Committee of Correspondence. Two years later, he was elected to the Continental Congress, where he became the only clergyman to sign the Declaration of Independence. He served in the congress until 1782, with appointments to more than one hundred committees. He was so well-loved by British Tories that he was memorialized in a piece of mocking doggerel:

> Whilst to myself I've humm'd in dismal tune,
> I'd rather be a dog than Witherspoon,
> Be patient reader—for the issue trust,
> His day will come—remember, heav'n is just.[4]

Such opposition did not stop Witherspoon. He went on to win election to the New Jersey state legislature in 1783 and again in 1789; in 1787, he helped craft the New Jersey state constitution.

Witherspoon was also deeply involved in church affairs, as would be expected; he prodded American Presbyterians to move toward a massive restructuring of the church. Even before the Revolutionary War, as early as 1774, many within the church recognized that changes were needed in Presbyterian structure to keep up with rapid

182

growth. In between the synod's annual meetings, a commission that exercised synodical powers met and issued disciplinary decisions, raising questions about polity and power. The war pushed issues related to polity to the back burner. But by 1783, discussion of polity issues began again in earnest. It seemed impractical to require presbyters from as far distant as South Carolina and eastern Tennessee to attend a synod meeting in Philadelphia, New Jersey, or New York. Two years later, concern about the state of the church reached a high point when nearly one hundred ministers were absent from synod and only six out of several hundred congregations were represented by ruling elders. Six entire presbyteries sent no one to synod. Also problematic was the loose church order, unregulated by any written code, which provided little structure to what was going on church-wide.

The solution was to divide the church into sixteen presbyteries, which would meet semi-regularly in three synods, which would then convene in one delegated General Assembly. In connection with this structure, Witherspoon and others helped to create the first Book of Church Order for the Presbyterian Church in this country. After three years of intense debate within synod and less than full interest from the existing presbyteries, the plan was adopted. The first Book of Church Order was published in 1788. The first General Assembly met in Philadelphia in 1789. In many ways, it is fitting that Philadelphia served as the site of the first General Assembly; it would be the center of much Presbyterian history in the years to come.

## »Questions for Thought and Review

1. Have you ever thought about the role that ethnicity played in Presbyterian history? How did the different ethnic backgrounds of the participants shape the early days of Presbyterianism?

2. How did Francis Makemie's stand against Lord Cornbury advance the cause of religious freedom?

3. Confessional subscription has long been an issue in Presbyterian history, as we will see. How did the ad hoc development of Presbyterianism affect the way the church thought about subscription?

4. At the heart of Jonathan Dickinson and John Thomson's disagreement on subscription was the purity of the church. Evaluate the two strategies for the purity of the church: do you agree more with Dickinson's emphasis upon personal piety or Thomson's upon doctrinal uniformity?

5. In thinking about theological education, was the church's solution to restrict licensure to graduates of an approved university a wise one? How did this solution reflect underlying theological and cultural tensions?

6. Often in the telling of Presbyterian history, one "side" in the division of 1741 is championed over the other. With which side are you more sympathetic? Can you understand the other side's point? How might there have been useful compromise between the two sides in order to avoid division?

7. This chapter states, "In a pattern that would be replicated many times throughout Presbyterian history, a war brought the two sides back together." In this case, the Seven Years' War was the catalyst. Think about other wars and church unions—how do national politics influence religious communions for good or for ill?

8. Describe John Witherspoon's role in the creation of American Presbyterianism. How did Witherspoon serve to unite the good of the church and the good of the emerging nation? How could this have given Presbyterians a sense of being "cultural custodians"?

9. Is it strange or amazing to you that the church operated for almost eighty years without a Book of Church Order? How did this developing polity shape Presbyterianism in both positive and negative ways?

184

*»For Further Reading*

Hall, David W., ed. *The Practice of Confessional Subscription*. Lanham, Md.: University Press of America, 1995.

Hodge, Charles. *The Constitutional History of the Presbyterian Church in the United States of America*. Philadelphia: William S. Martien, 1839–40.

Le Beau, Byron F. *Jonathan Dickinson and the Formative Years of American Presbyterianism*. Lexington: University Press of Kentucky, 1997.

Smylie, James H. *A Brief History of the Presbyterians*. Louisville, Ky.: Geneva, 1996.

Schlenther, Boyd, ed. *The Life and Writings of Francis Makemie*. Philadelphia: Presbyterian Historical Society, 1971.

Thompson, E. T. *Presbyterians in the South*. 3 vols. Richmond, Va.: John Knox, 1963–73.

Trinterud, Leonard. *The Forming of an American Tradition*. Philadelphia: Westminster, 1949.

Westerkamp, Marilyn. *Triumph of the Laity: Scots Irish Piety and the Great Awakening, 1625–1760*. New York: Oxford University Press, 1988.

# CHAPTER 11

# The Golden Age: American Presbyterians in the Nineteenth Century

WHEN WE THINK ABOUT the great Presbyterian theologians in America, we tend to think about the nineteenth century. From Charles Hodge to James Henley Thornwell, from Robert Lewis Dabney to A. A. Hodge, from B. B. Warfield to John L. Girardeau, the nineteenth century was when theological "giants roamed the earth." This was also one of the most formative periods for American Presbyterianism. Much of what we consider to be "historic Presbyterianism" hails from this period. Recognizing this brings on a two-fold responsibility. On the one hand, we should consider critically what we view to be "historic" or "traditional" Presbyterianism to determine whether it was produced by cultural forces or social location as opposed to biblical and theological reflection. On the other hand, we must recognize that, though there are aspects of our history that may be repugnant to us today (such as southern Presbyterian defenses of slavery), these events and people are part of our Presbyterian history, part of our family photograph album, if you will. To change the metaphor, while we may have scoundrels or skeletons in our closets, they are *our* scoundrels and skeletons; they testify to the power of God's grace to use flawed and sinful instruments for his own mighty redemptive purposes.

One thing to remember as we look at this period is that Presbyterianism in America was still developing. By the turn of the nineteenth century, American Presbyterians had only had a Book of Church Order

186

for fifteen years; the General Assembly had only gathered for twelve years and, at first, was not an annual event; a true theological seminary did not yet exist (the first Presbyterian seminaries were Union Seminary in Virginia, which started in 1807, and Princeton Seminary, which began in 1812); and Presbyterians were numerically one of the leading denominations in the country. In contrast, by the end of the century, Methodists and Baptists (not to mention Roman Catholics) far outstripped Presbyterians in terms of size; the church had divided three times and reunited twice; there were eight Presbyterian seminaries and a ninth began shortly after the century ended; and the centralization represented by the General Assembly and church boards had multiplied many-fold. Many of the characters and debates in this period contributed directly to what Presbyterianism in its many forms is today.

## PRESBYTERIANS AND CONGREGATIONALISTS TOGETHER

With the creation of the United States, the 1787 acquisition of the Old Northwest (western New York, Ohio, Indiana, and Michigan), and the 1803 Louisiana Purchase, a wide-open frontier called out for settlers from the established colonies. Hoards of newcomers poured into the new land to carve out farms, cities, and new states. As they went, these women and men took their religion with them. Both Presbyterians and Congregationalists were concerned that these travelers retain their traditional religious connections. Because of the similarity in doctrine and polity between the two denominations (Congregationalists by this time had developed presbytery-like structures), they agreed in 1801 to cooperate in evangelizing the Old Northwest.

Under the plan developed by Jonathan Edwards Jr., president of Union College in New York, each denomination promised "to promote mutual forbearance, and a spirit of accommodation" toward each other, particularly in each local congregation that might be constituted from both Presbyterian and Congregational elements. The plan provided means for adjudicating disputes between Congregational churches that desired to settle Presbyterian ministers, and vice versa, either by referring the matter to the appropriate association or presbytery that held the minister's ordination credentials, or by creating a joint committee made up of Congregationalists and Presbyterians to rule on the matter. The plan also provided an avenue for churches with "mixed" sympathies to join as a "united" congregation and to exercise discipline of church members by creating a session of ruling elders; members under discipline had the right of appeal either to presbytery or to the congregation. Finally, the plan potentially gave Congregationalist leaders "the same right to sit and act in the Presbytery as a ruling elder of the Presbyterian church."[1]

While on the surface the Plan of Union appeared to be a remarkable effort of ecumenical cooperation, it did create some knotty problems. First, by creating "union" churches, these local congregations would not have a fixed identity. Were they Presbyterian or Congregational? To whom were the churches ultimately responsible in terms of discipline or financial giving? Where would they secure ministers—from Congregationalist sources or Presbyterian ones? Also, the Plan of Union appeared to minimize polity as an essential element of church order. As we noted in chapter 8, church polity is an important practice that marks Presbyterians as different from Baptists and Congregationalists or Episcopalians and Methodists. The Plan of Union seemed to suggest that the differences between the polities were not large or important. Finally, the Plan appeared to assume that there was doctrinal similarity between the two groups and that this agreement would continue. These were bad assumptions, as we will soon see. In fact, by 1837, there were such differences between Congregationalists and Presbyterians in terms of identity, polity, and doctrine that the Plan of Union was no longer deemed to be tenable.

Another major cooperative effort was the revivalism that broke out throughout the frontier areas at the turn of the century. We often think of these revivals as being part of the so-called "Second Great Awakening," which is usually dated from around 1792 to 1835. In Virginia, North Carolina, and western New York, a number of local revivals took place in which men and women were converted. The most important (and notorious) of these efforts was the 1801 revival at the Presbyterian Church at Cane Ridge, near modern-day Paris, Kentucky. The occasion of the Cane Ridge Revival was the annual communion services held by a number of frontier Presbyterian churches. Barton W. Stone was the pastor of the Cane Ridge church, and he encouraged people from his own and other churches to come to Cane Ridge in order to participate in the communion service. In order to accommodate the crowds, Stone invited the travelers to camp out in the fields near the church house, thus beginning one of the first "camp meetings." Many others soon followed. Taking place over a four-day period, these services were mainly preaching events with the sacrament being offered on Sunday to those who had been examined by the elders. Baptist, Methodist, and Presbyterian ministers set up preaching booths around the camp grounds and held forth through most of the day and night in order to "prepare" the hearers for the sacrament. Because of the emotional strain of the events, physical reactions such as barking, shaking, and jerking were commonplace on the camp grounds. By the time the services ended, it was estimated that as many as twenty thousand people had attended. Out of this revival, a number of denominations and groups were born, including the Christian Church/Churches of Christ, which belonged to the Disciples of Christ for a time; the Cumberland Presbyterian Church; and the Shakers of Pleasant Hill, Kentucky.

## THE DIVISION OF 1837

Presbyterians continued to be involved in revivals throughout the early period of the republic, though perhaps none as unique as that at Cane Ridge. By the time of the late 1820s, a new revivalist came to the forefront in the northeast, symbolizing for many much that was going wrong within Presbyterianism: Charles Finney. Born in Connecticut and transplanted to western New York, Finney was a privately trained lawyer when he experienced conversion in 1821. After studying theology with his minister for two years, he was licensed and then ordained by his presbytery in 1824 as an evangelist and missionary in upstate New York. His preaching and methods were electrifying: he utilized what he called "new measures" in his revivalism, such as the "anxious bench," protracted meetings, and public roles for women. By the following year, he was causing a sensation in the leading cities of New York State.

Finney's innovations soon drew national attention. In the summer of 1827, a number of Finney supporters and opponents, including Ashael Nettleton and Lyman Beecher, gathered in New Lebanon to discuss their differences. Though little substantial agreement was reached at the conference, Finney so impressed his opponents that he emerged from the meeting as the new leader of evangelical revivalism, replacing Nettleton in that role. Finney went on to hold important revival campaigns in urban centers such as New York City, Philadelphia, Boston, and Rochester between 1827 and 1832. Because of his health, he was forced to curtail his itinerant ministry and settled in 1832 in a New York City pastorate. From his post at the Chatham Street Chapel, he delivered his most important series of messages, entitled *Lectures on Revivals of Religion* (1835).

Men like Finney deeply disturbed large portions of the Presbyterian church. Finney represented a developing "New School" branch within the church in four significant ways. First, of course, was his new and innovative approach to revivalism. Finney quite boldly proclaimed that revivals were not due to the miraculous outpouring of God's Spirit, but simply the result of the proper applications of means. This philosophy, coupled with several of the "new measures" that Finney pioneered, stood in marked contrast with the more "traditional" brand of revival that most Presbyterian ministers preferred, in which people waited for God to pour out his Spirit in his own time.

Second, Finney represented an interdenominational consciousness and practice that stood in marked distinction from the developing denominational identity that characterized other parts of the Presbyterian church. This interdenominational consciousness was evidenced in the various independent benevolence societies that were centered in New York City and used Finney's church building for their annual meetings: the American Home Missionary Society, the American Tract Society, the American Bible Society, the American Board of Commis-

190

sioners for Foreign Missions, the American Colonization Society, and the American Sunday School Union. By contrast, some Presbyterians were arguing that the church should create and support denominational boards to carry out many of these same functions.

The benevolence societies, and Finney's own ministry, represented a third issue that created tension in the church—social reform. Finney's brand of revivalism had important social consequences. For example, in 1831, merchants in Rochester invited Finney to bring revival to the immigrant masses that were flooding the city. The hope was that revival would make these immigrants sober and productive consumers for the city's businesses. One recent scholar has claimed that Finney's Rochester revival represented "a shopkeeper's millennium" because he was successful in "converting" the immigrants to an American way of life and practice, which happened to include temperance and a diligent work ethic.[2] However, the most important and divisive social reform was abolitionism. A number of New School leaders were strong advocates for African Americans and their freedoms: especially Theodore Weld, who led a number of "Lane Seminary Rebels" in protesting against slavery. Southern Presbyterians especially kept a wary eye on New School abolitionists, who were stirred by Finney's rhetoric and vision of millennial renewal.

Finally, and most importantly, Finney represented a different and innovative theological position from other Presbyterians. Drawing upon theological insights first associated with Jonathan Edwards but more fully developed by later disciples, such as Samuel Hopkins and Nathaniel William Taylor, Finney proclaimed a "new divinity" that was a powerful theology for revival. With a revised understanding of original sin, freedom of the will, regeneration, conversion, and sanctification, Finney popularized many of the New Divinity's positions as he and his fellow evangelists won large numbers of converts throughout the country. His positions, though, varied a great deal from the Westminster Standards and drew heavy criticism from many quarters of the church.

These four issues—doctrine, church polity, revivalism, and social reform—created two separate "schools" within the church. Those who sided with Finney and other leaders with similar views— such as Lyman Beecher and Albert Barnes—came to be called the "New School." Many of these leaders ministered to or were associated with churches that were planted under the 1801 Plan of Union. Their opponents—led by Ashbel Green, Charles Hodge, and R. J. Breckinridge— were called the "Old School." The division between the two schools became so rancorous that Finney claimed that "there is a jubilee in hell each year about the time of the meeting of the General Assembly."[3] Between 1832 and 1835, several prominent New School leaders were brought up on heresy charges; none were ever convicted.

Finally, by 1837, the Old School was able to force a solution. At the General Assembly meeting in Philadelphia, the Old School was able to elect their candidate as moderator, which was an important test of strength for their side. They then were able to pass an act, later called the "Abrogating Act," which officially cancelled the 1801 Plan of Union, claiming that it was unconstitutional and un-Presbyterian. The Old School's second move was to recommend that this abrogating act be retroactive to 1801. This action, later called the "Excising Act," eliminated four synods from the church (Western Reserve in Ohio and Utica, Geneva, and Genesee in New York); by this action, sixty thousand communicants were no longer members of the Presbyterian church. The following year, when General Assembly met again in Philadelphia, the former New School members were denied seats as commissioners in the church's court and went down the street to form the "true" General Assembly of the Presbyterian Church in the United States of America.

## THE NEW SCHOOL AND THE OLD SCHOOL

Thus, the Presbyterian church was now divided into two "schools." The New School was mainly a northern church, though it did have a few members from the South, located mainly in western Virginia, North Carolina, and eastern Tennessee. Most of the attacks against the New School during the height of the controversy had been doctrinal in nature. Therefore, once on its own, the New School attempted

192

to vindicate its orthodoxy. Already in 1837, the New School had crafted a document called the "Auburn Declaration," which sought to answer Old School strictures. In this document's sixteen points, the New School sought to establish its interpretation of the Westminster Standards as allowable within the bounds of orthodoxy. The New School was a tolerant branch of the church; while its adherents wanted to be viewed as orthodox when compared with the Old School, they also wanted some of their brethren who disagreed with the Westminster Standards to have a place within the church. Hence, they tended to advocate "system subscription" to the Standards, an approach that affirmed that the Standards taught the system of doctrine contained in the Scriptures, but that denied that every proposition or doctrine in the Standards was necessary for the system of doctrine to exist.

The New School also sought to demonstrate that it was more distinctively Presbyterian than previously thought. New School adherents began to withdraw from their alliances with the Congregationalists after 1838 and sought a more explicit Presbyterian identity. They created their own "standing committee on church extension" in 1852. They also demonstrated a greater vigilance against doctrinal deviation within interdenominational Protestantism, often sounding very much like their Old School brethren. And until 1857, the New Schoolers took no position on slavery, being unwilling to alienate their southern supporters; they wanted to maintain their character as a "national" church. These movements caused a number of erstwhile New England Presbyterians to return to their Congregational roots: Edward Beecher took a New England pulpit; George Cheever left his Presbyterian pulpit to serve Church of the Puritans in New York City in 1845; Lyman Beecher, in 1850, retired as president of Lane Seminary to return to the Congregational church led by his son, Henry Ward Beecher; and Charles Finney, who had not waited until the division, removed to Oberlin, Ohio, to serve as professor of systematic theology at Oberlin College and pastor of the Congregationalist church in that town.

Perhaps most important for the strengthening of the New School during this period was the creation of Union Theological Seminary in New York City in 1836. Union Seminary served as an important conduit of pastors into the New School church. Among its leading professors during the period were Edward Robinson, who taught biblical studies, and Henry Boynton Smith, who taught systematic theology. Union Seminary would later play an important part in the late nineteenth century's Fundamentalist-Modernist Controversy as a bastion of progressive theological thought, but during the Old School–New School division, Smith was particularly well respected by both sides as an accomplished theologian.

While the New School continued to sort out its identity, the Old School Presbyterian church represented the most sustained attempt at a confessional Presbyterianism in the nineteenth century. Sometimes it made for hard debating and confusing rhetoric; but the thirty-year period of the Old School's existence represents a fertile time for conservative Presbyterian theology. Perhaps chief among the Old School's leaders was Charles Hodge. Born in Philadelphia in 1797, Hodge studied at Princeton College and Princeton Seminary. He also studied in Europe, one of the few American theologians to have that opportunity as early as the 1820s. Upon his return, he took his position at Princeton next to his mentor, Archibald Alexander, as an exponent of what came to be called "The Princeton Theology," a blend of Westminster theology and Scottish moral philosophy. Hodge promoted his theology in the most influential theological journal of its day, *Biblical Repertory and Princeton Review*, which he edited for over forty years. Equally important for understanding Hodge's influence was the sheer number of students that he taught. From 1830 to 1869, for example, 2,260 different students attended Princeton Seminary. Assuming that most of these attended Hodge's systematic theology lectures, it is not too much to claim, following historians Peter Wallace and Mark Noll, that Hodge was the most influential educator in the United States.[4] Hodge's lectures were eventually published in his three volume *Systematic Theology* (1872–73), which remains in print and continues to exert a strong influence today. Finally, Hodge was

194

not an ivory tower theologian; he was a churchman profoundly engaged in the issues of his day. As we will see, he debated several issues facing the church on the floor of the assembly as well as in the pages of the *Princeton Review*. In recognition of his leadership, Hodge served as the moderator of the General Assembly in 1846.

Hodge's chief opponent in many of those debates was James Henley Thornwell, a South Carolinian who served both the church and the academy. After studying theology in the North at Harvard University and Andover Seminary, Thornwell returned to his native state to pastor a Presbyterian church in Lancaster in 1835. Three years later, he went to Columbia to serve as professor of philosophy at South Carolina College. He returned to the pastorate in 1839, serving First Presbyterian Church in Columbia as pastor, only to move back to the college in 1841 as chaplain and professor of sacred literature and Christian evidences. After serving as president of South Carolina College from 1852 to 1855, Thornwell returned to the service of the church as professor of theology at Columbia Seminary and pulpit supply at First Church until his death in 1862.

Thornwell was quite simply the most important churchman of the South. He served as moderator of the General Assembly in 1847, the youngest man to do so at the age of 35. He articulated a strong version of "divine right Presbyterianism," which demanded biblical warrant for the principles as well as many of the details of church polity. As a result, Hodge and Thornwell locked horns in several major battles over what the Bible said about the nature of Presbyterianism. One such debate was over church boards. Thornwell questioned the biblical warrant for boards that conducted the church's business. Instead of permanent boards that operated like miniature corporations, he advocated temporary committees that were charged to act on behalf of the church, preferably under the control of presbyteries rather than General Assembly. Hodge, by contrast, argued that the Bible only presented basic principles about church polity and that the details, such as church boards, were open to Spirit-directed discretion. Another debate was over ruling elders. Thornwell believed that there were two offices (elder and deacon) and two orders within the office of elder (teaching and ruling elders); he also held that there was essential parity between ruling and teaching elders in matters such as ordination and participation in presbytery. Hodge, on the other hand, held that there were three offices (minister, ruling elder, and deacons), that ruling elders operated as "representatives" of the people, and that ministers were a superior office for which the elders served as "checks and balances." These differences eventually led to real distinctions between northern Presbyterianism, represented by Hodge, and southern Presbyterians, exemplified by Thornwell, distinctions that continue in various conservative Presbyterian denominations today.

## A Nation and Church Divided and Reunited

Compared to other denominations, the two schools of the Presbyterian church were able to maintain their individual "unity" in the face of the sectional crisis for quite a long while. Methodists had divided in 1837 over slavery as did Baptists in 1845. And while slavery served as a context for the Old School–New School division in 1837, both schools were able to maintain their "national" character well into the 1850s. It was the New School that divided first. In 1856, at its General Assembly in New York, that body issued a report on "the constitutional power of the General Assembly over the subject of slaveholding in our churches."[5] The report implied that slaveholders were not in good standing in the church because the General Assembly deemed slaveholding to be a sin worthy of discipline. In addition, Albert Barnes, a leading New School pastor-theologian, wrote his *The Church and Slavery* in 1857, which called upon his church to recognize slavery as a sinful relation. By the time the 1857 General Assembly met, it was clear that the church was ready to say that slaveholders were not only in a sinful economic and social relation, but that they ought to be barred from church membership. Southerners knew that they would no longer be welcomed in the church; in August, they met in Richmond, Virginia, to form the United Synod of the South, a separate church from their New School brothers in the North.

The Old School Presbyterians maintained unity until the Civil War began. Though it was clear after Abraham Lincoln was elected president in November 1860 that portions of the South would secede, it was not until Fort Sumter was destroyed and the federal government issued its call for seventy-five thousand troops to crush the "rebellion" that the nation would truly be divided. In May 1861, the Old School General Assembly met in Philadelphia minus a large number of southern commissioners. Gardiner Spring, the minister at the Brick Presbyterian Church in New York City, proposed a resolution that committed churches to "do all in their power to strengthen, uphold, and encourage the federal government."[6] Though Charles Hodge argued against the "Spring Resolutions," claiming that they violated the doctrine of the church's spiritual nature, the resolutions passed overwhelmingly. Southerners were placed in the awkward position of living in states that had seceded from the federal union and belonging to a church that supported it. They soon resolved the tension, meeting at First Presbyterian Church, Augusta, Georgia, on December 4, 1861, to form the Presbyterian Church in the Confederate States of America. Thornwell and B. M. Palmer, pastor of First Presbyterian Church, New Orleans, Louisiana, were the leading voices at the assembly: Thornwell preached the opening sermon and wrote the first address on behalf of the church; Palmer was the first moderator.

In Thornwell's "Address to all the Churches of Jesus Christ throughout the Earth," he made the case for separation from northern Presbyterians by first emphasizing their breach of the doctrine of "the spirituality of the church." He complained that southerners were forced to separate because the northerners propounded a political theory "which made secession a crime, the seceding States rebellious, and the citizens who obeyed them traitors." This was a clear instance where the church "transcended her sphere, and usurped the duties of the State," he claimed. "It kissed the sceptre and bowed the knee to the mandates of Northern phrenzy." Thornwell also insisted that it was proper for the southern church to minister to the new nation in which she found herself, with its "peculiar institutions," such as slavery. Because the new southern nation believed that slavery was a permissible social relation, he argued that continued union with the northern church, with its inconsistent approach to the slavery issue, was "too dear a price to be paid for a nominal union." While the social and political issues related to slavery belonged to the state and were outside the purview of the church, when people considered slavery from a biblical perspective, "it would no more have entered into any human head to denounce slavery as a sin, than to denounce monarchy, aristocracy, or poverty." According to Thornwell, slavery had existed from the time of the patriarch Abraham on through the first days of the Christian church; God never condemned the institution at all. In fact, he held that slavery had been "overruled for the greatest good" to the slave in America by exposing him to the gospel. Finally, Thornwell justified the formation of the new church as an opportunity to "bring out the energies of our Presbyterian system of government" in the South Carolinian's "divine right" formulation.[7]

During the war, the four churches began to make overtures to their regional brethren for fraternal relations or reunion. The southern branches reunited first in 1864. This reunion was promoted and effected by Robert Lewis Dabney, one of the most prominent leaders and theologians in the southern church, over the objections of B. M. Palmer. Dabney desired the reunion to further his personal goal of creating one single southern Presbyterian church that would serve as a "bulwark" of morals and doctrine in the South. He also fought for the reunion because he feared the effects of a proposed New School seminary in Charlottesville, Virginia, so near his own seminary in Farmville; with a reunion, the money for the New School seminary would go to Union Seminary, he reasoned. Though Dabney chaired a conference of committees that prepared a statement on controverted doctrinal points between the New and Old Schools, in the end the reunion was consummated on the basis of subscription to the Westminster Standards "pure and simple."

After the war was over, the northern branches began exploring reunion. Many of the issues that had divided them seemed less important by 1869: the New School had become more "Presbyterian" in its identity; many of the innovative revival practices were now widely used in Old School churches; and the war had convinced Old School Presbyterians about the propriety of social reforms, such as abolitionism. The only substantive issue dividing the two bodies was doctrinal, and it was summed up in the question of confessional subscription. The theological leader of the New School, Henry Boynton Smith, promised that his side would be willing to subscribe to the Standards in their commonly understood form "without note or comment." But some Old School leaders, such as Hodge, worried that the two branches had substantively different understandings of what subscription meant—the Old School holding to a type of "strict subscription" in which all the truths of the Standards were affirmed, while the New School affirmed "system subscription" in which ministers subscribed to the fundamental system of doctrine contained in the Standards. However, the church was still basking in the glow of patriotism and the power of "union" to overcome all obstacles; and over Hodge's objections, the church reunited.

## THE NORTHERN PRESBYTERIAN CHURCH (PCUSA), 1870–1903

In hindsight, it does appear that at least some of Hodge's fears over subscription were well-founded. Almost immediately, the northern church was plunged into a series of doctrinal crises, beginning with the trial of David Swing in 1874. Swing, pastor of Westminster Presbyterian Church in Chicago, came under accusations of heresy for his book *Truths for Today* (1874). In the book, Swing denied basic Christian doctrines as summarized in the Westminster Standards. When brought to trial by Francis L. Patton, who later would serve as president of both Princeton College and Seminary, Swing claimed that creeds were simply the summary of the Christian experience of any particular generation; as such, they were only valid for the generation that produced them and were not binding on any future believer. Swing's presbytery acquitted him of all charges, but when Patton planned to appeal the case to the Northern Illinois Synod, Swing decided to leave the denomination and became pastor of an independent church in Chicago. "The Swing Trial" was the precursor of a number of heresy trials during the last thirty years of the century, as new theological and philosophical currents swept through the Presbyterian church; among the more celebrated were the trials of three Union Seminary professors: A. C. McGiffert, Henry Preserved Smith, and Charles Briggs.

To meet these new theological trends, the faculty at Princeton Seminary stood forthrightly for the old Princeton theology, which they felt adequately summarized the theology of the Westminster Standards. Once Charles Hodge retired, his son A. A. Hodge came to the chair of theology and taught at Princeton from 1878 until his death in 1886. Upon the younger Hodge's death, B. B. Warfield moved from New Testament into the systematic theology chair, where he would teach until 1921. Through these three men, the same theological perspective was taught to generations of students; indeed, until the reorganization of Princeton Seminary in 1929, the seminary faculty taught over seven thousand students, the overwhelming majority of whom ended up in the Presbyterian church as ministers. While there were other streams into the church—most notably Union Seminary in New York City, which was increasingly progressive in its view of biblical inspiration and theological formulation—Princeton stood as a bulwark against the new views of the day.

Still, the Princetonians were not able to stand against the church's move toward confessional revision. The impetus for revision of the Westminster Confession came from the increasing desire for "reunion" with the Cumberland Presbyterian Church. Cumberland Presbyterians owed their existence to the Cane Ridge revival at the beginning of the century; they emphasized human beings' freedom to choose to believe in Jesus Christ for salvation. Begun in 1810, they grew rapidly in rural areas, but the denomination had its predominate strength in western Kentucky and Tennessee. By the mid-1880s, northern Presbyterians sought reunion with their Cumberland brothers and sisters and began a process of confessional revision to accommodate the Cumberlands; this was unsuccessful and was ultimately abandoned in 1893. However, by 1903, the church moved to revise the Confession by adding two chapters to it, one on the love of God and one on the Holy Spirit. The net effect of the revisions, many believed, was that the chapter on God's decrees was contradicted and that historic belief in God's sovereignty in the election of a people for himself was impinged. Many in the Cumberland Presbyterian Church were pleased; that communion brought more than a thousand congregations into the church when merger occurred in 1906. But even some Cumberland Presbyterians were not convinced by the revisions; a continuing Cumberland Presbyterian Church exists to the present day, staunchly defending its more "Arminian" doctrines.

Another major issue that riled both the northern and southern branches of the church was evolution. With the publication of Charles Darwin's *The Origin of Species* (1859), evolution became a live issue for most Christians. Darwinism seemed to cast doubt upon the traditional view that God created the world in six "literal" days. Already, before Darwin, there were harmonization schemes that sought to reconcile Genesis with geology; but Darwin's theory, with its emphasis upon an apparently purposeless yet somewhat optimistic "survival of the fittest" through "random selection," brought a new challenge. Charles Hodge believed that, while aspects of Darwin's theory may be useful for science, it was ultimately "atheistic" because it posited an "ateleological" evolution. Others were not so certain. A. A. Hodge and B. B. Warfield both believed that it was possible to harmonize evolution with biblical revelation, claiming that, when God created the world, he, in his providence, worked through secondary means, which was evolution. These theologians did hold out for a special creation of Adam, based on Genesis 2. The whole evolution question would break out anew in the early part of the twentieth century as the church confronted "modernism" within its ranks.

## THE SOUTHERN PRESBYTERIAN CHURCH (PCUS), 1865–1900

When Lee's army surrendered at Appomattox, the southern church had a different outlook and character than it had four years prior at its founding. Its founding leader, Thornwell, had died in 1862; it was forced to change its name to the Presbyterian Church in the United States; and it had lost a great number of its laymen and ministers in the war. During the Reconstruction period, the southern church tried to get its bearings in a new world in which its people were under military control and their political rights were slowly being granted back to them. Because of its tenuous political circumstances, the church turned inward, focusing on rebuilding its institutions and stressing even more than before the spiritual nature of the church.

In this, the church was assisted by a border state defection. During the Civil War, Stuart Robinson, pastor of Second Presbyterian Church, Louisville, Kentucky, and editor of the *True Presbyterian* newspaper, upbraided both northerners and southerners for repeatedly violating the spiritual nature of the church. As a member of the Synod of Kentucky, which was affiliated with the northern church, Robinson despised the actions of his church after war, particularly the "Pittsburgh Orders," which declared "the civil rebellion for the perpetuation of negro slavery . . . a great crime" and the creation of the southern church to be "unwarranted, schismatical, and unconstitutional."[8] In addition, these "orders" based membership in the northern church on loyalty to the federal government and agreement with the resolutions passed by the church during the war against slavery. For Robinson, requiring loyalty to the federal government as a basis for church membership was a massive violation of the doctrine of the church's spirituality and made life in the northern church impossible. He was able to convince the majority of his synod to withdraw from the northern church and, after existing in an independent condition for a while, to unite with the southern church in 1868. In recognition of his leadership, the PCUS elected Robinson moderator of the General Assembly in 1869, and his church hosted the national gathering in 1870.

The Louisville General Assembly took place in 1870, the year after the northern Old School–New School reunion. The newly reunited northern church, which wanted to pursue fraternal relations and, ultimately, reunion with the southern church, sent a delegation to plead its case. Robert Lewis Dabney was moderator in 1870 and was disgusted that the assembly was even considering reunion. He moved the assembly into a committee of the whole and called another man to the chair so that he might speak against the action. His speech turned the tide against reunion:

> I hear brethren saying it is time to forgive. Mr. Chairman, I do not forgive. I do not try to forgive. What! Forgive these people, who have invaded our country, burned our cities, destroyed our homes, slain our young men, and spread desolation and ruin over our land! No, I do not forgive them. But you say, "They have changed their feelings toward us, are kind." And why should they not be kind? Have we ever done anything to make them feel unkind to us? Have we ever harmed or wronged them? They are amiable and peaceful, are they? And is not the gorged tiger amiable and peaceful? When he has filled himself with the calf he has devoured, he lies down in a kind, good humor; but wait till he has digested his meal, and will he not be fierce again? Will he not be a tiger again? They have gorged themselves with everything they could take from us. They have gained everything they tried to get, they have conquered us, they have destroyed us. Why should they not be amiable and kind? Do you believe that the same old tiger nature is not in them? Just wrest from them anything they have taken from us and see.[9]

Dabney had been a rising leader before the war, serving as professor of ecclesiastical history and polity and then of didactic and polemic theology at Union Seminary in Virginia for thirty years. During the Civil War, he was Stonewall Jackson's chief of staff for five months in 1862. After the war, Dabney represented southern conservative intransigence, both on ecclesiastical and political matters. While other leaders approved friendly relations with the northern church—fully ratified in 1882, though reunion between the two mainline branches would wait until 1983—Dabney never reconciled with his former northern brethren. This contrarian tack marginalized him within his own theological institution and eventually within the courts of the church. He would leave Union Seminary in 1883 to become a founding faculty member at the University of Texas at Austin; he also helped to start the institution that would eventually become Austin Presbyterian Theological Seminary.

Throughout the last thirty years of the nineteenth century, the southern Presbyterian church loudly proclaimed its doctrinal purity and solidarity. Such proclamations masked differences among leading theologians, such as Dabney and Palmer, as well as the increasing diversity within the seminaries and major pulpits that appeared in the 1880s and, especially, the 1890s. As the church sought to move increasingly from a rural to a more urban and cosmopolitan character, there was a corresponding shift in theological concern. For example, in 1898, James I. Vance, popular minister of the First Presbyterian Church, Nashville, Tennessee, preached a stirring sermon on the Presbyterian doctrine of predestination. Later published with the imprimatur of the Presbyterian Committee on Publication, Vance's sermon modified the classic Calvinism of the Westminster Standards in an attempt to make predestination palatable to modern sensibilities. Unlike theologians who divorced "God's decrees from God's heart," Vance rooted predestination firmly in God's love. "The tap-root of predestination," Vance observed, "grows out of the soil of divine love. God's decrees are not the manifestation primarily of power, wisdom, expediency, or foreknowledge, but OF ETERNAL AND UNCHANGEABLE LOVE." Far from being independent of his creation, "God is under obligation—the obligation of his love, of his mercy, of his nature." God was bound to save all his creation, to remake all the marred clay into vessels "for the Master's use . . . invested with imperishable beauty and worth." In the end, Vance's doctrine of predestination veered toward universalism. "God is not glorified by the damnation of his creatures . . . God's glory is his goodness, his grace; and if he can be glorified by the redemption of one soul, much more by all," he proclaimed. While Vance's teaching was friendly to modern thought, the fact that it was published by the denominational publishing house gave it a troubling credibility and authority, and signaled the growing strength of progressive thought within the southern church.[10]

## »Questions for Thought and Review

1. Now that you have read this chapter, reflect on the entire nineteenth century: What are some commonalities in the way Presbyterians approached religious life and ministry? What are some differences?

2. In your opinion, what were some benefits from the 1801 Plan of Union? What were some challenges? Could you imagine a similar "union" with other related groups today?

3. How did the description of Cane Ridge strike you? If an event like Cane Ridge were to happen in a Presbyterian church today, how would you react?

4. The four issues that led to tension in the church in the 1830s—revivalism, social reform, interdenominational cooperation, and theological innovation—are still with us today. How should contemporary Presbyterians evaluate the solutions that our forefathers developed?

5. Where do your sympathies lie—with the New School or with the Old School? What were some positive contributions made by the "other" school? What were some negative aspects of the school you favor?

6. As you think about the "Spring Resolutions," how would you react if the General Assembly were to pass a resolution requiring you to "do all in your power to strengthen, uphold, and encourage the federal government"? Biblically speaking, why would you react that way?

7. The reunions between the New School and Old School North and South were based on subscription to the Westminster Standards "pure and simple." Yet it does not appear that this worked out well in the North, as evidenced by the Swing trial. How does that historical situation inform the way contemporary Presbyterians should see ecumenical relations and even future unions with other Presbyterian denominations?

8. Did it surprise you to find out that the Princeton theologians—arch defenders of inerrancy—were also convinced evolutionists?

How should that fact nuance the way we approach differences on the days of creation, if at all?

9. What do you think about Dabney's reaction to the possibility of reunion with the northern church?

## »For Further Reading

In addition to the books by Smylie and Thompson mentioned in the previous chapter, the following materials would also be useful for this period.

Calhoun, David B. *Princeton Seminary: Faith and Learning, 1812–1868.* Carlisle, Pa.: Banner of Truth, 1994.

Conkin, Paul. *Cane Ridge: America's Pentecost.* Madison: University of Wisconsin Press, 1990.

Farmer, James O. *The Metaphysical Confederacy: James Henley Thornwell and the Synthesis of Southern Values.* Macon, Ga.: Mercer University Press, 1986.

Hambrick-Stowe, Charles. *Charles G. Finney and the Spirit of American Evangelicalism.* Grand Rapids, Mich.: Eerdmans, 1996.

Lucas, Sean Michael. *Robert Lewis Dabney: A Southern Presbyterian Life.* Phillipsburg, N.J.: P&R, 2005.

Maddex, Jack. "From Theocracy to Spirituality: The Southern Presbyterian Reversal on Church and State." *Journal of Presbyterian History* 54 (1976): 438–57.

Marsden, George M. *The Evangelical Mind and the New School Presbyterian Experience: A Case Study of Thought and Theology in Nineteenth Century America.* New Haven: Yale University Press, 1970.

Parker, Harold. *The United Synod of the South: The Southern New School Presbyterian Church.* New York: Greenwood, 1988.

Steward, John W., and James Moorhead, eds. *Charles Hodge Revisited: A Critical Appraisal of His Life and Work.* Grand Rapids, Mich.: Eerdmans, 2003.

# CHAPTER 2

# "A True Presbyterian Church":
# Twentieth-Century Presbyterianism
# in the American North

THE FIRST DECADES OF THE TWENTIETH CENTURY represented
an important era of change for American culture in general and for
American churches in particular. The overweening optimism at the
end of the previous century led one religious periodical to call itself
*The Christian Century,* so convinced were its editors that the progressive ideals of American Protestantism would triumph. The Presbyterian Church in the United States of America (PCUSA) was at the
center of the progressive cultural and intellectual trends. The church
was represented in presidential politics by Woodrow Wilson and
Calvin Coolidge, as well as by three-time losing candidate William
Jennings Bryan. Wilson and Bryan, in particular, were progressive
reformers, seeking to rectify the imbalance between capital and labor
as well as to control the teeming masses of immigrants through the
federal prohibition of alcohol, represented by the Volstead Act.

Though many in the church were committed to a "Social Gospel,"
which saw sin and salvation in structural and corporate terms, the
denomination itself moved toward increased bureaucracy and centralized control. In fact, the church's identity came to be centered on
its programs—PCUSA leaders sought to promote unity and identity
through common denominational activities, rather than through com-

mon belief. These denominational actions were particularly geared toward using institutional influence and leadership to restructure American society in order to bring about social justice. There was a genuine belief that denominational leadership could transform America into the kingdom of Christ.

As the PCUSA stressed loyalty to the denomination and its programs, it increasingly tolerated a wider spectrum of belief in its ministers. Though the church had disciplined three prominent seminary professors at Union Seminary, it did not stop the infusion of theologically progressive ministers into the church. For conservatives, the nadir of theological liberalism in the church was the Auburn Affirmation, published in early 1924 with 150 original signatures; eventually, the Affirmation was signed by nearly 1,300 ministers and elders in the PCUSA. The Affirmation argued that, while the church was committed confessionally to ideas such as Jesus' virgin birth, his atonement for sin, his resurrection from the dead, the reality of miracles, and the authority of Scripture, there were multiple theories for accounting for these ideas biblically. The Affirmationists held that the conservatives' were wrong in their insistence that the Confession committed ministers to believe in these traditional Christian doctrines, or to hold to the inerrancy of Scripture. Thus, these men urged the church to express its "unity" by recognizing as ministers in good standing those who held widely divergent understandings of the resurrection or of Christ's death on the cross. For many PCUSA conservatives, the Auburn Affirmation signaled "modernism's" aggressive attempt to take over the church. In order to fight against this relativistic theological attitude, both within the PCUSA and in other mainline denominations, northern church conservatives linked arms with those who came to be known as "fundamentalists."

## NORTHERN FUNDAMENTALISM AND THE PRESBYTERIAN CHURCH

American fundamentalism had its roots in the period directly after the Civil War. It was a uniquely American response to the new intellectual and religious trends of the day and a confluence of many appar-

208

ently disparate streams. One stream that helped to forge American fundamentalism was revivalism. In many ways, D. L. Moody represented the apogee of fundamentalist hopes and dreams—successful mass urban evangelism that led to the correction of morals. Moody, a Congregationalist layman, was able to take the old urban evangelism previously associated with antebellum evangelists such as Charles Finney and organize it on a much larger scale. In addition, Moody forged alliances across denominational boundaries on a simple theological platform: ruined by sin, redemption by Christ, and regeneration by the Holy Spirit. This platform enabled him to reach a larger number of churchgoers who may not have experienced conversion. Further, as the denominations united for evangelistic efforts under Moody's leadership, they also worked together for the elimination of vice. Chief on the list of social taboos that these urban evangelists sought to eliminate was alcohol use. Combining moral imperatives with a desire for social reform, fundamentalists looked to revivalistic enterprises—typified by Moody and his successors, especially Presbyterians J. Wilbur Chapman and Billy Sunday and Methodists Sam Jones and Bob Jones—as a means for maintaining Protestant hegemony in American culture.

The revivalists desired not only to reach people with the gospel, but also to help them grow in the Christian life. As a result, fundamentalists latched onto a particular approach to the Christian life, associated with a conference in England called the "Union Meetings for the Promotion of Practical Holiness." Eventually, this approach to holiness was named after the town in which this conference took place, Keswick (pronounced Keh-zek). Among the key teachings of Keswick holiness were, first, that the possibility of living without sin moment by moment as an individual depended completely on Christ, which would produce a "happy Christian life"; and, second, the necessity of a full surrender to Christ, which would bring a "second blessing" or "baptism of the Holy Ghost" that would empower one for service. These views found their way into Presbyterian churches through the influence of Charles G.

Trumball, editor of *The Sunday School Times,* and A. T. Pierson, foreign missions advocate and Presbyterian minister.

Fundamentalist revivalists were fired in their zeal to reach men and women for Christ by a particular view of the future. Convinced by a way of reading the Bible called dispensational premillennialism (which we discussed briefly in chapter 3) that the current church age was to degenerate until Jesus returned, revivalists such as Moody claimed that God had given them a lifeboat to rescue as many people as they could before the end. Actually, for these fundamentalists, the end was a succession of events—the secret return of Jesus to "rapture" believers to heaven; a seven-year period of tribulation in which Jews would initially fall for the antichrist but then recognize Jesus as the true Messiah; a major battle called Armageddon that would be fought between believing Jews and the rest of the apostate world; and the visible return of Jesus at the end of the seven-year period to triumph over his enemies and usher in a thousand-year period called the millennium, in which he would rule over the nations. Dispensational premillennialism was taught to many ministers and church members by two important American educational institutions, Moody Bible Institute and Dallas Theological Seminary. It was also codified and disseminated in Congregational minister C. I. Scofield's *Scofield Reference Bible* (1909).

Fundamentalist commitments to revivalism, premillennialism, and holiness led them to have a low view of denominations, which they saw as participating in the promised end-time apostasy. Hence, they increasingly came to be committed to interdenominational cooperation. Two major examples of this cooperation were a series of booklets called *The Fundamentals* and the organization called the World's Christian Fundamentals Association. Two wealthy laymen, Lyman and Milton Stewart, funded the production of twelve booklets containing articles from a wide range of scholars defending aspects of the Christian faith. Among the contributors were Presbyterians B. B. Warfield, W. J. Erdman, A. T. Pierson, Robert E. Speer, and Charles Erdman. These booklets were mailed to over three hundred thousand ministers and Christian leaders and helped to create a sense of common commitment to a set of fundamental beliefs that were under attack by liberal intellectuals in the denominations. The World's Christian Fundamentals Association (WCFA) was formed in 1919 and headed by prominent northern Baptist pastor W. B. Riley. The first meeting of the association in Philadelphia drew more than six thousand people, who rallied to the cause of conservative doctrine. Six years later, the WCFA became involved in the Scopes Trial, throwing its collective weight on the side of the Dayton, Tennessee, prosecution and its lead lawyer, William Jennings Bryan. In the aftermath of the trial, the organization lost strength and influence. Still, the WCFA was another example of the way in which fundamentalists operated in the first decades of the twentieth century.

Above all, fundamentalists held firmly to the inspiration, inerrancy, and authority of Scripture. They championed the understanding of the nature of Scripture defended at the Presbyterians' Princeton Seminary and articulated in a seminal 1881 article by B. B. Warfield and A. A. Hodge: that God the Holy Spirit so superintended the writing of Scripture that the original autographs were without error; yet this superintendence happened in such a way that each part of Scripture faithfully represented both the historical context and the writers' own personalities. More than this, fundamentalists were also committed to a particularly "literal" approach to Scripture. They tended to read the text of Scripture with certain "common sense" and sometimes uncritical commitments. On the one hand, this led them to read accounts of Jesus' resurrection as historical truth; on the other, they also tended to read parts of Revelation in fairly wooden ways.

Still, this commitment to scriptural authority led fundamentalists to stress supernaturalism. The miracles, the resurrection, the visible return of Jesus, the virgin birth—all of these doctrines were rooted in the belief that God the King worked supernaturally. Fundamentalists defended these doctrines against the more naturalistic approaches upheld by liberal pastors and theologians. As a result, they found ready allies within the northern Presbyterian church and particularly with the theologians on the faculty of Princeton Seminary.

## J. Gresham Machen's Defense of the Faith

One theologian who made common cause with fundamentalists in the defense of truth was J. Gresham Machen. Born in 1881, Machen received a thorough training in the Reformed faith as a child in the southern Presbyterian church. Eventually graduating from Johns Hopkins University with a degree in classics, he wrestled with his vocational choice. After receiving a graduate degree from Johns Hopkins University and taking classes in international banking at the University of Chicago, he entered Princeton Theological Seminary to test his interest in the ministry. Though he was a somewhat lackadaisical student, he excelled in New Testament, winning the fellowship competition in New Testament studies. The fellowship funded extended graduate studies in Germany, where Machen confronted the radical theological liberalism, studying with theologian Wilhelm Hermann and New Testament scholars Adolf Julicher, Johannes Weiss, and Wilhelm Bousset. Through a deep spiritual struggle, allured by the spirituality of the liberal scholars, Machen arrived at a commitment to the doctrines of the Westminster Standards and an abiding opposition to progressive theological thought.

Upon his return from Germany, Machen was offered an instructorship in New Testament at Princeton Seminary. Though still uncertain about whether he should move toward ordination, he excelled in the classroom. He came under the influence of William P. Armstrong, Francis L. Patton, and B. B. Warfield, each of whom helped to calm Machen's doubts and reassure him in the traditional theological tradition represented by the seminary. Machen eventually was ordained as a Presbyterian minister and took his place as professor in New Testament at the seminary.

Machen came to the church's notice through his opposition to liberal trends within the PCUSA. Alerted by PCUSA participation in ecumenical endeavors such as the Interchurch World Movement and the American Council on Organic Union, he worried that these organizations' commitment to a minimalist creed actually revealed more about their anti-intellectual and anti-biblical biases than about their

212

common love for truth. Fearful for the future of the Reformed faith, Machen wrote an important primer on Christian doctrine that exposed progressive Presbyterian perspectives and called for liberals to leave the church. *Christianity and Liberalism* (1923) received wide notice in both the church and secular circles. His compelling case that Christianity was not simply a life, but a way of life based on doctrinal norms that took seriously the historicity of the supernatural events of Scripture provided conservative Presbyterians and their fundamentalist fellow travelers with a well-wrought, scholarly argument against liberalism. While liberal Presbyterians reprobated the book's accusation that they had taken their ordination vows in a dishonest fashion, secular elites like Walter Lippman and H. L. Mencken praised Machen as one of the few truly honest and capable churchmen left.

*Christianity and Liberalism* also made Machen a leader among conservative Presbyterians and rallied a number of fellow ministers and elders to his cause. When progressives published their Auburn Affirmation in early 1924, which sought to defend the freedom of liberal Presbyterian ministers to teach varying interpretations of classical Christian doctrines, Machen led conservatives in response. He argued in the *New York Times* that

> the declaration as a whole is a deplorable attempt to obscure the issue. The plain fact is that two mutually exclusive religions are being proclaimed in the pulpits of the Presbyterian Church. . . . One is the great redemptive relation known as Christianity—a religion founded upon certain supernatural events in the first century; the other is naturalistic or agnostic modernism, anti-Christian to the core.[1]

Machen was convinced that the church's unity could only be maintained based on a common understanding of and adherence to the Westminster Standards.

But Machen was not only confronting doctrinal deviation on his left; he was also dealing with doctrinal indifferentism among fellow evangelicals within the PCUSA. He opposed his Princeton Seminary colleague Charles Erdman's bid to be elected as moderator in 1925 because Erdman was willing to cooperate with liberals for the sake of evangelism. Machen also refused to involve himself in various evangelical causes that moved him away from his central contentions with the church. For example, William Jennings Bryan requested that Machen serve as an expert witness during the Scopes Trial, an invitation from which Machen excused himself because of his lack of expertise in the first chapters of Genesis. Likewise, when W. B. Riley invited Machen to speak to the World's Christian Fundamentals Association, Machen was careful to distance himself from the organization's insistence on premillennialism as the way of understanding biblical prophecy. He could not understand how fundamentalists could get fixated on days of creation or the order of the end times when the real battle was over the historicity of the life, death, and resurrection of Jesus—the heart of the gospel itself.

Machen's instincts to fight for the preservation of the gospel led him into a major conflict within his own church over Presbyterian missions. The Presbyterian Board for Foreign Missions supported a study led by William Hocking; the final report, entitled *Re-thinking Missions: A Layman's Inquiry after One Hundred Years* (1932), denied the exclusivity of Christianity and recommended interreligious cooperation as an effective missions strategy. While the PCUSA Foreign Missions Board tried to distance itself from the Hocking report, one of their missionaries, author Pearl Buck, applauded the report. "I think this is the only book I have ever read which seems to me literally true in its every observation and right in its every conclusion," she wrote for *The Christian Century*. "It expresses too perfectly all that I have known and felt about Christianity in general and missions in particular." Later, in *Harper's* magazine, Buck claimed that, while some missionaries in China believed in Christ in line with traditional doctrinal formulations, "some of us do not know what he is, some of us care less. In the world of our life it does not matter perhaps what he is. If we are asked we shall say, I admire him of course. He was perhaps the best man who ever lived. But that is all he is."[2] The outrage caused by Buck's statements eventually caused the Board to ask for her resignation.

Machen and other Presbyterian conservatives were not satisfied with this resolution. Machen authored a booklet that took on the entire denominational missions venture. This booklet was meant to support an overture that he tried to pass in his own presbytery; when that failed, the overture was passed by the Philadelphia Presbytery and sent to the General Assembly. However, the church failed to take his warnings about modernism on the foreign fields seriously and rejected his overture in an overwhelming fashion. In response, Machen led in founding an independent missions organization that would promote Presbyterian missions on a confessional basis. Machen's presbytery saw this action as a violation of his ordination vows and a renunciation of the rules and authority of the church. The presbytery convicted him of these charges. After the charges were sustained by the 1936 General Assembly, Machen was deposed from ministry by the PCUSA.

## A True Presbyterian Church at Last: The Orthodox Presbyterian Church

That Machen was ousted from the church was no surprise to anyone, least of all to himself. He helped to form the Presbyterian Constitutional Covenant Union, which could serve as the basis for a new denomination, in June 1935; and on June 11, 1936, the meetings of the Covenant Union became the first General Assembly of the Presbyterian Church of America. The Adopting Act of the new denomination declared that the PCUSA had died, but that the new denomination represented "the true spiritual succession" of Presbyterianism in America. Hence, Machen declared that "we became members, at last, of a true Presbyterian church" without being schismatic in the least. In his view, the new denomination was simply the continuation of the historic Presbyterianism that the PCUSA had rejected.[3]

The fledgling church, however, had a difficult first eighteen months. Almost immediately, the PCUSA sued the new denomination for using the name Presbyterian Church of America. In order to avoid a lengthy lawsuit, the church decided to emphasize its orthodoxy by renaming itself as the Orthodox Presbyterian Church (OPC). Another challenge was that the leader of the new denomination, Machen, died in South Dakota on New Year's Day, 1937, six months after the church began. Machen's vision and leadership had led them out of the mainline church, but now he was dead and it was not yet clear who would provide the needed leadership.

The greatest challenge, however, was the swift realization that not everyone who had joined the new denomination had a similar vision or goal for the church. Almost immediately, "confessionalist" and "fundamentalist" parties emerged in the church, coming to the forefront in the six months between the denomination's founding and Machen's death. Two issues created tension and distrust: premillennialism and Christian liberty. On both issues the point men for the fundamentalist coalition in the new denomination were J. Oliver Buswell, president of Wheaton College, and Carl McIntire, pastor of the Presbyterian Church of Collingswood, New Jersey, and editor of the *Christian Beacon*. Before his death, Machen had tried to diffuse the growing tensions in the OPC by arguing that the bonds of unity were the shared commitment to the Westminster Standards and not interpretations of nonconfessional teaching in the realm of eschatology or personal holiness. Further, Machen had tried to promote unity through a political maneuver at the Second General Assembly; he had Cornelius Van Til, professor at Westminster Seminary and one of those in the confessionalist "party," nominate Buswell as the moderator of the assembly.

These maneuvers, in the end, only delayed the inevitable. A few weeks after the Second General Assembly, the elections for the Independent Board of Presbyterian Foreign Missions took place. Machen had served as president of the Independent Board since its inception in 1933. The constitution of the Board's membership, including both Presbyterians and nondenominational churchmen, proved to be its undoing. During the November 1936 meeting, the nondenominational churchmen joined forces with the discontented fundamentalist Presbyterians on the Board, led by Carl McIntire, to oust Machen from the presidency. Machen lost the vote, after a five-hour debate, being replaced by Harold S. Laird, pastor of the First Independent Church of Wilmington, Delaware. Machen was deeply disappointed that the organization whose founding had caused his departure from the mainline church had rejected his leadership; he was more distressed, however, that the board was now moving in the direction of independent leadership. The final division occurred at the third General Assembly, when Buswell threatened to withdraw from the new denomination if it did not go on record as renouncing "social drinking," a major issue of Christian liberty debated in the pages of the denomination's magazine, *Presbyterian Guardian*. When the church rejected Buswell's overture, fourteen ministers and three elders, led by Buswell and McIntire, left to form the Bible Presbyterian Synod.

## The Road Less Traveled: The OPC, American Evangelicalism, and Church Union

The "Division of 1937" between the OPC and the Bible Presbyterians indelibly shaped the way in which the OPC related to broader evangelicalism. Ned Stonehouse, professor of New Testament at Westminster Theological Seminary and editor of the *Presbyterian Guardian*, observed that "from the beginning, we have sought to foster *Presbyterianism*, the Presbyterianism, as we believe, of the Bible and of the historic creeds, not merely what might go under the name of Presbyterianism. The differences between Presbyterianism and Arminian fundamentalism we have never been able to regard as trifling."[4] Many of the remaining leaders of the OPC saw Buswell and McIntire as representing American fundamentalism and not the confessional Presbyterianism they desired. The scarring involved in the division of 1937 led many in the OPC to stress a general avoidance of cooperation with broader evangelicalism in areas that would compromise its testimony for Presbyterian confessionalism.

Several controversies in the church's life emphasized its "separatist, but not isolationist" approach to other evangelical believers. One such controversy that came to be viewed as a battle between confessionalist and fundamentalist parties centered on Gordon Clark, a ruling elder in the OPC. Formerly professor of philosophy at Wheaton College, Clark left the school when his protector, J. Oliver Buswell, was forced to resign the presidency of the college. By 1943, Clark was interested in teaching at the Reformed Episcopal Seminary in Philadelphia and sought ordination in the OPC. Though he didn't have theological training, his philosophical study and his activity in the church convinced the Philadelphia Presbytery to waive its ordination requirements and to proceed to examine his theological views. Clark failed to achieve the necessary three-fourths majority vote to sustain his examination at the 1943 meeting, but when he returned to try again the following year, he passed presbytery's muster and he was licensed and ordained at that meeting.

Clark's ordination, however, was challenged by thirteen members of Philadelphia Presbytery, including Westminster Seminary faculty members Ned Stonehouse, Cornelius Van Til, R. B. Kuiper, Paul Woolley, and E. J. Young. Their complaint centered on the irregularity of the presbytery meeting at which Clark was examined and on his views of human beings' knowledge of God. Clark held that human knowledge of God was identical to God's self-knowledge. In contrast, the Westminster faculty argued that human knowledge was never identical to God's knowledge, but only analogous to it. At stake in this seemingly esoteric debate was the possibility that Clark was denying the distinction between the Creator and the creature and that he was veering toward an unhealthy rationalism that would lead to a denial of the gospel he was claiming to defend. What made the situation more complicated was that Clark's defenders set the entire debate in a larger, more political context. They held that nothing less was at stake than the future of the OPC as a leader denomination in American Protestantism; to deny Clark ordination would irreparably damage the possibility of the church reaching an unsaved and irrational world. By contrast, Clark's opponents feared that this controversy would lead the OPC away from its core commitments forged in its first two years of separation from the oldline church and its division with Bible Presbyterians.

Philadelphia Presbytery allowed Clark to sit on a committee appointed to answer the complaint against his ordination. Clark's defense was not adopted by presbytery and the entire matter came before the 1945 General Assembly. This highest court decided that the presbytery had erred in ordaining Clark, not because his theology was deviant, but because presbytery had failed to follow the niceties of Presbyterian procedure; he had been licensed and ordained at the same meeting rather than at two consecutive meetings. Yet the General Assembly did not overturn Clark's ordination; rather, it appointed a study committee to investigate the theological issues raised by Clark. In 1946, the majority report from the study committee exonerated Clark's views. However, the minority report, authored by Westminster Seminary theologian John Murray, stated that presbytery had erred in not demanding a fuller explanation from Clark regarding his views. To Murray, the Clark controversy evidenced a lack of understanding of the nature of God's glory and how human beings related to this glorious, transcendent God. In response, the General Assembly appointed another study committee to examine the doctrines of God's incomprehensibility and other doctrinal matters raised by Clark.

This study committee, which included both Murray and Stonehouse, produced a massive fifty-four page report for the 1947 General Assembly. However, the committee was not able to make its report, because the controversy spilled over into a debate about sending Floyd Hamilton as a missionary to Korea. The Foreign Missions Committee, which included Murray, did not want to send Hamilton because of his role in defending Clark. When the General Assembly voted to sustain the missions committee, evidenced by re-electing Murray to his spot on it, the Clark-Hamilton defenders withdrew from the denomination. By this time, Clark had secured a position teaching philosophy at Butler University and eventually would join the United Presbyterian Church of North America. The entire controversy confirmed the OPC in a careful, patient confessionalism that was content not to be involved in the larger workings of American evangelicalism.

This stance was strengthened in the following years as the church wrestled with whether to affiliate with one of the larger interdenominational associations of Bible-believing evangelicals. In 1943, the OPC was invited to join with the National Association of Evangelicals. The church eventually rejected the invitation because of the group's apparently inconsistent position on affiliation with liberal denominations and its broadly evangelical constituency, which included Methodists, Baptists, Presbyterians, Pentecostals, and other fellow travelers. OPC leaders believed that such a broad representation could never be an effective witness against theological deviation. Much more attractive for the OPC was the American Council of Christian Churches (ACCC), formed in 1941 by Carl McIntire. The ACCC battled against modernism in all its forms, requiring all constituent members to separate from the left-leaning Federal Council of Churches. However, it took the OPC eight years before it decided not to join the ACCC. Part of the reason for this hesitation was simply the general deliberativeness with which the OPC approached every issue. The 1944 General Assembly, in the midst of the Clark controversy, set up a committee on interchurch relations and ecumenicity to investigate the issue of cooperation with the ACCC and other church bodies. In the end, the OPC decided that the American Council failed to keep separate the religious and political spheres, so that the council appeared to be "a political lobby . . . [in which] civil politics seem [to be] its very food and drink."[5] In the end, fears over losing its distinctively Reformed testimony kept the OPC from affiliating with any organization that appeared to lead toward American evangelicalism.

This is not to say, however, that the church was uninterested in ecumenical endeavors. The OPC frequently considered various church mergers, sometimes with the Christian Reformed Church, sometimes with the Bible Presbyterian Church (Columbus Synod). It was not until the 1970s that the possibility of merger was close to becoming a reality. In 1975, the OPC and the Reformed Presbyterian Church, Evangelical Synod (RPCES) voted on a Plan of Union that would have largely healed the "Division of 1937." The RPCES, as we will see, was a product of a variety of divisions and mergers that had roots back in the original Buswell-McIntire movement. Though the OPC voted by the necessary two-thirds majority to merge with the RPCES, the merger failed when the RPCES only tallied a fifty-seven percent favorable vote. This failure did not stop the OPC from later attempting to merge with another church body. In 1981, the OPC was part of a process of joining and receiving with the RPCES and the Presbyterian Church in America (PCA). While the PCA presbyteries approved joining and receiving with the RPCES, they narrowly rejected the OPC, the vote being defeated by two presbyteries. Again, in 1986, the PCA re-extended the invitation to the OPC, but this time the OPC decided against joining and receiving with the PCA, the vote falling well short of a three-fourths majority.

Each of these failed mergers highlights one of the deep contradictions in the identity of the OPC. On the one hand, the church has longed for a larger church fellowship and has stood consistently for a Reformed ecumenicity based on shared confessional standards. But on the other hand, the church has generally been unwilling to forsake its perception that it stands as the unique and unparalleled preserver of theological orthodoxy. As one OPC minister put it, "It is clear from anyone who knows the history of the OPC that our denomination is not popular because it has consistently been a Machen-type of contending church. Call it 'theological expertise' if you will; but I say, 'Thank God for it.' The OPC has never shunned doctrinal issues thrown at it."[6] While the OPC has always been more than willing to debate confessional issues, this posture of contention has sometimes made it difficult for other confessional Presbyterians to link arms with them in a genuine sense of brotherhood and common mission. That being said, the OPC has an enviable sense of being comfortable with itself as a denomination. Its members are content with being "a true Presbyterian church," even if such a church is a remnant, a pilgrim people, in the midst of this world.

"I've Been OP, BP, EPC, and RPCES": Other
Northern Presbyterian Denominations

The group that went with Carl McIntire and J. Oliver Buswell out of the OPC in 1937 soon settled into the regular patterns of Presbyterian church government as the Bible Presbyterian Synod. Convinced that they had made "a false start" in uniting with the group that had formed the OPC, the men who forged the Bible Presbyterian Synod desired to "form a testimony" that was more in line with the "historic attitudes of the Presbyterian Church in the U.S.A." Perhaps the greatest difference confessionally between the Bible Presbyterians and the OPC was the willingness of the former to tolerate premillennialism under the banner of "eschatological liberty." Another important issue for the Bible Presbyterians was total abstinence from alcohol, which was viewed as a test of living a holy life separated from "worldliness." At the first Bible Presbyterian Synod meeting in 1938, the church passed a resolution that called on the church "to pursue the course of total abstinence." In fact, these issues were summarized in the Bible Presbyterian testimony: a church that was to be "Calvinistic, fundamental, premillennial, and evangelistic."[7]

In order to further this testimony, the Bible Presbyterians took the Independent Board for Presbyterian Foreign Missions as their own missions agency and started their own seminary, Faith Theological Seminary. One of the students who left Westminster Seminary to go to Faith Seminary was Francis A. Schaeffer. Already, by the late 1930s and early 1940s, Schaeffer was regarded as a brilliant protégé of Carl McIntire. After pastorates in Grove City, Pennsylvania, and St. Louis, Missouri, Schaeffer became McIntire's right-hand man in the ACCC and, later, in the International Council of Christian Churches, a conservative counterpart to the more liberal World Council of Churches. While working for these councils, as well as for the Independent Board for Presbyterian Foreign Missions in Europe, Schaeffer determined to start a mission for children, which he began in 1948 in Lausanne, Switzerland. In the midst of this ministry, Schaeffer began interacting with art critics and theologians, developing his vision for a Christian cultural apologetic. Out of this vision came L'Abri, an independent ministry in Switzerland that emphasized a dynamic ministry to young people throughout Europe. Travelers would come to the Schaeffers' home to discuss philosophy and theology and to imbibe their hospitality and Christian worship.

Schaeffer was not the only influential younger Bible Presbyterian leader. Another important figure was Robert G. Rayburn. A student of J. Oliver Buswell at Wheaton College, Rayburn finished seminary in Omaha, Nebraska, and was ordained in the PCUSA in 1938. After a brief ministry in Bellevue, Nebraska, Rayburn enrolled in Dallas Theological Seminary, receiving the Th.D. degree in 1944. While attending Dallas, Rayburn served as pastor for a PCUSA church in Gainesville, Texas, and later enrolled as an army chaplain. Upon returning from Germany at the end of World War II, he discovered that his presbytery had begun process against him for violating his ordination vows on the basis of a letter that he had written which decried the liberalism in the northern church. He was eventually deposed from the ministry of the PCUSA and was received into the Bible Presbyterian Church. After returning briefly to Gainesville, Rayburn moved to Wheaton, Illinois, to serve as the pastor of the independent College Church for a little more than three years. When the Korean War began, Rayburn was returned to active status as an army chaplain and served for two years in Korea. He returned to the United States and accepted the presidency of Highland College in Pasadena, California, a Bible Presbyterian-related college. He also began to serve on the Bible Presbyterian Church's committee on the ACCC. While doing so, he found that the American Council was inflating its membership statistics; he reported this to the Bible Presbyterian Church, which in turn reprimanded the American Council. However, ACCC loyalists on the board of Highland College were able to fire Rayburn as president, which caused a majority of the faculty to resign. In response, Rayburn and his faculty then started Covenant College in 1955. Initially, the college was located in Pasadena, but in 1956 it moved to St. Louis to the present site of Covenant Seminary; that year, the seminary also began. Covenant College would eventually move in 1964 to Lookout Mountain, Georgia, while Covenant Seminary remained in St. Louis.

The various conflicts within the church, highlighted by the debacles over the American Council and Highland College, signaled deeper divisions. At the center of the conflict was Carl McIntire. He had been the driving force in the creation of the Bible Presbyterian Church, the American and International Councils, and Faith Seminary. His *Christian Beacon* newspaper was the symbol of unity among Presbyterian fundamentalists, both north and south. His radio show, books, and other activities were the public face of the movement for a "Twentieth-Century Reformation." To younger allies like Schaeffer and Rayburn, McIntire's personality was beginning to overwhelm the church. In addition, there was a movement within the church to be more explicitly Presbyterian in its approach to evangelism, missions, and theological education, using church agencies rather than independent ones. These two issues—McIntire's control of the organization and the ideological division between those who desired more Presbyterian approaches to ministry and those who were more Congregational in orientation—led to the division of the church in 1956. Ultimately, nearly forty percent of the church followed McIntire into a rival Bible Presbyterian Synod, based in Collingswood, New Jersey.

The group that remained eventually renamed itself as the Evangelical Presbyterian Church in 1961.[8] More important than the new name was the new attitude represented by those who continued on in the church. Gone was the angry separatism that was characteristic of their association with McIntire. Replacing that was a spirit of reconciliation with other conservative Presbyterians and with evangelicalism at large. While the church continued to stress personal and ecclesiastical separation, in practice there was a willingness to explore possible church mergers and the expansion of the church's testimony. Almost immediately, the church engaged in union discussions with the Reformed Presbyterian Church, General Synod. Although it took seven years to consummate the union and bring about the creation of the Reformed Presbyterian Church, Evangelical Synod (RPCES), the church was struggling mightily during this time to overcome its separatist background and transform itself in order to demonstrate the larger spirit of the body of Christ.

When the RPCES came into being in 1965, it continued to explore other ways in which it could bear a common testimony with other Presbyterian and Reformed believers. In that connection, the denomination became involved with southern Presbyterians in leading the National Presbyterian and Reformed Fellowship in 1971. Envisioned by some southern Presbyterians as a mechanism for "realigning" all of the Reformed and Presbyterian denominations into two large liberal and conservative churches, the fellowship became the venue in which southern Presbyterians and RPCES ministers learned more about one another. When the southern Presbyterians left the Presbyterian Church in the United States to form the Presbyterian Church in America (PCA) in 1973, these discussions took on a deep seriousness. Two years later, the RPCES considered a merger with the OPC, which failed. But in 1982, the denomination participated in a process of joining and receiving with the PCA, which brought nearly 190 churches and twenty-six thousand communicant members from the RPCES into the PCA. A truly national conservative Presbyterian church that was committed to the Scriptures and the Reformed faith had at last been born.

## »Questions for Thought and Review

1. In the early twentieth century, the Presbyterian Church in the United States of America began to secure its unity through shared programmatic and institutional endeavors, rather than through shared doctrinal commitments. How does that affect churches today in what is essentially a post-denominational age?
2. What were some positive effects of American fundamentalism? What were some negative effects? How do you see the streams that fed American fundamentalism still affecting conservative Presbyterians today?
3. J. Gresham Machen had to confront both doctrinal deviation and doctrinal indifferentism. How can this type of confrontation be done in a winsome fashion? How would you persuade those who do not believe that traditional doctrinal commitments are important?

4. One of the challenges for the OPC was that not everyone was expecting the denomination to be and to do the same thing. How might it be easy to join a movement that some think is fighting one thing (i.e., modernism) and find that others in that movement had something else in mind (i.e., confessionalism)?
5. How does the Clark controversy help to shape OPC identity? How might it have affected future merger negotiations with the Reformed Presbyterian Church, Evangelical Synod (RPCES) and the Presbyterian Church in America (PCA)?
6. What are some positive aspects of the OPC's identity as a "contending church"? What might be some negative aspects?
7. How does the Bible Presbyterian/RPCES story strike you? How does Presbyterianism deal with larger-than-life figures like Carl McIntire?

## »For Further Reading

Calhoun, David B. *Princeton Seminary: The Majestic Testimony, 1869–1929.* Carlisle, Pa.: Banner of Truth, 1996.

Carpenter, Joel. *Revive Us Again: The Reawakening of American Fundamentalism.* New York: Oxford University Press, 1997.

Hart, D. G. *Defending the Faith: J. Gresham Machen and the Crisis of Conservative Protestantism in Modern America.* Baltimore, Md.: Johns Hopkins University Press, 1994; reprint, Phillipsburg, N.J.: P&R, 2003.

———. *That Old Time Religion in Modern America: Evangelical Protestantism in the Twentieth Century.* Chicago: Ivan R. Dee, 2002.

Hart, D. G., and John Muether. *Fighting the Good Fight: A Brief History of the Orthodox Presbyterian Church.* Philadelphia: Orthodox Presbyterian Church, 1995.

Hutchinson, George P. *The History Behind the Reformed Presbyterian Church, Evangelical Synod.* Cherry Hill, N.J.: Mack, 1974.

Longfield, Bradley J. *The Presbyterian Controversy: Fundamentalists, Modernists, and Moderates.* New York: Oxford University Press, 1991.

Marsden, George M. *Fundamentalism and American Culture: The Shaping of Twentieth Century Evangelicalism, 1875–1925,* 2nd ed. New York: Oxford University Press, 2006.

# "A Continuing Presbyterian Church": Twentieth-Century Presbyterianism in the American South

CONSERVATIVE DISSENT PLAYED ITSELF OUT in markedly different ways in the northern and southern Presbyterian churches. In the northern Presbyterian Church in the United States of America (PCUSA), the conflict and resolution was relatively quick. There was a span of about thirteen years from the time Machen wrote *Christianity and Liberalism* to when the Orthodox Presbyterian Church was created in 1936. By contrast, in the southern Presbyterian Church in the United States (PCUS), conservative dissent boiled and roiled under the surface of the denomination for over forty years until the Presbyterian Church in America (PCA) was born in 1973. Some suggest that the reason for this is that liberalism did not widely infect the southern church until the late 1950s. But this is certainly not the case; as we will see, the church's leadership, particularly at Union Seminary in Virginia, had embraced progressive thought at about the same time that it was being embraced in the North. Another way of looking at the situation could be that many conservative ministers, elders, and laypeople were excruciatingly patient in attempting to turn the tide against liberalism in the southern church. Though by the mid-1960s it was almost certain that something would have to be done in terms of a new denomination, that did not stop conservatives from attempting a wide range of renewal efforts, from evangelism to new theological seminaries to prayer groups, in an attempt to turn the tide.

## DRIFT TOWARD PROGRESSIVE THOUGHT

As evidenced by James I. Vance's sermon on predestination, theological drift was already occurring in the PCUS by the last decade of the nineteenth century, even as the church was loudly proclaiming its orthodoxy. In the seminaries, a new generation of professors was taking over for Robert Lewis Dabney at Union Seminary and John L. Girardeau and J. B. Adger at Columbia Seminary. Some of these professors, such as Thomas Cary Johnson at Union and W. M. McPheeters at Columbia, were staunchly conservative in their theology and in their loyalty to the Reformed faith. Others, such as W. W. Moore, preferred to be described as "progressive conservatives." While holding to the inspiration of the Scriptures, men like Moore were open to the new scholarship coming from Germany and Scotland. This openness to new views cleared the way for the modern theological streams of the early twentieth century.

In particular, three progressive intellectual trends became prominent at the PCUS seminaries. The first, and most important, was the "Social Gospel." The phrase described the effort to relate biblical principles to social needs and challenges raised by the industrialization and urbanization of the early twentieth century. But the Social Gospel came to represent a major shift in the way important theological categories were used. In short, the Social Gospel represented a movement away from individual to corporate categories for theology. Sin was defined in social and systemic terms—the oppressive social structures that kept people from achieving their potential. Salvation, likewise, was the removal of those structures in order to maximize human potentialities and make a more just world. Also distinctive about the Social Gospel movement was a genuine embrace of the historical Jesus and his teaching as the norm for social action; "What would Jesus do?" was the question that Social Gospel promoters such as Charles Sheldon desired Christians to ask themselves. In particular, the question was what Jesus would do in order to realize the kingdom of God as an earthly reality, bringing social harmony in its wake. All natural and political processes that brought God's kingdom to closer fulfillment were seen as the work of God's Spirit; hence, the Social Gospel emphasized the immanence of God, going so far as to say that the spirit of the age was "the age of the Spirit." This optimistic progressivism was consonant with the American spirit in the decade before the First World War and it captured the hearts and minds of many young southern Presbyterians.

Though Union Seminary had already added to its curriculum a course in "Christian Sociology" in 1913—which was a class dedicated to the analysis of social problems from a Christian point of view— the early advocate for the Social Gospel in the PCUS was Walter L. Lingle. When Lingle was a professor at Union Seminary from 1911 to 1924, he was introduced to the writings of Walter Rauschenbusch, one of the leading Social Gospel theologians. After reading Rauschenbusch's seminal *Christianity and the Social Crisis*, Lingle admitted that "since that time I have read many volumes on the same general subject, but no other book has stirred my soul as" that one. After reviewing several Rauschenbusch books for the *Union Seminary Review*, Lingle gave an address at the 1916 North Carolina Conference for Social Service, which was later published in the seminary's journal. He identified the kingdom of God as "the solution which we find for our social problems," a solution that would solve the world's problems "if men everywhere could catch a vision of this ideal and devote all the energies of their lives to its realization." One of the means for making the kingdom of God a reality in American culture, Lingle held, was the application of the Golden Rule in all business dealings. Another means was the recognition that all public office is a position of service to God and humanity. A third was a commitment to self-sacrifice for the good of others. Also important, according to Lingle, was the Sermon on the Mount, which represented "Jesus' ideal for the world" and the true answer to modern social problems.[1]

While many of Lingle's beliefs appear today to be naïve and senti-mental, in the decade of the Great War and Wilsonian progressivism, his vision fired a number of young PCUS ministers. Chief among them was E. T. Thompson. It is not hyperbole to claim that Thompson was probably the most important churchman in the history of the PCUS. He served as a professor at Union Theological Seminary from 1922 to 1964, was elected moderator of the General Assembly in 1959, edited or co-edited the *Presbyterian Outlook* magazine for nearly fifty years, and wrote a Sunday school column for longer than that. Thomp-son took Lingle's Social Gospel teaching seriously and sought to move the church from its historic position emphasizing its "spiritual nature" to a prophetic engagement with American culture. The chief mani-festation of Thompson's efforts was the creation of the permanent committee on social and moral welfare, established at the General Assembly level in 1934. Throughout this committee's existence in its different forms, it sought to use Scripture to speak to contemporary social issues, including war, business inequities, marriage and divorce, and, especially, racial relations. The committee came to represent the way progressive Presbyterians desired to advance the cause of the church: through the transformation of culture and the advancement of God's kingdom on earth.

A second major trend during the 1920s and 1930s was evolution. As early as 1884, the church had taken a strong stance against evo-lution as an allowable belief for ministers, declaring that the teach-ing of evolution in theological seminaries, "except in a purely expos-itory manner, without intention of inculcating its truth is hereby disapproved."[2] Forty years later, Hay Watson Smith, pastor of Sec-ond Presbyterian Church, Little Rock, Arkansas, openly defended evolution in a pamphlet, which brought the ire of his own presby-tery and stalwart defenders of the faith like McPheeters and John-son. McPheeters was able to pass an overture at the 1929 General Assembly instructing Smith's presbytery to investigate the rumors abroad regarding Smith's orthodoxy. However, Smith was acquitted of heresy charges when the presbytery found the rumors to be unfounded without ever questioning Smith himself about his views.

230

The third intellectual trend in the PCUS was neo-orthodoxy, a theological movement that represented both a restatement of the older liberal theology as well as a major revision of it. Associated primarily with Continental theologians Karl Barth and Emil Brunner, neo-orthodoxy came to America as the antidote for Protestant progressivism and optimism, which had been shattered by the First World War. Barth, in particular, emphasized the absolute opposition of the transcendent God and sinful humanity, and the priority of God in the revelation of Jesus Christ. Barth's position stood in contrast to the older liberal approach of meeting the culture's questions with abiding religious experiences in ever-changing categories. However, neo-orthodoxy had several theological difficulties, such as an admittance of the Bible's fallibility, an apparent openness to universalism, and a major revision of theological categories such as justification and atonement. As with the Social Gospel, neo-orthodoxy came to the PCUS by way of Union Seminary. In the 1930s, Thompson took over as *Union Seminary Review*'s book review editor and immediately began exposing the southern church to the latest theological scholarship from Germany. Also, in the seminary classroom, John Newton Thomas came as professor of systematic theology in 1940 and immediately stopped using Robert Lewis Dabney's textbook on systematic theology; instead, he required students to read Barth. Even in moderate Presbyterian newspapers, such as *Christian Observer*, Karl Barth's theology received positive notices during the 1930s. When the church moved toward confessional revision in that decade, though the move was not directly motivated by neo-orthodoxy, the theological climate of change created by the seminary's embrace of the new theology was an undeniable influence.

## THE CRYSTALLIZATION OF CONSERVATIVE DISSENT

Conservative Presbyterian churchmen were alive to what was going on. In the letter columns of the Presbyterian newspapers, they registered their dissent against the growing progressive trend. In particular, these ministers protested the growing movement away from the inerrancy of Scripture and the spirituality of the church. They worried about the effects of the new committee on social and moral welfare. They were concerned about the church's on-again, off-again relationship with the Federal Council of Churches, the forerunner to the modern-day National Council of Churches. They fretted over the effects of confessional revision. And they opposed strongly any movement toward reunion with the northern Presbyterian church, which had shown itself inhospitable toward conservative orthodoxy as represented by J. Gresham Machen.

For conservatives, these problems came to head in what came to be called "the Thompson-Glasgow affair." Tom Glasgow, a ruling elder from Myers Park Presbyterian Church, Charlotte, North Carolina, and a nephew of W. M. McPheeters, became increasingly concerned about the direction of his southern Presbyterian church during the late 1930s. Like his uncle, he became convinced that the source of the trouble in the church was the theological seminaries, and particularly, Union Seminary. Glasgow took the floor as a commissioner to the 1940 General Assembly and proposed that the assembly examine the church's seminaries to determine whether they were orthodox. When his proposal received no action, he mailed out a pamphlet he had written attacking Thompson's theology, charging that it deviated both from the standards of theology as taught in the past at Union Seminary and from the Westminster Standards.

Glasgow's charges failed to receive much notice from the southern Presbyterian newspapers. *Christian Observer* rejected any article that brought his charges to light, and the *Presbyterian of the South*, which Thompson edited, closed its columns to him as well. Though Glasgow tried to find other outlets, running his claims in Bible Presbyterian leader Carl McIntire's paper, his attack on Thompson found little place or support in the southern church. In addition, there was a groundswell of support for Thompson, who was well-respected for his generally kind demeanor. The Synod of Virginia unanimously reelected Thompson as moderator, and the other synods that had oversight of Union Seminary lent him support as well. In fact, the professor was so certain of his final vindication that he petitioned his home presbytery to investigate Glasgow's charges. As expected, presbytery's committee delivered a full vindication of Thompson's orthodoxy and the presbytery approved the report unanimously.

Glasgow's final hope was his Mecklenburg presbytery, which overtured General Assembly to investigate the matter. The presbytery was joined by Central Mississippi, Roanoke, Knoxville, and Harmony presbyteries in requesting such an investigation; not surprisingly, these presbyteries would represent a large portion of conservative Presbyterianism's strength in the decades to come. When the 1941 General Assembly met, it was clear that the progressive element in the church had the stronger constitutional case: Thompson's case had been decided by his own presbytery, which was the court of original jurisdiction; hence, General Assembly could not consider these charges, regardless of whether other presbyteries petitioned the assembly to do so. In the end, General Assembly voted by a two-to-one ratio to support Thompson's position in the case. As one historian has noted, by protecting Thompson, the church extended "a new sense of protection" that would "encourage church progressives" in the days to come.[3]

Conservatives believed that their failure was the result of being shut out completely from the Presbyterian papers. During the summer of 1941, L. Nelson Bell, a medical missionary to China who was forced home because of the Second World War, began sounding out fellow conservatives on the possibility of starting a conservative journal for the church. In March 1942, Bell brought together eight leaders as the first planning group for what would become the *Southern Presbyterian Journal* (later *Presbyterian Journal*). Nelson Bell was the leading figure and main editorial writer for the *Journal*, though Henry Dendy, a pastor in Weaverville, North Carolina, served as "editor." Bell not only shaped the editorial policy of the magazine, but also became the leading conservative in the church in the 1940s and 1950s. His daughter, Ruth, would marry Billy Graham, then a young student at Wheaton College; the marriage was influential not only in Graham's life, but also in Bell's. The older man promoted his son-in-law's ministry relentlessly in the pages of the *Southern Pres-byterian Journal*, and together the two founded *Christianity Today* as a means of engaging the culture and serving as a rallying point for conservatives from all denominations.

The *Journal* was the clearinghouse for conservative Presbyterian opinion in the South and served as a means for networking. Particu-larly important were the "Journal Days" that were hosted in Weaverville, North Carolina, each August. Part Bible conference, part homecoming weekend, Journal Day served to introduce conservatives to one another in face-to-face venues. When the denominational situ-ation became particularly depressing in the early 1960s, Journal Day provided needed fellowship for conservative ministers to continue to stand firm for the inerrancy of Scripture and the truth of the Reformed faith. It was not by accident that the initial plans for a "continuing Pres-byterian church" were announced at the 1970 and 1971 Journal Days.

FAILED REUNION, CONTINUED DEVOLUTION,
AND THE CONTINUING CHURCH MOVEMENT

Almost immediately, the *Journal* had a significant issue to unite conservatives together. Though reunion between the PCUS and the northern church had been discussed ever since the northern Old School–New School reunion in 1870, the idea of such a reunion had moved to a front burner position in 1937. Six years later, the perma-nent committee on cooperation and union submitted the first draft of a plan of union between the northern and southern Presbyterian churches. At that point, the *Journal* began to agitate for putting in place a continuing Presbyterian church structure to perpetuate the southern Presbyterian church in case of reunion. The magazine also fought tooth and nail against reunion for a variety of reasons: the "doctrinal infidelity" of the northern church; the more centralized polity of the northerners; church property issues; the northern com-mitment to the Social Gospel; and the loss of southern Presbyterian identity that it was feared the reunion would bring about. Finally, in 1949, the majority of the permanent committee recommended that

234

the plan of union be docketed for that year's General Assembly meeting. The minority, led by Nelson Bell, offered a substitute that the question of union be set aside for five years. This substitute was adopted by progressive members who favored reunion with the northern church; they believed that the delay would lead to a final victory for the reunion plan by allowing them time to urge the question privately in the church. At General Assembly that year, the recommendation was overwhelmingly adopted.

When the progressive members of the committee continued to explore reunion during the moratorium period, the conservatives cried foul. They immediately began to campaign aggressively against the plan of union. For five long years, the issue was agitated in the pages of the *Journal*, in church courts, and in local congregations. The Continuing Church Committee was ready to leave the church if reunion with the northern church succeeded. By 1954, when the plan was sent down, the union was to include the United Presbyterian Church, a small northern denomination with Scots Presbyterian roots. Complicating matters was the Supreme Court's landmark *Brown v. Board of Education* decision, which made government-enforced racial integration in the public schools a real possibility in the South. The PCUS General Assembly urged the entire church to support racial integration. With presbyteries considering both the integration advice and the reunion plan—each one an incendiary issue in itself—the plan of reunion failed. The presbyteries defeated reunion by the count of 42 in favor and 43 opposed, well short of the two-thirds majority needed to pass.

Though reunion had been defeated, the church was by no means saved. Indeed, the fundamental difference between the progressives and the conservatives remained in place. The progressives believed that the best way to transform America was to educate Presbyterian laypeople about the social issues facing the country and foster gradual, long-term social and cultural change led by denominational leaders. By contrast, conservatives held that the primary mission of the church was spiritual in orientation—the evangelization of lost men and women. While this would necessarily lead to transformed house-

235

holds, social transformation was merely a by-product of men and women being born again and entering God's kingdom. Perhaps this was why conservatives supported Billy Graham and his style of evangelism; this appeared to offer the best means of bringing people into a life-changing encounter with the gospel. It was also why Bill Hill, long-time pastor of West End Presbyterian Church, Hopewell, Virginia, started Presbyterian Evangelistic Fellowship (PEF) in 1964. Hill was convinced that the only hope for American culture was the old-time, "soul-winning" evangelistic ministry rooted in the inerrant Word of God. PEF eventually started a home missions branch, called Mission to the United States, and an overseas ministry called Executive Committee on Overseas Evangelism (ECOE—pronounced "echo"). These organizations would eventually become Mission to North America and Mission to the World when the PCA was founded in 1973.

This evangelistic commitment was important because it was clear to conservatives that the PCUS, with its focus on cultural engagement and transformation, had become too identified with the culture. Whether it was youth gatherings at the PCUS Montreat Assembly Grounds that appeared to contradict traditional ideas of propriety, advocating marijuana use in the PCUS-sponsored youth magazine, or supporting the legalized right to abortion in 1972, conservatives believed that the trends in the church were leading to apostasy and the dissolution not simply of the PCUS, but of Christianity in America. These progressive views had an effect in turning the church away from evangelism both at home and abroad. Conservatives were very concerned when C. Darby Fulton retired as secretary of the Board for World Mission in 1962 and was replaced by T. Watson Street, who would defend syncretism as an appropriate missions strategy. In response, conservative churches began to sponsor missionaries through independent mission boards, diverting their money away from denominational causes to ones they could support in good conscience.

Theologically, the church continued to stray from its moorings as it aggressively adopted the current theological trends. In the seminaries, more radical versions of progressive theology were promoted, represented by theologians such as Paul Tillich, Harvey Cox, and

Thomas J. J. Altizer. Some faculty members at the seminaries were even accused of having ties to Communist front organizations. While Union Seminary in Virginia and Louisville Seminary were viewed as the most radical seminaries during the 1960s, even Columbia Seminary was not immune to these new trends. Many had come to believe that a new conservative seminary was needed to supply ministers for the PCUS. Using seed money supplied by First Presbyterian Church, Jackson, Mississippi, Reformed Theological Seminary was started in 1966; conservative churches began supporting this seminary and sending their money and students to it.

Most problematic for conservatives was the fact that the progressive theology was not simply cloistered in the seminaries; it was also being promoted in the Sunday school literature. The Covenant Life Curriculum, which debuted in 1958, offered a blend of neo-orthodox views of Scripture and a progressive social vision. Promoting pacifism, racial integration, and feminism as legitimate and "revolutionary" applications of the gospel, the Covenant Life Curriculum drove many churches to stop using the denominational literature. They turned instead to independent evangelical publishers, such as David C. Cook and Gospel Light.

Thus, as a result of the social and theological trends in the PCUS, conservative churches experienced a profound loss of trust in the denominational causes and began supporting independent ministries. They also founded organizations within the church in an attempt to arrest the theological decline that they perceived. Kenneth Keyes, a successful Miami real estate developer, helped to start Concerned Presbyterians in 1965, intended to organize conservative laymen in the church; eventually, the group advocated withholding all funding of denominational activities. Ministers, too, organized themselves into a group for prayer, encouragement, and networking. Presbyterian Churchmen United began in 1969; this group was coordinated by John E. Richards, the pastor of First Presbyterian Church, Macon, Georgia. These two organizations, along with PEF and *Presbyterian Journal*, would provide leadership for conservative Presbyterians as they moved toward the creation of a new denomination.

During this period, conservatives found themselves battling over far more than some of the nuances of the Reformed faith; rather, evangelical doctrine itself was at stake. As Kennedy Smartt, pastor of West End Presbyterian Church during the 1960s, observed, "In the days of and following World War II the issue was not allegiance to the Reformed faith, but . . . the historicity and deity of Jesus, the inspiration and inerrancy of the Scriptures, and whether men were lost and going to hell apart from faith in Jesus Christ as Savior and Lord."[4] Because these conservatives were dissenting from the mainstream, progressive theological positions, they tended to define themselves in terms of the historic fundamentals of the faith as well as in terms of what they were *against* (theological and social liberalism). Perhaps this is why, as we will see, conservative Presbyterians have had such a difficult time sorting out what we actually do believe and practice, and hence what our identity truly is.

## "TO THE GLORY OF GOD": THE CREATION OF THE PRESBYTERIAN CHURCH IN AMERICA

At the 1968 Journal Day, conservative leaders decided to act. They invited representatives from *Presbyterian Journal*, Concerned Presbyterians, and the PEF to meet in Atlanta to chart a strategy that would either lead to the reformation of the PCUS or the creation of a continuing church. At that meeting, these leaders produced "A Declaration of Commitment" that defended the infallibility of Scripture and the necessity of faith in Christ for salvation; committed its supporters to "love, concern and neighborliness toward all races of men without partiality and without prejudice"; and demanded the preservation of "a confessional Church, thoroughly Reformed and Presbyterian."[5] For these men, a confessional church meant a church with a commitment to the Westminster Standards and to historic Presbyterian polity. The declaration was mailed to over a thousand ministers in the PCUS requesting their support; over five hundred eventually signed the document. Those who had signed the "Declaration," as well as other interested parties, were invited to a rally in Atlanta in

December 1968. Over seventeen hundred ministers and elders attended the rally, and 260 sessions signaled their agreement with the "Declaration" and the Continuing Church movement.

However, the good feelings generated from this rally soon faded. The leaders of the Continuing Church movement had attempted to translate this agreement into political action at the 1971 General Assembly, running D. James Kennedy, pastor of Coral Ridge Presbyterian Church, Fort Lauderdale, Florida, for moderator and other conservatives for key positions in the church. All their work ended in failure. And so the conservative leaders decided to regroup in Atlanta. There they set out "a plan for the continuation of a Presbyterian church loyal to Scripture and the Reformed faith." The plan included a resolution to identify conservative presbyteries and churches, to assist them in taking a stand for "Scripture and the Reformed faith," and "to accept the inevitability of division of the PCUS and to move now toward a continuing body of congregations and presbyteries."[6] These leaders agreed to be formed into an executive committee, which was introduced along with the plan at the 1971 Journal Day. Yet not all of the conservative leadership agreed with this movement; Nelson Bell, who had done so much for conservative Presbyterians and who had written in the *Journal* for almost thirty years, withdrew his support from the Continuing Church movement and resigned from the *Journal*.

What made division so difficult was the variety of opinions about a timetable for departure. Paul Settle, a longtime PCA pastor, observed that there were three groups within the leadership: the "sooners," who were ready to leave after the 1972 General Assembly; the "keepers," who wanted to wait until after the following year's General Assembly; and the "planners," who did not want to leave until the Plan of Union was adopted or some other definitive issue surfaced. What complicated matters further was that, as conservative leaders were planning to leave the PCUS, the denomination was once again engaged in union discussions with the northern church. The progressive leadership had told conservatives that there would be an "escape clause" similar to the one in the 1954 plan that would allow those who did not want to be part of the new united church to leave the denomination, taking their church property with them. This caused some who might have wanted to press ahead with separation to wait and see if they might be able to leave more easily via the escape clause. In the end, the plan of union was scrapped and the entire process was to begin again. Eventually, though, reunion did take place between the northern and southern branches, with the creation of the Presbyterian Church (USA) in 1983.

Meanwhile, the conservative leadership continued to make plans for the continuing church. They meet with ministers and ruling elders in Atlanta in September 1971, where they issued "A Declaration of Intent," which committed these men to "a Church in the United States, Presbyterian in government, Reformed in doctrine, fervent in evangelism and concerned for human welfare."[7] The steering committee met again in March 1972 to plan for the upcoming General Assembly. Though the assembly elected Nelson Bell as moderator, a sop to conservatives who were willing to stay in the denomination, the meeting was a continuation of the same progressive trends—the approval of abortion for economic reasons, the defense of universalism, and continued unconstitutional cooperation with the northern church.

By 1973, the momentum picked up for the Continuing Church movement. Once it was clear that there would be no escape clause, or even a plan of union, for several years, many of the "planners" were willing to move more quickly toward a separation. In February, the steering committee hosted a rally in Atlanta where evangelical apologist Francis Schaeffer told them, "When it is no longer possible to practice discipline in the church courts, then you must practice discipline in reverse and leave. But your leaving must be with tears, not with flags flying and bands playing."[8] In May, the steering committee called for a Convocation of Sessions at Westminster Presbyterian Church, Atlanta, at which time the committee transferred responsibility over to an organizing committee. In August, an advisory committee gathered in Asheville, North Carolina, where members heard reports on the initial committees for missions; on the versions of the Westminster Standards and Book of Church Order that would be adopted; and on Christian education matters, including a committee for Women in the Church.

When the commissioners gathered at Briarwood Presbyterian Church, Birmingham, Alabama, in December 1973, the structures of the Continuing Presbyterian Church were in place. At that first General Assembly, W. Jack Williamson, a ruling elder from Alabama, was elected the first moderator; Morton Smith, a professor at Reformed Theological Seminary, was the first stated clerk. The commissioners also chose the name of the new denomination: the National Presbyterian Church. This name would bring the church into conflict with a local congregation in Washington, D.C., with the same name; so, at its Second General Assembly, the new denomination would change its name to the Presbyterian Church in America. A spirit of peace and harmony pervaded that first assembly as commissioners felt a sense of relief in belonging to a church that was "true to Scripture and the Reformed faith and obedient to the Great Commission of Jesus Christ."

LEARNING TO BE PRESBYTERIAN: THE HISTORY OF
THE PCA, 1973–2003

This harmony did not last long. G. Aiken Taylor, editor of the *Presbyterian Journal*, observed in a 1974 article for *Christianity Today*, that "ever since the organizing assembly in December in Birmingham, where the original lines had been drawn between hardliner followers of latter-day Calvinists and those referred to by the hardliners as 'evangelical,' the trenches had been dug and the guns loaded."[9] And this was a mere ten months after the denomination had been founded! This struggle over identity within the PCA has lasted for thirty years. As Aiken Taylor's comment indicates, if one were to take the PCA's motto—"faithful to the Scriptures, true to the Reformed faith, and obedient to the Great Commission of Jesus Christ"—it could easily be said that, while everyone affirms the first, some might identify themselves more with the second statement and others more with the third.

Clearly, after forty years of not trusting denominational leadership (and perhaps one another), trying to figure out what it meant to be

"Presbyterian" was going to be a challenge. Throughout its first thirty years, the PCA has wrestled with some major issues, any one of which could conceivably have lead to a major division. By God's grace, the denomination has hung together and has now become the largest conservative Presbyterian body in the United States with over three hundred thousand members. It even received an entire denomination into its midst, the Reformed Presbyterian Church, Evangelical Synod, in 1982, and managed to maintain its unity.

This has not been easy, however. In fact, there have been (at least) four big issues with which the church has wrestled in its brief history. The first had to do with charismatic gifts and continuing revelation. The PCA was born in the 1970s when the charismatic movement was bringing the Holy Spirit back to the center of evangelical theology's agenda. The first General Assembly set up a committee to study the issue of charismatic gifts, covering issues such as "the extent to which any must certainly have permanently ceased, the possibility that any may perhaps exist today and, if so, the nature of such gifts as they may be practiced today." The resultant pastoral letter was one of the best pieces of work done by the church. Carefully distinguishing biblical material, the pastoral letter taught that there was not a "baptism of the Holy Spirit" that occurred subsequently to conversion; that the "filling of the Spirit" meant the "dominion of Christ in our lives and occurs when one is led willingly by the Word through which the Spirit works"; and that all believers receive spiritual gifts. However, on the debated issue of speaking in tongues, the pastoral letter pointedly denied "any view of tongues as experienced in our time which conceives of it as an experience by which revelation is received from God" and "any view of tongues which sees this phenomenon as an essential sign of the baptism of the Spirit." The letter also denied that revelatory miracles continued today, "since revelation was completed with the closing of the Canon in the New Testament era."[10]

A second debated topic has been theonomy. At its most basic, theonomy means "God's law." But in the mid-1970s, theonomy (or "Christian reconstruction") became a way of relating the Old Testament law to contemporary social, political, and economic issues in

242

order to manifest the dominion of Christ. Associated mainly with the work of theologians Rousas Rushdoony and Greg Bahnsen, theonomy became a major intellectual part of the Christian Right for a time, when even charismatic leader Pat Robertson appeared to embrace aspects of its thinking. But theonomy always has had the most allure for those Reformed believers for whom a stress on the continuity of the Old and New Testaments and on a "world and life view" have great appeal. As a result, a number of local churches wrestled with theonomy when church members or pastors adopted this perspective. The issue came to the attention of the General Assembly on repeated occasions. Rather than answering the question head on, General Assembly has, through the years, been content to allow lower courts to think through the implications of these views. For example, in 1979, the church said that it affirmed "that no particular view of the application of the judicial law for today should be made a basis for orthodoxy or excluded as heresy." In 1983, when a constitutional inquiry came before the assembly, the court was careful to note that "since there are differences of opinion with regard to the application and 'general equity' of the various penal sanctions, this declaration shall not be used by the courts of the Church to bind the conscience of elders in the PCA." While such actions manifested brotherly love and kindness, they also had the effect of allowing the issue to fester in many congregations. In addition, there has not been a definitive answer by the church on what the Westminster Confession means when it claims that "to them also, as a body politic, He gave sundry judicial laws, which expired together with the State of that people; not obliging any other now, further than the general equity thereof may require" (WCF 19.4).[11]

Strikingly, many of the same people who desired to reread the Confession on the issue of the continuing validity of the Old Testament civil laws for contemporary American politics did not want to allow this same latitude to those who questioned whether God created all things "in the space of six days" (WCF 4.1). The "creation day" debate raged for a number of years as some within the church made it a test case for confessional subscription among PCA ministers and elders.

Others believed that, because the church historically has allowed for a diversity of views on the meaning of Genesis 1, the PCA should allow a similar diversity. In 1999, the General Assembly appointed a study committee, which reported back two years later. In the end, the committee wisely urged that all officers affirm the basic tenets of the orthodox view of creation, including "that Scripture is the inerrant Word of God and self-interpreting; the full historicity of Genesis 1–3; the unique creation of Adam and Eve in God's image as our first parents; and Adam as the covenant head of the human race." While this answer has not satisfied some, it did bring a potentially divisive issue to a necessary conclusion.[12]

The most divisive and difficult question that the church has faced in its history, however, was undoubtedly that having to do with the nature of subscription to the Westminster Standards. As we have seen, this has long been a debated issue in the history of American Presbyterianism. In the PCA, the issue first came to notice in 1982; perhaps not coincidentally, that was the year that the RPCES joined and was received by the PCA. The initial questions were offered in a personal resolution: do ministers' ordination vows require them "to embrace as Bible truth each and every statement in our confessional standards?" If not, then which statements in the Standards should be seen as "fundamentals of the system of doctrine," which must be held in order to be an officer in the PCA?[13] These questions were debated and considered for over twenty years in the courts of the church as well as in the various church periodicals. In 2003, the church adopted a procedure that mandated ministerial candidates to give written declaration of any differences ("scruples" or "exceptions") they have with the Westminster Standards. Presbyteries then have to determine whether these differences are "out of accord with any fundamental of our system of doctrine." If the difference is deemed not to be "hostile to the system nor strikes at the vitals of religion," then the presbytery would allow the candidate to hold that difference (BCO 21-4). These differences, written down and entered into the presbytery minutes, are then subject to the review of the General Assembly. This procedure, sometimes called "good faith subscription," was meant to provide a way to manifest the unity of the church as well as provide the means for its peace and purity. While the church continues to work out some of the issues related to how this procedure works, it does seem to have answered the larger concerns about confessional subscription.

Each of these questions, from one angle of vision, could be construed as attempts to sort out what it means to be Presbyterian in the postmodern age. By defining what it means to subscribe to the Standards, the denomination tried to say what it means to claim Presbyterian beliefs as our own. By sorting out doctrinal issues such as creation days and theonomy, we attempted to be clear about how certain theological commitments may or may not be necessary for fellowship. By staking out a position on charismatic gifts, not only did we evaluate certain beliefs, but we also considered whether we would allow charismatic practices within Presbyterian churches. Finally, we were determining what would and would not be part of the Presbyterian story as it entered into the twentieth-first century. As a result, many of the disagreements within the PCA have dealt with the fundamental nature of our identity.

And yet, in the midst of these substantive and often difficult controversies, the PCA not only has maintained the unity of the church of Christ, but has consistently been one of the fastest growing denominations in North America. In the five-year span from 1999 to 2003, the denomination added seventy-two churches and saw an increase in mission churches from 199 to 287. The total membership increased over 7 percent in those five years, and total contributions were up 18 percent. In 2003, the denominational seminary, Covenant Theological Seminary in St. Louis, Missouri, enrolled nearly 950 students, and the denominational college, Covenant College in Lookout Mountain, Georgia, claimed over 1,250 full-time equivalent students. In addition, in this same five-year period, Mission to the World's full-time missionary force increased over 18 percent. In short, the heartbeat of the church is very strong, and God has kindly used this denomination to advance his reign in the world. As ministers and missionaries go into the world to preach the good news of Jesus Christ, men and women, boys and girls, are coming to know real peace with God in

Christ. In the fulfillment of the Great Commission, God's Word is being taught and the Reformed faith is being upheld. It may very well be that the PCA is on the brink of experiencing a new season of usefulness and fruitfulness in the outworking story of God's redemption. If so, it is by the grace and for the glory of God! Thanks be to God that he would use us in the furtherance of his gospel work!

## »Questions for Thought and Review

1. How should contemporary Presbyterians respond to the Social Gospel? Is it possible to hold on to the need for an individual relationship with Jesus and still manifest that relationship through working for social justice? What are some examples you know about where this has happened?

2. What was the failure of the church in the 1920s and 1930s? How do the Smith and Thompson cases illustrate this failure?

3. What was Nelson Bell's role in the development of conservative dissent?

4. Would it have been possible that the issues surrounding *Brown v. Board of Education* could have ended up providing the necessary impetus to scuttle reunion? How do we think through the relationship between cultural and social justice and ecclesiastical relationships?

5. This chapter describes the fundamental difference between conservatives and progressives as being their attitude toward evangelism and the personal appropriation of saving faith in Jesus Christ. Do you think that is a fair assessment? How do we go about ensuring that conservative Presbyterianism continues to demonstrate "obedience to the Great Commission"?

6. PCUS progressives succeeded in disseminating their views through the Sunday school literature, leading conservatives to fund independent educational ministries. How might that affect later attempts to sponsor Christian education and publishing in the PCA?

246

7. Do you see any parallels between the OPC story and the PCA story? How did the constituency involved in the organization of each denomination affect their early histories?
8. As you think about the controversies that have shaped the PCA, how have they led to the further refinement of Presbyterian identity?

## »For Further Reading

Chapell, Bryan. "Perspective on the Presbyterian Church in America's Subscription Standards." *Presbyterion* 27 (Fall 2001): 67–119.

Gilchrist, Paul, ed. *PCA Digest.* 3 vols. Atlanta: PCA Administrative Committee, 1993–1998. These position papers can be found on the Internet at http://www.pcahistory.org/pca/index.html.

Nutt, Rick. "The Tie That No Longer Binds: The Origins of the Presbyterian Church in America." In *The Confessional Mosaic: Presbyterians and Twentieth-Century Theology.* Edited by Milton J. Coalter, John M. Mulder, and Louis B. Weeks, 236–56. Louisville, Ky.: Westminster John Knox, 1990.

Settle, Paul. *To God All Praise and Glory: 1973 to 1998—The First 25 Years.* Atlanta: PCA Administrative Committee, 1998.

Smartt, Kennedy. *I Am Reminded: An Autobiographical Anecdotal History of the PCA.* n.p.: n.d..

Thompson, E. T. *Presbyterians in the South*, vol. 3: *1890–1972*. Richmond: John Knox, 1973.

# Epilogue: Becoming Presbyterian

I HAVE TRIED TO MAKE the argument that being Presbyterian involves certain beliefs, practices, and stories that intersect to forge a web of personal identity. This Presbyterian identity may involve overlap with other evangelical believers (for example, most Christians would affirm belief in the priority of grace and many would agree with the necessity of Scripture to regulate worship). However, Presbyterians tend to emphasize these beliefs and practices in certain ways influenced by the stories that we have told about ourselves and our beliefs and practices. To put it more technically, beliefs and practices are embedded in the stories, and these stories provide the narrative structures that make the beliefs and practices understandable.

Obviously, I have not said everything that could be said in any one of these sections. For example, Presbyterians have had a lot to say on a range of more "public" issues: church and state, education, and gender relations, for example. By not talking about these things, I'm actually making an important statement: namely, that Presbyterianism, at its best, focuses on spiritual issues—one's relationship with God through Jesus and a life of service to others. It doesn't (or shouldn't) identify with particular political stances or regional particularities. The fact that it has done so in the past actually reinforces Presbyterian teaching about the continuing reality of sin in the lives of men and women.

In addition, there are other Presbyterian stories on which I have said little. For example, there is a whole tradition of Scots Presbyterianism that has received limited mention in this book: namely, the Covenanters. They were hardy souls who withstood the attempts by seventeenth century Anglicans to impose the Book of Common Prayer upon the Church of Scotland. These believers had certain beliefs about the relationship between church and state, but as important were their beliefs about psalm singing. Their descendents continue to promote "exclusive psalmody" and are represented by the Reformed Presbyterian Church of North America. Another story that hasn't been mentioned is the secession from the PC (USA) in the early 1980s that led to the creation of the (current-day) Evangelical Presbyterian Church. This denomination is found mainly in the northern United States and has as its motto, "in essentials, unity; in non-essentials, liberty; and in all things, charity." Their motto is one of their primary justifications for allowing churches to elect and ordain women as elders.

Clearly there is much, much more about which I could have written. But to do so would have produced a much longer and a less useful book. While some might wonder whether it is possible to represent "vanilla Presbyterianism" (or what I like to call, "Plain Ol' Presbyterianism"), what I have tried to do in this book is to keep our focus on the broad middle of what conservative Presbyterians in America have believed for over three hundred years.

Now, perhaps you have been reading these pages because you are considering membership in a Presbyterian church, particularly a church that belongs to the PCA. Or perhaps you are an outsider to Presbyterianism, but would like to be part of a PCA church. And the question with which you are confronted is this: How does someone become Presbyterian?

There are two answers to that question, one that is procedural and the other more psychological. The *procedures* required to become a member of a PCA congregation are actually fairly straightforward. The one basic requirement is to "give a testimony of [your] Christian experience to the Session" (BCO 57-6). What the elders will be listening for is a credible profession of your faith. And this credible profession of faith for which the elders will listen is well summarized in the membership vows that you will be asked to take:

- Do you acknowledge yourselves to be sinners in the sight of God, justly deserving His displeasure, and without hope save in His sovereign mercy?
- Do you believe in the Lord Jesus Christ as the Son of God, and Savior of sinners, and do you receive and rest upon Him alone for salvation as He is offered in the Gospel?
- Do you now resolve and promise, in humble reliance upon the grace of the Holy Spirit, that you will endeavor to live as becomes the followers of Christ?
- Do you promise to support the Church in its worship and work to the best of your ability?
- Do you submit yourselves to the government and discipline of the Church, and promise to study its purity and peace? (BCO 57-5)

These questions actually represent the heart of the Christian faith. The first vow asks whether you will acknowledge that you are a sinner deserving divine condemnation. Following that, the second membership vow asks whether you are receiving and resting upon Christ alone for salvation as he is offered in the gospel. The third and fourth questions probe whether you are willing to live a life of Christian discipleship, both individually as motivated and transformed by the Spirit and corporately in the worship and work of the PCA. The final vow asks whether you will submit to the government and discipline of the PCA, as summarized in the BCO.

This final point is important: when you become a member of a Presbyterian church, your name is listed on a local church's membership roll, but you are actually a member of the Presbyterian Church in America. You submit to the discipline of the PCA as manifested in a particular local congregation—but because what we said in the government chapter is true (remember: the parts are in the whole and the whole is in the parts), your "loyalty" is not to a particular set of elders, and even less to a particular pastor, but to the church as a whole and Christ the King above all.

That's basically all that is required to become a Presbyterian: some churches may have a new members' class; other churches may have you take these vows in front of the congregation. But the procedure for becoming Presbyterian is fairly straightforward. It's the *psychology* of becoming Presbyterian that may be more difficult. What do I mean? It all goes back to the issue of identity. Think back to the ways in which you identify yourself: those labels are actually identity markers that may have profound psychological weight. Some labels can be changed with little difficulty: I've moved so much, for example, that the change from a Philadelphia Phillies fan to a St. Louis Cardinals fan was made with little effort. Other self-identifications can only be changed with great difficulty: a career change ("I was a lawyer, but now I am a school teacher"); a political party affiliation; or religious adherence.

That is why to move from seeing yourself as a Baptist or Roman Catholic to being Presbyterian can involve great cost to the psyche, both personal and familial. The personal cost can involve intense mental effort; sometimes I tell people it involves imagining yourself in a different kind of clothes. If you are used to seeing yourself a certain way, in a certain set of clothes (as a Southern Baptist, for example), it can be challenging to change those clothes and view yourself in a new way (as a Presbyterian). But for many people, the familial cost can be more challenging. Parents or siblings can wonder why the church in which you grew up wasn't "good enough" for you. Spouses can become very uncomfortable when you are on a journey they haven't joined. Children can struggle with the thought of leaving a particular church to go to a different one, particularly if it has a different "feel" in terms of worship or church structures.

I want to acknowledge that these psychological challenges are real and often quite painful. But if you find a deep resonance with the Presbyterian beliefs, practices, and stories that I have described in this book, you probably won't be satisfied until you embrace a Presbyterian identity fully and joyfully. Further, there are a number of people in PCA churches who have made the same journey and who are ready to love you and welcome you with open arms. And finally, there is a sense of relief that you will feel when you are finally in a church that believes and practices Christianity in the way you see it reflected in Holy Scripture. While the cost may feel high, the benefits are worth the journey.

And so, I would invite you to join us on this journey of becoming Presbyterian. In doing so, you may feel uncomfortable at first, as you would be in learning anything new and unfamiliar. But in the end, being with a people that longs to be "faithful to the Scriptures, true to the Reformed faith, and obedient to the Great Commission" will bring you great joy. And above all else, you will share a way of life that will bring great glory to God alone: to him be all praise and glory!

# Notes

### Introduction: Presbyterian Identity in the Postmodern Age

1. Robert Lewis Dabney, "A Thoroughly Educated Ministry," in *Discussions*, ed. C. R. Vaughan, 4 vols. (1890–97; reprint, Harrisonburg, Va.: Sprinkle, 1982), 2:676.

### Chapter 1: God Is King: The Sovereignty of God

1. "O Father, You Are Sovereign." Words by Margaret Clarkson. © 1982 Hope Publishing Company, Carol Stream, Ill. 60188. All rights reserved. Used by permission.

2. Jonathan Edwards, "Personal Narrative," in *The Works of Jonathan Edwards*, vol. 16, *Letters and Personal Writings*, ed. George S. Claghorn (New Haven: Yale University Press, 1998), 792.

3. Samuel Rodigast, "Whate'er My God Ordains Is Right," trans. Catherine Winkworth, in *Trinity Hymnal* (1990), #108.

4. Abraham Kuyper, "Sphere Sovereignty," in *Abraham Kuyper: A Centennial Reader*, ed. James D. Bratt (Grand Rapids: Eerdmans, 1998), 488.

5. Abraham Kuyper, *Lectures on Calvinism* (1931; reprint, Grand Rapids: Eerdmans, 1994), 163.

6. Isaac Watts, "How Sweet and Awesome Is the Place," in *Trinity Hymnal* (1990), #469.

### Chapter 2: The Priority of Amazing Grace

1. Steve Turner, *Amazing Grace: The Story of America's Most Beloved Song* (New York: Harper Collins, 2002), xxvii, xxxii, 217–18.

2. John Newton, "Amazing Grace," in *Trinity Hymnal* (Suwanee, Ga.: Great Commission Publications, 1990), #460.

3. Robert A. Peterson and Michael D. Williams, *Why I Am Not an Arminian* (Downers Grove, Ill.: InterVarsity, 2004), 207.

4. Newton, "Amazing Grace."

5. Augustus M. Toplady, "Rock of Ages, Cleft for Me," in *Trinity Hymnal* (1990), #499.

6. John Calvin, *Golden Booklet of the True Christian Life*, trans. Henry J. Van Andel (Grand Rapids: Baker, 1952), 25–26.

7. Newton, "Amazing Grace."

8. John Bunyan, *The Pilgrim's Progress* (1895; reprint, Carlisle, Pa.: Banner of Truth, 1977), 183.

## Chapter 3: God's Story, Promise, Reign: Covenant and Kingdom

1. Richard Phillips, "Covenant Confusion," http://www.alliancenet.org/part ner/Article_Display_Page/0,,PTID307086%7CCHID559376%7CCIID1787572,0 0.html.

2. John Murray, *The Covenant of Grace* (London: Tyndale Press, 1954; reprint, Phillipsburg, N.J.: Presbyterian and Reformed, 1988), 31.

3. Anne R. Cousin, "The Sands of Time Are Sinking," in *Trinity Hymnal* (Suwanee, Ga.: Great Commission Publications, 1990), #546.

## Chapter 4: What in the World Is the Church?

1. "The Church" by Derek Webb. © 2002 Derek Webb Music (admin. by Music Services). All rights reserved. Used by permission.

2. Much of what I say follows Edmund P. Clowney, *The Church* (Downers Grove, Ill.: InterVarsity Press, 1995).

3. John Murray, "The Church: Its Definition in Terms of 'Visible' and 'Invisible' Invalid," in *The Collected Writings of John Murray*, 4 vols. (Carlisle, Pa.: Banner of Truth, 1976), 1:234–35.

4. Samuel Stone, "The Church's One Foundation," in *Trinity Hymnal* (Suwanee, Ga.: Great Commission Publications, 1990), #347.

## Chapter 6: A Heart Aflame: Presbyterian and Reformed Piety

1. Hughes Oliphant Old, "What Is Reformed Spirituality?" *Perspectives: A Journal of Reformed Thought* 9 (January 1994): 8.

2. Ibid., 9.

3. Augustus Toplady, "Rock of Ages, Cleft for Me," in *Trinity Hymnal* (Suwanee, Ga.: Great Commission Publications, 1990), #499.

4. James Montgomery Boice, "Give Praise to God," in James Montgomery Boice and Paul Jones, *Hymns for a Modern Reformation* (Philadelphia: Tenth Presbyterian Church, 2000), #1. Used by permission.

## Chapter 7: Gospel-Driven Presbyterian Worship

1. I borrow this language from Dr. Mark Dalbey, dean of students and assistant professor of practical theology at Covenant Theological Seminary.

2. Hughes Oliphant Old, *Worship: Reformed according to Scripture*, rev. ed. (Louisville: Westminster John Knox, 2002), 6.

3. These questions receive full explanation in John D. Witvliet, "Beyond Style: Rethinking the Role of Music in Worship," in *The Conviction of Things Not Seen:*

*Worship and Ministry in the 21ˢᵗ Century*, ed. Todd E. Johnson (Grand Rapids: Brazos, 2002), 70–80.

4. Ibid., 72.

5. Anne Steele, "Thou lovely source of true delight."

### Chapter 8: "Decently and in Order": Presbyterian Church Government

1. James Bannerman, *The Church of Christ*, 2 vols. (1869; reprint, Carlisle, Pa.: Banner of Truth, 1974), 1:195.

2. Ibid., 271.

### Chapter 9: The Glorious Reformation: Calvin, Knox, and the Beginnings of Presbyterianism

1. John Calvin, "Calvin's Catechism of 1538," in *Calvin's First Catechism: A Commentary*, trans. Ford Lewis Battles, ed. I. John Hesselink (Louisville: Westminster John Knox, 1997), 21.

2. I. John Hesselink, "Calvin, Theologian of the Holy Spirit," in *Calvin's First Catechism*, 178.

3. Jasper Ridley, *John Knox* (New York: Oxford University Press, 1968), 219.

4. "The Solemn League and Covenant," in *Westminster Confession of Faith* (Glasgow: Free Presbyterian Publications, 1994), 359.

5. J. Gresham Machen, "The Creeds and Doctrinal Advance," in *God Transcendent*, ed. Ned B. Stonehouse (Grand Rapids: Eerdmans, 1949), 151.

### Chapter 10: Errand into the Wilderness: Early American Presbyterianism

1. Letter of Francis Makemie to Benjamin Colman, 28 March 1707, in C. A. Briggs, *American Presbyterianism* (New York: Charles Scribner's Sons, 1885); quoted in E. T. Thompson, *Presbyterians in the South*, 3 vols. (Richmond: John Knox, 1963–73), 1:23.

2. Gilbert Tennent, "The Dangers of an Unconverted Ministry," in *The Great Awakening*, ed. Alan Heimert and Perry Miller (Indianapolis: Bobbs-Merrill, 1967), 85.

3. Letter of Jonathan Edwards to John Erskine, 5 July 1750, in Jonathan Edwards, *The Works of Jonathan Edwards*, vol. 16, *Letters and Personal Writings*, ed. George S. Claghorn (New Haven: Yale University Press, 1998), 355.

4. James H. Smylie, *A Brief History of the Presbyterians* (Louisville: Westminster John Knox, 1996), 60.

### Chapter 11: The Golden Age: American Presbyterians in the Nineteenth Century

1. "Plan of Union," in *The Presbyterian Enterprise: Sources of American Presbyterian History*, ed. Maurice W. Armstrong, Lefferts A. Loetscher, and Charles A. Anderson (Philadelphia: Westminster, 1956), 104.

2. Paul E. Johnson, *A Shopkeeper's Millennium: Society and Revivals in Rochester, New York, 1815–1837* (New York: Hill and Wang, 1978).

3. Charles Grandison Finney, *Lectures on Revivals of Religion*, ed. William G. McLoughlin (Cambridge, Mass.: Harvard University Press, 1960), 291.

4. Peter Wallace and Mark Noll, "The Students of Princeton Seminary, 1812–1929: A Research Note," *American Presbyterians* 72 (Fall 1994): 203–15.

5. Harold M. Parker Jr., *The United Synod of the South: The Southern New School Presbyterian Church* (Newport, Conn.: Greenwood, 1988), 129.

6. Lewis G. Vander Velde, *The Presbyterian Churches and the Federal Union, 1861–1869* (Cambridge, Mass.: Harvard University Press, 1932), 50.

7. James Henley Thornwell, "Address to All Churches of Christ," in *The Collected Writings of James Henley Thornwell*, ed. B. M. Palmer (1870–73; reprint, Carlisle, Pa.: Banner of Truth, 1974), 446–64 (quotations on pp. 451, 455, 456, 460, and 463).

8. Joseph M. Wilson, ed., *The Presbyterian Historical Almanac and Annual Remembrancer of the Church for 1866* (Philadelphia: Joseph M. Wilson, 1866), 43–45.

9. Dabney's speech can be found in Thomas Cary Johnson, *Life and Letters of Robert Lewis Dabney* (1903; reprint, Carlisle, Pa.: Banner of Truth, 1977), 352.

10. James I. Vance, *Predestination: A Sermon* (Richmond: Presbyterian Committee of Publication, 1898), 14, 17, 19, 26, 29.

## Chapter 12: "A True Presbyterian Church": Twentieth-Century Presbyterianism in the American North

1. "Moderns Agnostic, Says Dr. Machen," *New York Times*, 10 January 1924, 4.

2. Pearl S. Buck, "The Layman's Mission Report," *Christian Century* 49 (23 November 1932): 1434; Buck, "Is There a Case for Foreign Missions," *Harper's* 166 (January 1933): 143–55.

3. J. Gresham Machen, "A True Presbyterian Church at Last," *Presbyterian Guardian* 2 (22 June 1936): 110.

4. Ned B. Stonehouse, "Taking Inventory," *Presbyterian Guardian* 17 (10 January 1948): 4.

5. Arthur W. Kuschke Jr., "Stay Out of the American Council!" *Presbyterian Guardian* 18 (April 1949) 64, 68–69.

6. D. G. Hart and John Muether, *Fighting the Good Fight: A Brief History of the Orthodox Presbyterian Church* (Philadelphia: Orthodox Presbyterian Church, 1995), 138.

7. George P. Hutchinson, *The History behind the Reformed Presbyterian Church, Evangelical Synod* (Cherry Hill, N.J.: Mack Publishing, 1974), 246–68.

8. This church should not be confused with the current Evangelical Presbyterian Church, which formed in 1981 in response to liberalism in northern Presbyterianism and the approaching reunion of the northern and southern Presbyterian churches.

Chapter 13: "A Continuing Presbyterian Church": Twentieth-Century Presbyterianism in the American South

1. Walter L. Lingle, "The Teachings of Jesus and Modern Social Problems," *Union Seminary Review* 27 (1916): 191–205.

2. E. T. Thompson, *Presbyterians in the South*, 3 vols. (Richmond: John Knox, 1963–73), 2:473.

3. Peter H. Hobbie, "Prophet under Fire: Ernest Trice Thompson and the Glasgow Case," *Affirmation* 6:2 (Fall 1993): 129–45.

4. Kennedy Smartt, *I Am Reminded* (Chestnut Mountain, Ga.: n.p., n.d.), 22.

5. "A Declaration of Commitment," *Presbyterian Outlook* (29 September 1969), 24.

6. "Plans for Continuing Church Announced," *Presbyterian Journal* (25 August 1971): 4–5.

7. "Declaration of Intent," Paul Settle Papers, Box 257, Folder 6, Presbyterian Church in America Historical Center, St. Louis, Mo. I thank Wayne Sparkman for tracking this down for me.

8. Smartt, *I am Reminded*, 83.

9. G. Aiken Taylor, "Presbyterian Church in America: In Quest of Name and Niche," *Christianity Today* 19 (11 October 1974): 48.

10. "Pastoral Letter Concerning the Experience of the Holy Spirit in the Church Today," http://www.pcanet.org/history/documents/pastoralletter.html.

11. "Theonomy" in *PCA Position Papers, 1973–1993*, http://www.pcahistory.org/pca/2-555.html.

12. "Report of the Creation Study Committee." http://www.pcahistory.org/creation/report.html.

13. *Minutes of the Tenth General Assembly of the Presbyterian Church in America* (Decatur, Ga.: Presbyterian Church in America, 1982), 220-24.

# Index of Subjects and Names

College of New Jersey,
177–78, 179–81
Collins, Judy, 33
colonial Presbyterians,
169–81
Columbia Bible College,
209
Columbia Seminary, 194,
227, 236
common grace, 39–40
Common Sense Realism,
181
communion. *See* Lord's
Supper
communion tokens,
93–94
communion with God,
102–3, 104
communion with other
believers, 103
Communism, 236
complaint, 145
Concerned Presbyterians,
236
confessional subscrip-
tion, 4, 171–73,
179, 192, 197–98,
243–44
confessionalism, 215
Congregationalists, 165,
166, 173, 186–87,
192
connectional nature of
church, 133, 145–46
consistory, 157
contemporary worship,
115–16, 123, 127
Continuing Church
movement, 233, 238
continuing revelation,
241
conversion, 190
Coolidge, Calvin, 206
Cornbury, Lord, 170–71
corporate worship, 8–9,
107, 109, 110, 125

Council of Orange, 154
Council of Trent, 155
Counter Reformation,
155
courts, of the church,
144
covenant, 6, 51–53
as irrevocable promise,
59–62
and kingdom, 52, 62
and redemption,
53–59
Covenant College, 146,
222, 244
Covenant Life Curricu-
lum, 236
covenant of grace, 6, 52
covenant of works, 54
covenant renewal, wor-
ship as, 121–23
Covenant Theological
Seminary, 146, 222,
244
covenant theology, 53,
58–59
Covenanters, 164, 247
Cox, Harvey, 235
Craig, John, 164, 178
creation, 19–20, 200
creation days debate,
243–44
Cross, Robert, 171–72
cultural apologetic, 221
Cumberland Presbyterian
Church, 188,
199–200

Dabney, Robert Lewis,
185, 197, 201–3,
227, 230
Dallas Theological Semi-
nary, 209, 222
Darwin, Charles, 200
David, 56, 57, 59
David C. Cook (pub-
lisher), 236

Davies, Samuel, 178, 180
Day of the Lord, 63
deacons, 109, 142–43,
160
"decently and in order,"
9, 10, 133
Declaration of Commit-
ment, 237–38
Declaration of Indepen-
dence, 181
Declaration of Intent,
239
deeds of mercy, 143
definite atonement, 38
Dendy, Henry, 232
denominational "ask-
ings," 11
denominations, 134, 209
depravity, 37
Deuteronomy, 124
dialogue, in worship,
122–23
Dickinson, John, 181
Dickinson, Jonathan,
172–73, 177
discerning Christ's body,
93
Disciples of Christ, 188
discipline, 137, 157, 249
discipline in reverse, 239
dispensationalism,
58–59, 209
Dively, David, 23
divine right Presbyterianism, 194, 197
doctors (church office),
160
doctrine, 4, 136, 166
doctrines of grace, 36
Dutch pietism, 176
dying well, 48–49

Eastern Orthodoxy, 101
ecumenicity, 220
Edward VI, 161

spirituality, 67, 99
Spring, Gardiner, 196
Spring Resolutions, 196
Stewart, Lyman and Milton, 209
Stone, Barton W., 188
Stonehouse, Ned, 216, 217
stories, 2–4
Strasbourg, 157
Street, T. Watson, 235
strict subscription, 198
subscription. *See* confessional subscription
Sunday, Billy, 208
Sunday school literature, 236
supernaturalism, 210
surface truths, 40
Swin, David, 198
Swiss Reformation, 156–60
Synod of Dort, 36–37
Synod of New York, 177, 179, 180
Synod of Philadelphia, 179
system subscription, 192, 198

Taylor, G. Aiken, 240
Taylor, Nathaniel William, 190
teaching elders, 142
Tennent, Gilbert, 175–76, 178, 180
Tennent, William, Sr., 175, 180
thankfulness, 112
theological education, 145, 174–75
theonomy, 241–42, 244
theosis, 101
Thirty-nine Articles, 165
Thompson, E. T., 229, 231–32

Thomson, John, 172–73, 178
Thornwell, James Henley, 185, 194–95, 196–97, 200
Tillich, Paul, 235
Tinkling Spring Presbyterian Church (Fishersville, VA), 178
tongues, 241
Toplady, Augustus, 42
total depravity, 37
traditional worship, 115–16, 123, 127
transcendence, 20
transforming grace, 41
transubstantiation, 90
tribulation, 58, 209
Trinity, 5, 69, 163
    and baptism, 86
    in Calvin, 158
    and worship, 117, 126
true church and false church, 71
*True Presbyterian*, 201
Trumball, Charles G., 208–9
truth, 40
Tuckney, Anthony, 165
TULIP, 37
Turner, Steve, 33
types, 62

ubiquity, of Christ's body, 90
unconditional election, 37
Union Seminary in New York, 193, 199, 207
Union Seminary in Virginia, 186, 197, 202, 226, 227, 228, 229, 230, 231, 236
union with Christ, 11, 41–42, 44, 45, 60
    Calvin on, 158–59
    and Christian life, 100

and church, 70
and connectionalism, 134
and Reformed piety, 101–3
and sacraments, 105–6
Unitarianism, 166
United Presbyterian Church of North America, 218, 234
United Synod of the South, 195
unity, of church, 70
universal church, 72, 133
universalism, 203
University of Glasgow, 180
University of Texas at Austin, 203
Ussher, James, 165

Van Til, Cornelius, 215, 217
Vance, James I., 203, 227
Virginia, 178
visible church, 7, 73–77, 88
vocations, 25, 65

Wallace, Peter, 193
Wallis, John, 165
Warfield, B. B., 185, 199, 200, 209, 210, 211
Watts, Isaac, 30
Webb, Derek, 68
Weiss, Johannes, 211
Weld, Theodore, 190
Wesley, John and Charles, 176
Westminster Assembly, 10, 119, 164–66
Westminster Confession of Faith, 4–5, 163, 165. *See also* confessional subscription

# Index of Scripture

# Index of the Westminster Standards

**Sean Michael Lucas** (Ph.D., Westminster Theological Seminary) is senior pastor of First Presbyterian Church in Hattiesburg, Mississippi. He was previously dean of faculty and assistant professor of church history at Covenant Theological Seminary. Lucas is author of *What Is Church Government?* and *Robert Lewis Dabney: A Southern Presbyterian Life*. With D. G. Hart, he is the co-editor of the American Reformed Biographies series.